Worth the Pain

Published by Kansas City Star Books

First edition
ISBN-13:
978-1508845645
ISBN-10:
1508845646

Editor: Monroe Dodd
Book designer: Jean D. Dodd

Cover photograph: Andy Marso at the University of Kansas Medical Center, June 2004. Photo courtesy *University Daily Kansan*.

Photographs, pp. 2, 4, 137-140 and back cover, courtesy Andy Marso.

Worth the Pain

How Meningitis Nearly Killed Me — Then Changed My Life for the Better

Andy Marso

KANSAS CITY STAR BOOKS
KANSAS CITY, MISSOURI

Contents

FOREWORD 7
PREFACE 9

1 .... A Single Shiver 13
2 .... A Rude Awakening 19
3 .... A Parent's Worst Nightmare 37
4 .... The Lost Days 47
5 .... Between Life and Death 55
6 .... Back to Reality 69
7 .... Moving Day 79
8 .... Two Graduations 83
9 .... Floating Flesh 91
10 .... The Search For Living Tissue 103
11 .... The Toes Come Off 117
12 .... The Advocates 123
Photographs 137
13 .... Let's Make a Deal 141
14 .... A Birthday Pouch 149
15 .... Finding Happy Places 155
16 .... The Visitors 163
17 .... A New Pouch, and Then Another 169
18 .... Of Basketballs and Bladders 177
19 .... Post Pouch, Farewell to Burn Unit 185
20 .... Rehab Unit 193
21 .... In the Cuckoo's Nest 203
22 .... One Last Scare 209
23 .... The Outside World 221
24 .... The Final Choice 229
25 .... Going Home 241
26 .... The New Life 249

EPILOGUE 253
ACKNOWLEDGMENTS 267

FOREWORD

By Bonnie Henrickson
Head coach, Women's Basketball
University of Kansas

As a head coach, you are trained to prepare for anything that an opponent can throw at you. I have spent countless hours throughout my coaching career preparing for games, recruiting visits and university events. However, nothing could prepare me for the journey I would take in the spring of 2002 with meningococcal meningitis. Through this journey, I saw firsthand the power of the human spirit. That year, Rayna DuBose was stricken with meningitis — as Andy Marso would be stricken two years later. Through tremendous courage and tenacity, both these young adults have overcome the odds and gone on to lead inspiring lives.

Rayna DuBose was a promising freshman on our Virginia Tech women's basketball team in spring 2002. A Columbia, Maryland native, she was highly recruited and became a spirited member of our program. With the first phone call, which brought news that Rayna had passed out in study hall, I found myself on a plane back to Blacksburg, Virginia, from the NCAA Women's Final Four in San Antonio. Doctors would release Rayna, thinking that she was dehydrated and weak from the common flu. The next morning though, Rayna's condition deteriorated and she was taken to the Student Health Center on campus and then on to our local hospital. A spinal tap and numerous tests would follow and doctors concluded she was suffering from meningococcal meningitis.

The next phone call came in the middle of the night from the hospital with news that Rayna's condition had worsened and that she was being taken by life flight from Blacksburg to the University of Virginia Medical Center in Charlottesville. A drive that normally would have taken two hours took me barely an hour; my foot never left the floorboard, and I ended up beating the helicopter to the hospital. While she was on the way in the helicopter, Rayna suffered a heart attack.

Doctors worked furiously to try to save Rayna's life. She was in a drug-induced coma — her organs failing and the blood no longer circulating to her limbs — but she was still alive and fighting. Her only chance for survival was an experimental drug. That was the longest 24 hours of my life, but thanks to Rayna's perseverance, she survived! The celebration was short-lived, though, when doctors broke the news that all four of her limbs would need to be amputated because of the damage. After 96 days at the Medical Center in Charlottesville, Rayna returned home to begin her quest for independence as a bilateral amputee.

Two years later, as the new head coach for the University of Kansas women's basketball program, I received a phone call asking to me reach out to Andy Marso, a promising journalism student at KU who had contracted meningococcal meningitis. Knowing what his family and friends were going through, I welcomed the opportunity to share Rayna's story in hopes that it would provide comfort to Andy and his family. After meeting Andy in his hospital room, I knew that he would win his battle. Andy is a fighter, and waged his own war for survival.

Despite their life-changing experiences, both Rayna and Andy refuse to be defined or limited by the after-effects. Instead, these experiences renewed their purpose in life and provided them an opportunity to help others. Both Rayna and Andy have gone on to complete their undergraduate degrees. They have become active members in their communities. Both are helping to raise awareness of meningococcal meningitis by sharing their stories and educating others. They are true examples of the human spirit and its everlasting resilience.

PREFACE

A warm breeze blew over my bare chest as I dug what was left of my feet into the sand of Copacabana Beach. Fine white grains rolled away from the stumps that ended just before where my toes used to be. For a moment, I pretended they were still there, buried under the sand.

The sand on my feet and the wind on my arms were feelings I remembered only vaguely. When I left the hospital four years earlier, the doctors told me to keep what remained of my arms and legs covered outdoors. The scar tissue and skin grafts would not be able to take much sun. Until they matured, UV rays were the enemy.

I had followed their advice religiously, but not only for medical reasons. I wasn't eager to show off those scars, especially the thick, ropy one along my left elbow. It had taken months of stretching exercises to loosen it enough so I could fully extend my arm.

But now I was in Rio de Janeiro, sitting on a beach with the Atlantic Ocean laid out before me, and the old rules didn't seem to apply. Bronze-skinned women in barely-there bathing suits strutted by, tiptoeing across the warm sand. Kids pulling wagons hawked everything from bottled water to knock-off luxury sunglasses. Seagulls screeched overhead in the calm moments between the crashing of waves and samba music coming from one of the huts selling fresh coconuts. It did not seem like a place for long sleeves.

So I took off my shirt, slathered on SPF 45 sunscreen and sat with my arms exposed, scars and all. Over my bathing suit I wore a pair of nylon warm-up pants, with snaps all the way up the sides. They were made for basketball players; they could be pulled off in a flash when the coach called you off the bench and ordered you to get in the game. I hadn't worn them for basketball in years.

"Are you going in?" Rebecca asked, returning to the beach with water dripping off her long black hair. She sat down on a towel nearby, next to her boyfriend Geoff.

"I don't know, how's the water?" I asked casually.

"Oh, it's great," she said, wringing water from her hair into the sand.

I had met Rebecca and Geoff the night before. They knew there was something wrong with my feet and hands. They could see the scars and they could see where my fingers and toes were supposed to be. Minutes earlier they had watched me take off the carbon fiber leg braces that came up almost to my knees and place them carefully beside me, upright so the things wouldn't get sand in them.

Rebecca and Geoff did not know that four years earlier I had almost died battling the bacterial infection that gave me those scars. They did not know that several doctors had told me I would never walk on those legs again. They did not know that it had taken me a year to stand and walk with those braces, going from a wheelchair to a crutch to finally being able to balance without toes. They did not know that right then I was wondering if it was even possible to get across those 20 feet of sand to the sparkling turquoise water without the braces.

It was this kind of situation that had made me wonder whether I should come to Rio or not when my old college roommate, Gustavo, sent me his wedding invitation months earlier. I wanted to go. I wanted to see the rainforest, the ocean, the women, the gigantic statue of Jesus up on the hill with his arms outstretched. But there were a million things to consider in my new, fingerless, toeless life. Would I be a target for thieves? What if my braces broke and there was no prosthetic technician to be found? What would I do when I found myself on the beach and wanted to go in?

"So what do you think, are you going to go in?" Rebecca asked.

Yes, I was going to go in, or at least I was going to try. I didn't really know how I was going to get into the water without my leg braces. I didn't know whether I could walk or I'd have to crawl. I didn't know how much effort it would take, or how I would look doing it. But one thing I did know after four years of living with the aftereffects of bacterial meningitis: that surf would not come to me. I was not entitled to it. If I wanted it, I had to go get it.

I unbuttoned the pants one snap at a time, giving myself more time to gather my courage. I had lost soft tissue on the bottoms of my feet along with my toes and, though I had gradually built up callus and strength, the first few years of walking had sent shivers of pain through the bones that were just a little too tight against the skin. The braces usually provided padding. But the sand seemed soft enough.

I rose to my knees first, then tentatively placed my right foot flat on the sand, as if genuflecting. How was it that one rose to a standing position from the ground? Oh yeah, push off one leg until you got upright enough to straighten the other. I took a deep breath and gave it a try.

It was deceptively easy at first. With my right hand on my right knee, I drove up off the sand, then planted my left foot. So far, so good. Then I felt myself start to sway. First I went backward, then, as I splayed my arms out for balance, I overcompensated and began to tip forward. This was the moment of truth. No toes to catch me. I'd have to move one leg to change my center of balance, or fall on my face.

My right leg swung forward and I jammed it back into the sand in front of me. Now my legs were spread wide apart, staggered, and I felt more stable, bracing against the sand a bit. I didn't want to glance back at Rebecca and Geoff and see what I was fairly certain would be looks of concern — better to pretend I did this all the time.

Again I put one foot in front of the other and then I was moving. Forward momentum made balancing easier. My small, stumpy feet and atrophied calf muscles made my legs look stick-like below my black swim trunks, but I was doing it. I was walking barefoot, and aside from some mild pressure pain at having my full weight on those foot stumps, it felt OK.

At the water's edge the sand was compact and hard from waves washing over it, and the pressure was worse. One step at a time, I stumbled in. The sandy bottom was rippled by the waves, waves that pushed at the front of my shins, then my knees, then my thighs, with increasing force. With each step, it got harder to stay upright, so once I was waist-deep, I just let myself fall.

The water was lukewarm and pleasant. I had gone swimming in the safety of a couple of pools in the years since my amputations and now I turned onto my back and took a few tentative strokes, looking up into a brilliant blue sky. Waves crashed against the top of my head and onto my face and I tasted salt. But I made progress and after going what I figured was a few dozen yards, I stopped swimming, straightened up and found the ocean floor.

I let myself float free briefly and looked out to sea, my feet barely brushing the bottom. Then I turned around.

"Wow," I gasped.

In front of me were miles of beach, dotted with people and coconut stands. Beyond that were high-rise apartments and luxury hotels, glittering in the sun. Beyond that were mountains covered in lush, leafy rainforest that seemed to rise out of the backs of the buildings. Tropical birds soared overhead. Even the favelas, or slums, that clung perilously to the mountainside behind the high-rises looked beautiful — their multi-colored roofs like splashes of paint.

I saw Rebecca and Geoff on the beach waving to me and I grinned and waved back. I didn't give any thought to my mangled right hand with its shrunken thumb, my only remaining digit. I just waved, and marveled at how far I had come to walk those few dozen steps on the beach.

CHAPTER 1
A SINGLE SHIVER

My first life ended on April 27, 2004.

The wind gusted hard over the Kansas prairie that day, with no trees or buildings to slow it as it passed through the complex of four baseball diamonds where I was sitting. But the sun warmed my face and the metal bleachers. I was comfortable in short sleeves, having transplanted myself from the much colder winds of Minnesota almost four years earlier.

A notebook sat open in my lap, and I alternated between it and a separate, spiral-bound scorebook lying next to me on the bench, trying to record every possible statistic from the Basehor-Linwood High School softball game. Basehor was a small but growing suburb west of Kansas City. Linwood was even smaller — so small, in fact, that the school was often referred to simply as "Basehor." The Bobcats were having a tough year in most sports and the *Basehor Sentinel*, which was printed weekly, didn't have many readers. But I was a "sportswriter," making $8 an hour. At the time that was enough to puff out my chest a little. The job had more or less fallen into my lap — I showed up for the interview and was told the position was mine if I wanted it based on the recommendation of one of my professors. This did not seem particularly strange to me. After all, I was extremely talented and creative. My mom had told me so repeatedly.

The green-clad Lady Bobcats trotted back to their dugout and I briefly allowed my mind to wander, leaning back and feeling the familiar sensation of the bleacher behind me on my shoulder blades. I had a lot to daydream about. I was in my senior year at the University of Kansas, just three weeks away from holding my journalism degree on graduation day. I had my job at the *Sentinel*, and I was also the Student Senate reporter for the university newspaper. I wasn't sure anyone outside of Senate actually read those articles, but they were good enough for the other student journalists and the paper's faculty adviser, Malcolm Gibson.

Malcolm was a short, energetic professor with thinning hair and a face that was often flushed with excitement. He was a well-traveled newspaper veteran who mercilessly pointed out every mistake, but was quick to offer praise for a job well done. I lapped up every compliment.

The future I'd envisioned for years seemed almost a given. I was going to be a writer, I was going to travel the world rooting out stories, just as I had dreamed about doing since seventh grade. That was the year I decided that life as a professional athlete probably wasn't in the cards for a kid who was a little short, a little slow and carried about 30 pounds of extra weight.

My body had always been a source of some discomfort for me. I was healthy and active, but had never been slim. My older brother, Josh, and my younger brother, Dan, were both rail-thin and their brotherly teasing had gotten to me more than it should have. I loved playing pick-up basketball, but the very mention of "shirts and skins" made me nervous because of the jiggly spare tire above my waistband. I had similar apprehensions about going to the beach.

But even that was getting better in that spring of 2004, my last year of college. KU had finished construction on a large, modern fitness center. Multiple weight machines and benches meant no waiting and extended gym hours meant I could pop down and lift whenever I had a spare hour. I had finally gotten into a regular workout routine, and my body had started to respond. I walked with my head higher as my flabby physique began to harden, especially in the arms and upper chest. The gut was still a problem area, but after seeing some results, I was more and more excited about going to the gym and trying to work it off — as long as I didn't have to work too hard.

I had grown up as the classic suburban kid, blessed in both nature and nurture with two intelligent, attentive parents. I coasted through school, leaning on my reading and writing ability to push me to the top in most subjects without much effort and avoiding the more challenging math and science courses, or relying on my equally bright friends to help me with the heavy lifting.

I continued to take the path of least resistance in college. I had been accepted by an Ivy League school but quickly cast that aside. It sounded expensive, and hard. At Kansas I wouldn't have to strain to stay on top, and the place handed me a full scholarship based on my standardized test scores.

The softball game ended with another hard-fought loss for Basehor. I flipped the pages of the notebook, preparing for the second game of the doubleheader. I hoped it would end in a Basehor victory so I'd have something cheerful to write about.

Then I felt a shiver go up my back. It was an odd sensation. The wind was gusting, but I was comfortably warm.

I tried to concentrate as the next game started. But the shivering continued and I started to think that maybe the breeze was too much for my bare arms. At the next break, I folded up my notebook and slipped off the bleachers, walking slowly along the field's fence to the parking lot. My legs felt heavy.

I slid into the driver's seat of the old, white minivan that my parents had handed down to me, glad to be out of the wind for a moment. There was a purple fleece sweatshirt in the passenger seat and I silently congratulated myself for being so well-prepared as I pulled it over my head. A sudden spell of nausea washed over me and my stomach turned. I spent a few minutes sitting there in the van, breathing slowly and trying to fight it off. Eventually I returned to the bleachers, but it wasn't long before I could no longer ignore what my body was telling me.

The game had advanced to the third inning, but I hadn't made a single scratch in the notebook. My thoughts were swimming in my head and the only thing I could focus on was the sick feeling growing in my stomach. I was shivering with cold, but a clammy sheen of sweat shone on my hands. I felt like doing nothing but lying down, and decided it was time to go.

Back in the van, I was barely on the highway before I had my cell phone out.

"Marso residence," my mom answered, back in Minnesota.

"Hi Mom," I mumbled.

"Andrew!" she said, her voice rising into a happy, singsong pitch, "How are you?"

"Not so good," I said. "What does it mean if you're sweating but you can't stop shivering?"

"Oh-h-h," she said, her voice dropping. "You probably have the flu. Does your stomach hurt?"

"Yeah, it feels like I have to throw up," I said. "Do you think I should go to Watkins?"

Watkins Memorial Health Center was the on-campus medical clinic for KU students.

A moment of silence followed as Mom tried to gauge the seriousness of my symptoms from 500 miles away.

"Well, why don't you get some sleep and then go in the morning if you still feel sick," she said.

This seemed like a reasonable plan, especially because I had little desire to go to Watkins. I had only been there a couple times in my college career, but the place had the reputation of telling most patients they were either pregnant or had a sexually transmitted disease, no matter their symptoms.

Back at campus, I eased the van into a spot in the parking lot just down the hill from Pearson Hall, taking another moment to sit, breathe and try to settle my stomach. I glanced into the back of the van to see if there was anything I needed to take in with me. Windbreaker, nylon warm-up pants, a few Nutri-Grain bars and a small mound of trash — nope, nothing crucial. I slid my notebook under my arm and started to trudge up the hill.

Pearson was a scholarship hall, something that, as far as I knew, was unique to KU. It was 47 other academically focused guys and I living in relative harmony. We all did a share of the cooking and cleaning to keep room and board low and we had to maintain a certain GPA to stay in the hall. I liked to call it a fraternity for nerds.

As I came through the front door I was greeted by the hall director, a grad student in charge of keeping order. His room opened onto the foyer so he could monitor comings and goings.

He told me to come see him if I got worse and felt I had to see a doctor. I said I would, but as I climbed the stairs to my room, I was determined not to come back down until I was better.

As a freshman I had let a simple case of the flu balloon into severe dehydration and a trip to the hospital. I figured that this time I'd be fine if I just got enough fluids.

Turning left into the second floor hallway, I entered my dorm room and tossed the notebook down on the small sofa in the middle of the floor. The living space was only about 10 feet by 12 feet, but Gustavo and I had stuffed it full of every luxury we could — including part of a sofa I had found at a thrift store for $50.

I shifted a pile of dirty clothes from the bed to the sofa and lay down with one hand on my forehead. Gustavo's mass of curly black hair flipped to the side as he spun around in his desk chair and looked at me.

"Hey man, what's wrong?" he asked, his thick accent causing me to pause for a second.

"I'm not sure," I said slowly. "I was fine a couple hours ago and now I just feel really sick."

"Do you need anything?" he asked.

"I don't know. I guess you could empty that trash can and put it here by the bed in case I need to throw up," I answered.

As Gus took the trash out, I tried to go over a mental checklist of what I had to do the next day. There were stories for Basehor — I'd have to get up early to finish them — a Student Senate meeting in the evening … and something else, I thought. I couldn't put my finger on it. Man, it was hard to focus all of a sudden.

There was a knock at the door and a head poked in, along with the eye-popping, slightly maniacal grin of my buddy Randy.

"Hey, man, you're back already. Wanna play 1080?"

1080 was a snowboarding game on the Nintendo 64. Randy and I, and our friend Clay, were hooked on it, but I wasn't even feeling up for video games.

"Naw, man, I'm sick," I mumbled, shielding my eyes from the light of the hallway.

"Oh shoot," Randy said, the grin quickly disappearing. "Do you want me to get you anything?"

"No, it's cool, Gus is taking care of me."

"All right. I'll come check on you tomorrow."

Randy shut the door and I tried to force my mind back to tomorrow's responsibilities. I wasn't sure I'd be up for covering that Senate meeting.

"Hey Gus, could you make a phone call for me?" I asked as Gustavo returned with the empty wastebasket.

Even talking on the phone seemed as if it would take more energy than I could muster. So I tossed him my cell and told him to call Michelle, the editor at *The University Daily Kansan*, and let her know she might have to find someone else to go to the meeting.

But as his conversation with her went in circles, I realized she had no idea I had a foreign roommate and that his accent probably made her think the call was some kind of joke.

I motioned for Gustavo to give me the phone and my suspicion was confirmed when I heard an amused Michelle ask what was going on.

"I'm feeling really sick," I said. "I don't think I'll be able to cover Senate tomorrow."

"Really?" she asked. "Is it that bad?"

"Honestly, I can't remember the last time I felt this bad," I mumbled.

"OK, that's fine, don't worry about Senate," she answered. "Just get better. I'll bring you over some chicken soup tomorrow."

I set the phone on the bookshelf next to the bed and decided I had done all I could to set things aside for the next day. After shifting around a bit to try to find the best position for my roiling stomach, I drifted off.

Hours later, something broke through my haze of sleep; my hands were cold. Ugh, it was so strange — I was sweating, yet shivery at the same time, and now my fingers felt icy. I brought my arms under the covers and jammed them between my thighs to try to warm them up. I glanced at the clock next to the bed and the red digital numbers glared "1:25." There was an odd clicking noise coming from behind the sofa and I realized that Gus had taken his laptop over there and was sitting on the floor, typing away. A soft glow emanated from that area. Apparently he also had his desk lamp back there. He must have been typing something from hard copy and had taken it behind the sofa so the light wouldn't disturb me.

My hands began to warm up and I was able to close my eyes and drift off again.

CHAPTER 2

A RUDE AWAKENING

The next time I woke up and looked over at the clock, it read "5:04." My throat was parched. God, I was thirsty. As I rolled the covers off and dropped my feet to the floor, I got a prickly sensation, as if my feet were asleep. I figured it would pass. Gustavo was nowhere to be seen.

As I made my way downstairs to the kitchen, the prickling in my feet remained and I had to step carefully and lean on the railing just to keep from collapsing. There was something else, too: hundreds of tiny purple pinpricks, like some kind of rash, all across my forearms. Strange. But I didn't really feel that much sicker. My head still hurt and the nausea was still there, but no worse than the night before. My most pressing concern at the moment was wetting my throat.

In the kitchen, the cabinet that usually held clean cups was barren. Slamming it shut, I grabbed a blue plastic cup from a pile of dirty ones next to the gleaming, stainless steel, industrial dishwasher. I took it to the sink, swished in a tiny pool of water and rinsed it out. I filled the cup nearly to the brim with orange juice from the fridge, then sat down at one of the dining tables and began to gulp down the cool liquid.

In a few hours the room would be full of guys stumbling in for some cereal before going to class, but that early in the morning it was just me and my thoughts. For some reason those thoughts were hard to pin down. I knew I had articles to write for Basehor, but I couldn't seem to remember what they were about. One was about that softball game, but the others were hazy. I couldn't focus. Probably still half-asleep, I figured.

I returned the empty cup to the pile of dirty dishes and began to trudge back upstairs. If the trip downstairs was hard, going up was nearly impossible. Putting pressure on each stair gave me shooting pains up and down my legs, and I found myself leaning on the railing more heavily and taking each step slowly.

When I got back to my room, I sat down at the computer with my notebook open and tried to type. I wanted to get at least one or two articles done before I went back to bed. But something was wrong with my brain. I could read my notes, but they didn't seem to mean anything. One sentence wouldn't connect to the next. I tried to type out a lead for the softball story, but it just wouldn't come. The words were swimming around in my head and I couldn't figure out how to fit them together.

It was a feeling I'd never experienced — not writer's block, just a complete inability to concentrate. I couldn't imagine doing anything but going back to bed. I got up from the chair and stumbled around the sofa, gripping the back of it for support because my feet wouldn't fully cooperate. When I finally got around to the bed, I fell back in it and was asleep almost immediately.

I was dozing restlessly when a knock at the door woke me. The clock blinked "11:14."

"Andy," a voice on the other side of the door said. "It's Clay."

"Yeah, come in," I groaned.

Clay opened the door slowly and stepped inside. He wore khaki shorts and a polo shirt and his blond hair was neatly combed and parted — he'd already been to class that morning.

Clay and I had been friends since our first day on campus, freshman year. There was a dance out in the street in front of the hall that night, a social event to kick off the new school year. Thing was, neither Clay nor I were particularly keen on being social with a huge group of people we didn't know. That wasn't the way we were wired.

The two of us ended up on a small hill across the street, watching other guys flirt with girls in tight jeans and low-cut tops — the kind of girls we wished we had the nerve to talk to. Instead we talked to each other, yelling over the thump of the music. A week later I spent Labor Day weekend at his parents' house in nearby Olathe and we went to a Kansas City Chiefs game. From then on he, Randy and I had been a tight group. We had recently signed a lease on a three-bedroom apartment in Kansas City, where we planned to live together after graduation.

That was far from either of our minds at the time, though.

"Dude, Randy told me you were sick," Clay said, eyeing the empty trash can next to the bed. "How you feelin?"

I took one arm out from under the covers and looked at it. The rash was worse; the purple blotches seemed bigger and more densely packed.

"Man, I can't remember the last time I felt this bad," I said through clenched teeth. I held out my arm. "Look at this rash. Isn't it weird?"

Clay took a few steps toward the bed and leaned in for a better look. His brow furrowed and his lips pursed into a thin line. Then he straightened back up and looked me in the eye.

"Have you called Watkins?" he asked.

"No," I said. "I can't get out of bed. My feet hurt too much."

I rolled from my side onto my back and stared up at the metal bars under Gustavo's mattress. My face burned and a thin layer of sweat covered my body, but the shivers persisted. I didn't know what was going on — all I knew was that I wanted to rest and feel better.

But Clay had made a decision.

"We're going to Watkins," he said, picking up the phone by my desk to call to let them know we were coming, and throwing me my black shower sandals that sat by the door.

After a bit of gentle prodding, he was able to get me to sit up in bed. Dressed only in my boxers and a T-shirt, I tried to pull on a pair of jeans. For some reason, my fingers wouldn't work on the button.

"I need my warm-up pants," I said. "They're in the van. It's parked down by Sellards."

Clay frowned, but he grabbed the keys off my desk and hurried out of the room. Minutes later he came back with the navy blue nylon pants, and I slowly pulled them on.

"I pulled my car up in front of the hall," he said.

I slipped my feet into the sandals, feeling a strong tingling between my toes where the strap hit my skin. Holding Clay's arm for support, I tried to stand.

Daggers of pain shot up my legs as I put my full weight through my feet. Gasping, I collapsed back into bed, my head in my hands.

"I can't walk," I moaned.

"Just sit tight," Clay said. "I'll go downstairs and find somebody to help."

Clay strode quickly into the hallway and headed down to the dining room, taking the stairs two at a time. All his instincts were telling him something was really wrong here. I had class that morning and he knew it wasn't like me to skip. Then there was that rash, which was just strange. But the most frightening thing for him was my immobility. Clay had seen people who were exhausted, dehydrated or hungover and didn't *want* to get out of bed. But he had never seen someone our age who wanted to get up and walk, but physically couldn't do it.

Clay had seen Joe, a Brillo-haired friend of ours, eating lunch downstairs and figured Joe would be able to help him get me to the car. But he had to take care to let Joe know this was for real. Guys in the hall were known to prank each other and he didn't have time to convince Joe that he wasn't trying to set him up.

The dining room was nearly deserted, but Joe sat munching a sandwich and reading one of the many newspapers strewn on the four long, rectangular tables.

"Joe, Andy's sick," Clay said, putting as much gravity in his voice as he could. "I'm going to take him to Watkins, but he can't get out of bed. I need you to help me get him down to the car."

Joe looked up from his paper, his eyes narrowed in suspicion. But he saw no trace of mischief on Clay's face, only an anxious stare.

"OK," Joe said, and stood up.

As he and Clay climbed the stairs, though, he couldn't help but make one little dig.

"Clay, if I get whatever Andy's got, I'm holding you personally responsible," he deadpanned.

Clay just quickened his pace.

I was still sitting on the edge of the bed when Clay and Joe entered the room. My chin was slumped down near my chest and I breathed slowly and deeply, trying to stave off the nausea.

"Ready to go?" Clay asked tentatively.

I nodded and he and Joe positioned themselves to my right and left. I gripped their shoulders and hoisted myself upright, slinging one arm around each of their necks. Now I could put one foot in front of the other, as long as I leaned heavily on my friends.

Clay was steady on my right side, but Joe was a couple inches shorter, and slightly built. He stumbled under my weight, but managed to keep his balance even as we descended the stairs. We met no one on our way down and I was vaguely glad of it — thinking it would have been embarrassing for someone to see me like that.

Clay had propped open the heavy front door and when we reached the foyer, the midday sun was streaming through.

"It's nice and warm out," he said. "You'll feel better once we get outside."

I nodded, but I was skeptical. My whole body was starting to ache and I could see no way a little fresh air would pull me out of it. But when we stepped out the door, I did feel a little better. The sun beat down like a soothing splash of warm water on my clammy forearms. Maybe I wasn't so sick after all. Maybe this would all pass soon enough.

Clay and Joe got me to the passenger door and I slumped into the car, not bothering with my seat belt. Clay got in the driver's side and as we began to pull away from the hall Joe's small figure receded in the rearview mirror.

The drive to Watkins was brief. I left the window open and tried to suck up more of the sunlight, but the burst of well-being I had felt moments earlier was already gone. The trip down the stairs had taken more out of me than it should have and I might have fallen asleep in the car if not for my sweaty, achy discomfort. A string of stomach acid seared my throat on its way up to my mouth and I spat it out the open window.

Clay looked over. He was saying something to me, but it didn't seem important, and at the moment I couldn't quite grasp what an appropriate response would be. I mumbled something back, hoping he would let me be.

When we arrived at Watkins, my head was tilted back against the headrest and I was breathing heavily through my mouth. My hands felt tingly and I wondered if I was hyperventilating. Clay asked if I could get inside with his help alone. I shook my head.

He rushed in and returned moments later with a wheelchair. Soon he was wheeling me in, up to the check-in counters where a young man, probably a student employee, looked at me from his office chair.

"I called earlier about my friend," Clay said. "He's really feeling sick. I've never been here before, so I don't know what the process is, but I think he needs to see someone right now."

The young guy motioned us to a circular, wooden desk where the nurses sat. There, Clay tried to reiterate the seriousness of the situation.

"My friend is really sick," he said. I looked up mournfully at the midde-aged woman with short blond hair behind the desk, as if to illustrate his point.

The nurse looked down at me from her high swivel chair. My head lolled around. My eyes were half-closed, my face was slightly bluish and my arms were covered with purple polka dots that were now dime size. Her eyes widened.

"I'm going to take you back to Urgent Care," she said, hurrying around the desk to take Clay's place behind the wheelchair.

While I was being wheeled to Urgent Care, Dr. Leah Luckeroth was in her office at Watkins, untying her brown work shoes. She was about to change into sneakers and take a short walk on her lunch break.

Dr. Luckeroth was a small-town Kansas homecoming queen who went on to college and later medical school, inspired in part by her veterinarian father. She was a diligent student and could have made a lot of money in private practice, but accepted a job at Watkins instead because she shared custody of two daughters with her ex-husband and liked the flexible hours. Her tenure at Watkins included recognition for a ground-breaking tuberculosis screening program for international students.

Just as she was about to slip off her untied shoes, the phone on her desk rang.

"Dr. Luckeroth speaking."

"Leah, it's Kim," the voice on the other end said. "I'm in Urgent Care and I really think you need to see this student who just came in. His friend brought him in in a wheelchair and he's blue in the face."

"OK, I'll meet you there."

Dr. Luckeroth hung up the phone and quickly retied her work shoes. Standing up, she snatched a white lab coat off the back of her chair and swung her arms through the sleeves, stopping briefly in the hallway to spray some antibiotic liquid on her hands and grab a pair of gloves out of a box on the counter. Then she was off to Urgent Care, which at Watkins was just a few beds separated by curtains. I was the only patient there, so the curtains weren't drawn and she could see me clearly as soon as she walked into the room. Two nurses had already helped me into the bed and I was lying back on the plain white sheets.

I looked up from the bed to see a woman in a lab coat with light brown hair approaching me. Clay was now quarantined in a small office nearby, and I was by myself. But this woman in the lab coat gave me a reassuring smile.

"I'm Dr. Luckeroth," she said. "And your name is…?"

"Andy Marso."

Her eyes fell to my right arm. She picked it up, studied it, gave it a little squeeze.

"How long have you had this rash, Andy?" she asked.

I tried to think. How long had it been there? Had I seen it at all the night before, even faintly? I didn't think so.

"I think it kind of just popped up this morning," I replied.

Dr. Luckeroth turned to Kim, the nurse.

"Call 9-1-1," she said.

She said it in a calm, almost matter-of-fact way, but there was a firmness to her voice.

"I want an ambulance over here and I want him taken to Lawrence Memorial as soon as possible," she added. "And get Dr. Brown and anybody else who's available in here, too."

At that point everything started moving very quickly.

Kim immediately rushed out of the room.

Dr. Luckeroth turned to the other nurse.

"We need to get an IV started," she said.

The other nurse went over to a drawer across the room and started rustling inside it.

Dr. Luckeroth turned back to me.

"Andy, do your parents live around here?" she asked.

I shook my head.

"I'm from Minnesota."

"OK, well we need to call them," she said, taking a pen and paper out of the front pocket of her lab coat. "What's their number?"

It was a simple question, but I blanked. Panic rose inside me. Why couldn't I remember my own home phone number? Then, in a flash of clarity, I remembered the area code and the rest flowed out.

"My grandma will probably answer," I said. "Her name is Dorothy."

My mom's mother lived with us in a cozy apartment attached to our house. A long-time widow, grandma had served as nanny to me and my brothers, reading to us and taking us to the park almost every day we weren't in school so Mom and Dad could work. It had occurred to me that she would likely be the only one home.

For some reason, I didn't think to ask Dr. Luckeroth what was wrong with me. She continued asking me questions — how long had I been feeling ill, where was I the night before, where I lived — while other activity swirled around the two of us. Dr. Brown, who looked vaguely familiar, came in and Dr. Luckeroth turned and said something softly in his ear, handing him the pad of paper with my parents' number on it. He quickly left the room. Kim returned and told Dr. Luckeroth an ambulance was on its way. Then she helped the other nurse poke an IV needle into my arm. I winced. The nurse placed an oxygen mask over my nose and mouth and held it there, telling me to breathe deeply.

Despite all the activity, I felt an odd sense of relief. Now that I was here, at least I didn't have to worry about whether I was sick enough to go to the doctor. I didn't have to worry about walking on my hurting feet. They could just wheel me wherever I needed to go on this bed. It was out of my hands and in the hands of medical professionals. They were going to take care of me and I had no doubt they'd make me feel better.

Even as two paramedics arrived, wheeled me out a side door and put me in an ambulance, I wasn't particularly worried. Just sick. Just sick and aching and nauseated and tired and wanting to feel better.

Dr. Luckeroth, on the other hand, was worried. She had managed to keep her emotions under wraps and do her job. But as she stood at the side door with Kim watching the ambulance pull away, she looked down at her hands and realized they were shaking. My purple rash was a nearly unmistakable symptom, especially if it had really come on as quickly as I'd said it had. The blue tint of my face was also a bad sign. It suggested that my lungs were compromised and I wasn't getting enough oxygen in my blood. She had never seen meningococcal sepsis in person, but she was pretty sure that's what I had.

At that moment, Dr. Robert Brown was trying to get my parents on the phone to tell them I was being taken to the emergency room at Lawrence Memorial Hospital. Dr. Luckeroth tried to calculate in her head just how far away Minnesota was and how long it would take my parents to arrive. She imagined what sort of condition I might be in by then and shuddered, thinking of her daughters. She would give them each an extra-long hug when she got home that night.

While I was in an ambulance, my dad was 500 miles away, in the kitchen of our house in St. Cloud, Minnesota, making a sardine sandwich. Dad worked as a collections analyst at Fingerhut, a mail-order catalog retail outlet. In more than 20 years with the company he rarely missed a day and he usually rushed through his lunch break, if he came home at noon at all. This particular day was no different. He ate standing up, leaning his chin out over the counter to keep stray food from falling on his button-down shirt and dark slacks. Wire-rim glasses bounced up and down as he chewed and he ran his free hand through his black hair, trying to place it over a growing bald spot.

When he had pulled into the driveway minutes earlier, he'd noticed that Grandma's car wasn't there — she was possibly buying groceries or at the senior center playing cards. He reminded himself to lock the door on the way out because he would be leaving the house empty.

Then the phone rang.

"Hello," Dad said in the soft, deep telephone voice that always made him sound tired.

"Um-m, hello," a male voice on the other end said. "Is this Mr. Marso?"

"Yes, this is Harry," Dad said with just a touch of impatience, assuming it was a telemarketer.

"Oh, um-m, this is Dr. Brown from Watkins Health Center at KU," he said. "Your son, Andrew, came to see me a few months ago for a toenail fungus. I don't know if he mentioned me or not."

"Well, no, sorry," Dad said.

"Oh, OK," Dr. Brown said. "Well, Andrew was just here; one of his friends brought him in. We think he might have meningitis."

"Meningitis?" Dad said.

"Well, yes, he has the purple rash," Dr. Brown replied.

Dad had heard of meningitis, but didn't know much about it and he was not sure what to make of this phone call. So his son had come to Watkins with a rash. Andrew was 22 years old and could probably handle it. Was there some question of insurance or something? Why did it seem like this doctor was being evasive?

"Can I talk to Andrew?" he asked. "Can you put him on the phone?"

"No, I'm afraid he's already left," Dr. Brown said. "He's being transferred to Lawrence Memorial Hospital. But we've already informed the head of infectious disease over there about what's going on and we've given him your phone number. So I suspect you'll be getting a call from him soon."

"Um-m-m, OK," Dad said, still a little confused. "So I should just wait for him to call?"

"Yes, I'd stay by the phone," Dr. Brown said. "It shouldn't be long."

Dad hung up and stood in the kitchen for a second, not sure what to do next. Then he crossed the dining room to a four-tiered wooden shelf in the corner that had a set of old Funk & Wagnalls encyclopedias on it.

Bending down, Dad extracted volume 17, which went from "Marin" to

"Monad." He flipped to page 176, where he came to the half-page entry for "Meningitis."

"... inflammatory condition of the meninges or membranes investing the brain and spinal cord," it said.

He skimmed down a few paragraphs until the words "school dormitory" caught his eye. Apparently there was a form of this disease that was more common to people living in close quarters, like dorms or army barracks.

"Most cases of meningitis, particularly those caused by bacteria, have an abrupt onset, with symptoms including headache, stiff neck, fever, nausea, vomiting, listlessness, and irritability, often leading to stupor and coma. It progresses rapidly and may lead to death if untreated in 24 to 72 hours. Bacterial meningitis is effectively treated by early administration of antibiotics."

Dad closed the book and set it on the dining room table slowly. He could hear his heart beating hard and fast, throbbing in his ears. He took a few breaths and told himself to relax. This book said that if Andrew got early treatment, the prognosis was good and Andrew was getting early treatment, right? After all, it was just the night before he had called home and told his mother he was starting to feel ill. So he was well within the 24- to 72-hour window and everything should be fine, right?

Now Dad was anxious for the phone to ring again. He got out of the chair and headed for the spare bedroom to fire up the computer. He needed to know more about meningitis.

About the time Dad was logging on, my ambulance arrived at Lawrence Memorial and I was rolled through the hallways on a gurney. The medics wheeled me into an exam room and put me on a table that was arched slightly, like a recliner. A nurse came in and helped me remove my shirt. She slipped a hospital gown over my shoulders and attached a fresh IV bag to the tube that protruded from my arm.

"Do you need a blanket?" she asked.

I nodded vigorously. My entire body shook.

Teeth chattering, I looked around the room. It was slightly larger than the exam room I'd visited the previous summer at the St. Cloud Hospital. On that sultry evening, I'd received a concussion in a collision at second base during a bar-league softball game, one of the most serious medical incidents of my life to that point. My brain was similarly hazy then, but without all this nausea and cold sweats.

I leaned back on the hard table and focused on breathing. In and out, in and out, trying to ward off the dark spots at the edges of my vision. My heart was racing and sweat covered me under the wool blanket the nurse had provided. I clenched my jaw against a growing pain in my hands and feet, which felt as if they were being pricked with needles.

It wasn't long before the doctor opened the glass door to the room and pulled aside the curtain that surrounded my bed. He was young for a doctor — dark-haired and wearing light green scrubs with a V-neck that exposed just a wisp of chest hair. He was trailed by two other people in light blue scrubs, one a girl, one a large guy.

The doc was staring at a chart but looked up quickly and put his hand on my shoulder.

"Andrew, right?" he said.

Only my family called me "Andrew," but I nodded anyway, eager to get to the part where he made me feel better.

"I'm Dr. Christopher Penn," he said. "We think you may have meningitis. Do you know if anyone you live with, or work with, has been sick recently?"

I couldn't come up with anything and again just wanted him to get on with the treatment. I shook my head.

"OK, well, we're going to run some tests, all right?" he said. "We have to do a CT scan because sometimes meningitis can infect your brain and we want to make sure that isn't happening, all right?"

I nodded again and soon the two in the blue scrubs were helping me onto another gurney. As they wheeled me into the hallway, I tried to pull meningitis information out of my memory banks.

What did I know about it? Where had I seen that word before?

There was a brochure about meningitis pinned up on the message board at Pearson. I must have passed it a thousand times and seen the word "**MENINGITIS**" in bold letters, all caps. But I'd never stopped to read it.

I remembered hearing about meningitis in the news once, though. As I recalled, one of the Spice Girls had it over in England. Funny how you remember stupid things like that. I thought that it was like mono or strep throat, nothing too serious. I was at the hospital now, so the doctors would make me better. That's what they do, right?

As I entered the CT tube, I thought of an old childhood friend back in Minnesota, Rick Reisdorf. He had a benign brain tumor in 10th grade.

Surgeons removed it and he made a full recovery, but still had to go back and have another scan every now and then. I tried to recall whether I had gotten a scan when I had that concussion, but I had trouble accessing the memory. My brain was getting more fuzzy.

The machine whirred and clicked. Lights flashed over and over. I kept sweating and shivering and the technician outside reminded me to keep my head still. I slowed my breathing again and closed my eyes. I was tired, so tired, but I was too miserable to fall asleep.

Soon the test was over and the technician was wheeling me out to the hall, where the two people in the light blue scrubs were waiting. The tech was young, too, with a light beard and blue eyes. He smiled down at me and put a hand on my shoulder.

"Your scans look good," he said. "I know you're scared, but you're gonna be all right."

I nodded and tried to smile back. Actually I wasn't all that scared. I just wanted to stop shaking so I could rest. I just wanted someone to give me something to warm up — something more than this damn thin blanket.

We returned to the glass-door room, the guy and the girl in the scrubs and I. They reached under my gown, attached some electrodes to my chest and plugged me into the machines that were against the back wall of the room. Soon Dr. Penn was back, sliding open the glass door and pulling aside the curtain again.

"Your scans came back negative," he said. "That's a good sign."

I nodded. Whatever. I was still shaking and sweating, my teeth were knocking together and my chest heaved as I breathed in and out rapidly, still nauseated.

A voice inside me screamed, "Just get to the part where you make me feel better!"

"We need to run one more test," he said. "We need to draw some fluid out of your spine to check it for bacteria, OK?"

I didn't like the sound of that.

"My sp-sp-spine?" I choked, through the clattering of my teeth.

He nodded solemnly.

"It sounds scary, but it's actually quite safe. And we need to do it to find out for sure what's making you sick."

I would rather not have a needle in my spine, but this guy could do whatever he had to do, as long as it would help him make me feel better.

"OK," I said.

I had second thoughts almost immediately as I watched the girl in the scrubs begin to unwrap the needle from its plastic covering. It looked huge, like a pelican's beak with a little cylindrical canister on the end. I gritted my teeth and tried to steel myself against what was coming.

"OK, Andrew, I need you to turn onto your side and curl up in a ball for me," the doc said, taking the giant syringe from the girl.

Still shaking, I slowly did as I was told and found that getting in the fetal position was kind of comforting. Someone pulled up the back of my gown and rubbed something cold and wet on my lower back.

"This is going to burn a little, but I need you to stay very still, OK?" Dr. Penn said.

I nodded. As long as my spine was involved I was going to stay as still as death. I tried to slow down my breathing and hold back the shivers.

When the needle went in, breathing was no longer something I could control. I gasped, held my breath, clenched my jaw and tried to keep from crying out. It was a white-hot poker, burning a hole in my back. My eyes bugged out and my tingly toes curled. It seemed to take an eternity, but finally the flaming sword withdrew, leaving just a dull ache. I exhaled.

"There, all done," Dr. Penn said. "Good job."

I felt a cotton ball being pressed against my back and I resumed shaking and hyperventilating. The pain of the lumbar puncture or "spinal tap" cut a clear path through my hazy thoughts. They just stuck a needle in my *spine*. They would not do that for just anything. This is not the flu; this is not even mono or strep throat. This is bad. I am in trouble here.

I rolled over onto my back. My shaking worsened. My teeth clanged together and my breath came in short, rapid-fire bursts. My chest was starting to burn. Waves of panic washed over me and I felt tears forming in the corners of my eyes.

"What's happening?" I moaned.

"We're doing everything we can to help you, Andrew," Dr. Penn said.

He had the fluid-filled vial from the syringe in his hand and was staring at it. Then he looked up and turned to the scrub-girl.

"Get him some oxygen and get him started on Rocephin," he said, then turned and hurried out of the room.

The girl put a clear plastic mask over my face, securing it with nylon straps that pulled at the hair on the back of my head and around my ears. I sucked in greedily, my breath fogging the mask, but the air kept coming in short, quick bursts. I hadn't run a step, I was just lying there in bed, and I couldn't catch my breath. This is bad, I thought.

Dr. Penn soon returned.

"We've decided to transfer you to KU Med in Kansas City," he said. "They're better equipped to help you there. I'd like to get you there as soon as possible, so I'm waiting to hear if they have a helicopter available. Otherwise we'll put you on an ambulance."

I moaned inside the oxygen mask. Even with the lights and sirens of an ambulance, it could take 45 minutes to drive from Lawrence to Kansas City. The thought of spending that much time on the road while I shivered and struggled for breath seemed hellish. If they could make me feel better in Kansas City, then I wanted to get there as soon as possible. I needed that helicopter.

The next few minutes were an eternity. I breathed rapidly inside the mask, tasting plastic, and stared up at the TV bolted to the wall in front of me. It wasn't on. The screen was blank, but for some reason I kept looking into that blackness. It was comfortingly mundane in a room otherwise full of beeping, blinking machines that were starting to scare me.

Dr. Penn watched those machines, wrote notes on a clipboard and occasionally came over and pressed the skin on my arm. When he touched me, I tore my eyes away from the TV and tried to look at what he was doing. My arms were swollen, light purple all over. They throbbed.

Finally another guy in blue scrubs opened the glass door a crack. He poked his head in, motioned the doctor over and spoke to him briefly. I couldn't hear what they were saying. My breathing seemed really loud inside the mask. The guy slid the door closed again and the doctor came back to the bedside.

"The helicopter is on its way," he said.

Good, I thought, and turned my head to stare at the TV screen again. Just take me to where they can make me feel better.

"I need to get on the phone with the doctors there to let them know you're coming, OK?" Dr. Penn said. "I'll be right back."

I nodded.

He left, but the girl in the scrubs stayed. I guessed she was a nurse or something. Maybe another doctor. She was slim with straight brown hair. Kind of plain-looking, but her eyes were warm. She stood next to the bed.

She looked at the machines, then she looked back at me. I breathed hard and fast, my chest heaving and the air rasping shallowly in my throat. She reached down and grabbed my hand with one of hers, which was encased in a rubber glove. My hand was prickly. I tried to squeeze hers, but my fingers were tired. The room seemed out of focus.

I lay like that for awhile, aching all over, just trying to breathe. Should I have thrown up by now? Would I feel better if I threw up? What would happen if I threw up inside this mask? That would be gross. Keep breathing.

The relative quiet was soon broken by a surge of chaos. The glass door slid open, Dr. Penn strode back in, two people followed him, and the girl in the scrubs let go of my hand and got out of their way. The new people, one man and one woman, both wore jumpsuits. The doc was talking to them, talking to them fast and saying a lot of numbers. They kept nodding. I couldn't catch all his words. I didn't know what he was talking about, anyway.

Another gurney was wheeled in and placed next to the examining table. The people in the jumpsuits helped me onto it, lifting me up and setting me down. I couldn't help them. My arms and legs hung limp.

Then they were wheeling me out of the room.

"Have you ever ridden in a helicopter before?" the woman asked.

I tried to remember. When I was little, my family occasionally went to an amusement park in northern Minnesota called Paul Bunyan Land. I remembered that they used to sell helicopter rides there. I remembered asking Dad if we could take one. I didn't remember if we ever did or not. The more I reached for the memory, the harder it became to access. Why couldn't I remember? The panic came back at me. I shook my head, frantically, not knowing what else to do.

"Don't worry, we're going to take good care of you," the woman said.

Soon we were outside and it was loud. The helicopter was running, the rotors thundering overhead and drowning out all other noise. The sun hurt my eyes. I shut them, but then forced them open again. I was afraid to fall asleep.

I felt the gurney being lifted off the ground and then sliding into the back of the helicopter. The man in the jumpsuit disappeared; the woman stayed by my side. The back of the helicopter was cramped. There were all sorts of electrical machines hanging from the ceiling. Buttons, dials, lights, like the ones in the room I was just in. The woman pulled a helmet over her head, a big one with a plastic visor on the front, the kind you see in the movies. The electrodes were still on my chest, with wires running from them. She plugged the other ends of those wires into the machines overhead and I felt us begin to lift off the ground.

Inside the cabin the roar of the chopper was muffled just enough that I could barely make out the beeping of the machines. I wondered what it meant, what they were saying. It was getting harder to breathe. I was panting, but it seemed that no air was getting in. When I was younger, I'd go to the lake with my friends and we'd submerge ourselves and see who could hold their breath the longest. We stayed down there until we got light-headed and our chests burned, and then sprang to the surface and sucked the sweet air.

I was light-headed. The lights and dials and the woman in the jumpsuit were starting to get blurry. My chest burned. I wanted to spring to the surface and breathe.

I looked at the woman. She just kept staring at the machines, occasionally reaching up to push a button or turn a dial. Why wouldn't she look at me? What was happening? I needed help! Why wouldn't she look me in the eyes?

My eyes shut again. I was tired. No, I didn't want to go to sleep.

I started to pray inside my head: "Our Father, who art in heaven..." over and over. The words started to run together. I lost my place, and suddenly I couldn't remember the prayer I had recited thousands of times since childhood. I switched: "Hail Mary, full of grace...."

Then we were on the ground and I was being carried out of the helicopter. The sun hit me again and it seemed bright enough to pierce through my eyes. All I could see was a flash of white and yellow. All I could hear was the deafening "whoosh" of the chopper's rotors. All I could feel was the daggers of pain shooting through my chest, my arms, my legs. All I could smell and taste was the stale air inside the plastic oxygen mask.

As we rolled toward the door, I saw darkness creeping into the edges of my vision again. I realized I couldn't fight it anymore. I was tired of holding on to the pain, tired of gasping for breath. So I let the darkness come.

I had no near-death experience. I didn't see any lights, or float through a tunnel, or hear the voices of loved ones who'd gone before me. There was just darkness. But it wasn't frightening or evil. It was a soft, warm darkness, as if I were wrapped in a pitch-black, velvet blanket. The pain melted away, all was quiet and I wasn't scared anymore.

It never occurred to me that those might be my last conscious moments on earth. I had realized that this was more than your average flu, but for some reason I never thought I might be dying. Part of that was probably because my fever was clouding my judgment; otherwise the inability to breathe and the helicopter ride would have been tip-offs.

But I also didn't think I could die. I was 22 years old and had never had a major illness or injury — I had never been in the hospital overnight. I was doing everything I had learned in health class. I didn't smoke, I'd never drunk enough to make myself vomit. I didn't have unprotected sex or use drugs. All the things I was warned about, I had them covered.

Yet there I was, rolling across the helipad at KU Med on a stretcher, my body disintegrating with each turn of the wheels. My pulse was racing and my blood pressure had skyrocketed. My heart was frantically trying to pump blood through ravaged vessels and was losing the battle. My lungs, not getting the amount of blood they usually relied on, were gasping at nearly 150 breaths a minute. I still wasn't getting enough oxygen, even at that desperate rate. I had what doctors call "disseminated intravascular coagulation," an often-deadly combination of widespread internal bleeding and out-of-control clotting.

I was melting down, and every internal alarm was going off in my body. It would have taken months for cancer and years for HIV to do what bacterial meningitis had done to me in a matter of hours.

CHAPTER 3

A PARENT'S WORST NIGHTMARE

How had things broken down so fast that a healthy 22-year-old was in organ failure within 24 hours?

It started a week or two earlier, when I came into contact with Neisseria meningitidis. To scientists, Neisseria meningitidis is a gram-negative diplococcal bacterium. To everyone else, it is a germ — one of trillions of tiny organisms that share this planet with us. Except this one, if given the chance, is a stone-cold killer. It lives comfortably in the human throat and upper nasal passages and doctors estimate that about 15 percent of the population carries it around at any given time.

At some point in April 2004, someone passed it to me, possibly when I used a dirty cup or spoon, or took a sip from someone else's beer bottle. It was probably not the first time I'd come in contact with it. I'd possibly received the bacterium several times before and it had just stayed in my throat where it's harmless, as it does in most cases. But this time something was different.

Maybe it was because I hadn't been sleeping enough or eating right. Maybe I'd had a cold and my immune system was compromised. Maybe I should have taken some zinc or vitamin C. For whatever reason, this time that little bug was able to burrow through the protective lining of my throat and get into my spinal cord. At that moment I became one of the approximately 3,000 Americans who suffer a Neisseria meningitidis infection every year.

On April 27, as I sat in class and listened to lectures and stopped by the *Kansan* newsroom to crack jokes with the other reporters and pretend to work, Neisseria meningitidis was inside my spinal cord, eating and breeding. After a few hours, there were billions of those tiny bugs swarming around in my spine and my body finally took notice, sending that shiver up my back as I sat on the bleachers in Basehor.

From then on, things became quite serious, quite quickly. Having spread throughout my spinal cord, the bacteria looked to move into new venues. In other cases it might push into the brain, leaving its victim at risk for brain damage, hearing loss, vision loss or death.

I wasn't that fortunate. In my case, it entered my bloodstream.

The little bugs flowed to all corners of my body, piggybacking through the system of veins and arteries I depended on to live. Each Neisseria meningitidis cell was covered with a layer of caustic endotoxin, and it shed microscopic bits of the poison as it traveled along. Those tiny bits burned holes in the walls of every blood vessel they touched. My white blood cells, wise to the foreign invader, attacked with full force. In the case of Neisseria meningitidis, though, this was a double-edged sword. Every time a white blood cell killed one of the germs, it burst open, spewing more acidic toxins. It was a catch-22: I needed my white blood cells to kill off the bacteria, but with every bacterium's death my condition worsened a bit. It was a little like carpet-bombing your own city to destroy an invading army.

Blood poured out of those holes in my blood vessels and pooled in the soft tissues of my arms and legs. That purple rash I saw when I woke up in the morning was actually thousands of tiny bruises — a telltale sign of what the medical community calls septicemia. Septicemia comes from the word "sepsis," which is Latin for "blood poisoning." Septicemia often leads to septic shock, in which a patient's organs begin to fail. That's the condition I was in when I arrived at KU Med.

The mortality rate for septic shock is about 50 percent.

When I got off that helicopter, I was essentially bleeding to death on the inside. My blood vessels were turning to Swiss cheese and my circulation was ebbing fast. Hours earlier my feet had become cold and tingly, the blood-starved nerves protesting painfully. My fingers lost their flex, to the point where I struggled to fasten the button on a pair of jeans. Now my internal organs had also begun to cry out for more blood. My heart, my lungs, my liver, my kidneys — all were finding it harder to do their jobs properly with every passing minute.

It's not that my body wasn't trying. It was frantically clotting up the mess of holes that had suddenly appeared. But in some cases there were so many holes that entire vessels were clotting and closing over, especially the small, delicate passages in my hands and feet. It was a cascade of events, a rolling snowball headed for a cliff. It was now up to the doctors at KU Med to stop the avalanche.

My parents only knew that their son was sick with some strange affliction they had barely heard of. That he was lying in a hospital bed far away and they needed to get there as soon as possible.

Dr. Penn had called my dad shortly after administering the spinal tap. He told Dad that it usually took at least two hours to get the results of the test back from the lab, but in my case he didn't need to wait. Spinal fluid is translucent when healthy, but mine was so murky with bacteria he could tell just from looking in the syringe that I was severely infected. He told Dad I was being airlifted to KU Med because it had a Level 1 trauma center.

"So, this is quite serious?" Dad asked, still hoping he might be misunderstanding.

"Oh yes," Dr. Penn said. "There's a chance he might not make it through this."

That left no ambiguity. Dad left a frantic message at my mom's law office. Soon Mom was canceling all her appointments and rushing home, and the two of them were headed to Kansas City. With no idea how long they'd be gone, they packed enough to get them through the weekend and caught the first flight out of Minneapolis.

They were met at the Kansas City airport by Clay's mom.

A few hours earlier, while Clay was waiting in that small office at Watkins, Dr. Brown came in and told him that I probably had bacterial meningitis, a contagious and potentially fatal disease. He gave Clay a dose of the antibiotic Cipro in case he had been exposed to the bacteria and told him to gather all the other Pearson guys for a meeting that night. The director of Watkins would be coming by to explain the situation and encourage them all to take antibiotics. Clay asked about me and was told that I was being taken to the hospital, and that I would get the best care possible. The most important thing for him to do, he was told, was try to make sure no one I had been in contact with also got sick.

Clay had every intention of doing that, and he set up the hall meeting later that afternoon. But first he called over to Pearson, told Randy I was being transferred to Lawrence Memorial, and drove straight to the hospital himself.

When he arrived at LMH, he was told he was not allowed to see me, but could sit in the waiting room. Within a few minutes other Pearson guys started to arrive — confused, worried, asking Clay what was going on. Then they heard the roar of the helicopter touching down outside and watched as two paramedics in jumpsuits hurriedly wheeled a prone figure with a hospital gown, an oxygen mask and a thick head of brown hair out to the chopper. They recognized that figure was me.

So it happened that as I lifted off in that chopper, as scared and alone as I'd ever been, a group of guys including Clay, Randy and Gustavo stood outside watching, the wind of the rotors whipping their hair and clothes in all directions. Until then Clay had held out hope that maybe this was all some sort of misunderstanding. That after a round of IV drugs and a big glass of orange juice, I might just spring out of that bed and tell him it was time to go back to the hall and play 1080.

But as he watched the chopper disappear, Clay had his own moment of clarity. His friend wasn't just sick in the everyday sense. No, somewhere along the way this seemingly normal day had gone horribly wrong. His friend was now in a helicopter, on his way to the biggest hospital in the region and he might not be coming back.

Clay allowed himself one brief moment to let that sink in. Then he reached into his pocket, pulled out his cell phone, and set about making sure my parents knew where I was going and how they could get there.

Clay's mom dropped my parents off at KU Med close to 6 p.m. and they were immediately directed to the Medical Intensive Care Unit on the top floor. There they were greeted by a young man — no older than 40 — with a round face and a white lab coat, and an even younger woman in light blue scrubs.

"Hello, I'm Dr. Southwell, but you can call me Jim," the young man said. "I'm a resident here. And this is Rebecca, one of our MIC-U nurses."

"Where's Andrew?" Mom said, leaning around to try to see past the doctor. There were glass rooms with drawn curtains along one side of the hall and a long desk with several nurses behind it on the other.

"We're going to take you to see him," Nurse Rebecca said. "But you need to be prepared. He's undergone a lot of swelling and he's heavily sedated."

Mom and Dad nodded quickly and were led back to one of the corner rooms. Beeping came seemingly from all sides. Dr. Jim approached the room and the glass doors slid open automatically. He walked in and drew back the curtain.

Mom gasped.

I was in a hospital bed, but the back of it was propped up so I was almost in a sitting position. Slings held up each of my arms, which were stretched out in front of me, zombie-like. My hands hung off the ends of the slings limply, puffed-up and purple. My head lay back against the pillow, eyes half-open, pupils wandering aimlessly, an oxygen mask fixed over my mouth and nose. My face was also swollen, with purple blotches dotting each cheek and the tip of my nose. Mom reached for Dad's hand and started to cry.

"He isn't very responsive, but there's a chance he can still hear you," Dr. Jim said quietly, anticipating my parents' first question.

Mom and Dad went to the bedside and bent over me. Mom stroked my hair and thought she heard me groan softly. I may have had some level of consciousness at the time, but I would remember none of this later. For all intents and purposes, I was in the middle of a blackout that would linger for weeks.

"It's OK, honey," Mom said, her tears dripping onto my pillow. "We're here. Mom and Dad are here."

Dad didn't know where he could touch me at first. There were tubes running from my arms, my neck, my mouth and places he couldn't see underneath the hospital gown. He counted eight in all, attached to my body on one end and to the room's many beeping, blinking machines on the other. Finally he reached over and gripped my left shoulder.

"Andrew, it's Dad," he said, his voice cracking. "You've got to hang in there. You've got to fight this thing, OK?"

He choked up.

Mom turned to face Dr. Jim and Nurse Rebecca.

"Is he going to be OK?" she asked through her tears.

"We're doing everything we can," Dr. Jim said. "My colleague and I met Andrew on the helipad outside. Dr. Simpson is the head of critical care here and very experienced with treating septic shock, which is Andrew's greatest danger right now."

Mom turned back to my bed and shook her head in disbelief.

"I guess all we can do is pray," she said.

Dr. Jim took a step closer and laid his hand gently on Mom's arm. He could see the rosary beads gripped in her hand, the one Dad wasn't holding.

"I'm a Christian too," he said. "Would you like me to pray with you?"

Mom nodded, and she, Dad, Dr. Jim and Nurse Rebecca all joined hands at my bedside. Mom was expecting a rote, rehearsed prayer, but when Dr. Jim started speaking, they were his own words.

"Lord Jesus, please watch over Andrew...."

"Amen," everyone repeated when he'd finished.

There was silence for a brief moment as Dr. Jim let his words sink in. Then he gently led Mom and Dad away from my bed.

"I need to take you to one of our counseling rooms," he said. "Dr. Simpson will be there shortly and he can tell you more about what's going on. Rebecca will stay here and notify us immediately if anything changes."

My parents sat in padded wooden chairs in a room barely bigger than a closet. They were facing a desk that was nearly as wide as the room itself, anxiously watching the door.

When Dr. Simpson entered the room, he wasn't quite what my parents were expecting. He wore the familiar long, white coat, but his broad shoulders and full beard brought to mind a lumberjack more than a doctor. The beard was thick and brown, without a trace of gray. While not as young as Dr. Southwell, he seemed too green to be in charge of critical care at such a big hospital.

But Dr. Simpson was more experienced than his appearance suggested. He knew he had to shoot straight with my parents, tell them exactly what I was up against. Then they could all fight it together. But it wouldn't hurt to start with the good news.

"First of all," he began, "your son's vital signs seem to have stabilized somewhat and he's not deteriorating at the rate he was when he arrived here. His CT scans look normal, so there's no indication of brain damage, which can be a common result with meningitis.

"We're giving him a full course of antibiotics to fight the bacteria and he's also receiving a relatively new drug called Xigris, which I think will ease the effects of his sepsis. I called the hospital in Lawrence to get his weight so that I could prepare a dose for him immediately and I administered it as soon as he got off the helicopter, something I've never done before."

He paused.

"I just want you to know that we're doing all we can, even beyond our usual critical care procedures, to help your son."

Dr. Simpson saw my parents' features begin to relax slightly and knew that he had to press on to the bad news before he led them too far. He tried to break down the complex cascade of internal processes that had led to this point in terms they could understand.

"I want to stress," he finished, "that this is still a very serious situation. Your son is getting the best care available, but I can't make any guarantee that he will survive this. In fact, many people with an infection as severe as his would have already succumbed. I fully expect that by tomorrow he will be on dialysis because his kidneys will have failed. He's in lung failure already. We held off putting him on a ventilator until you could get here, but we need to intubate him as soon as possible. There's a possibility he will suffer a heart attack also — it happens in some cases of severe sepsis. And, even if his organ function recovers and his vitals stabilize completely, he's almost certain to lose parts of his extremities."

Mom and Dad were back up on the edge of their chairs now.

"What do you mean by 'parts of his extremities?'" Mom asked.

"The toxins that the bacteria are releasing, and his body's response to them, are cutting off the circulation to his arms and legs," Dr. Simpson said. "At best, he will lose some toes and fingertips. At worst, he could lose both his arms and legs."

Mom sank back, devastated. But Dad still couldn't quite process it.

"You're not giving us much to hold on to here," he said. "Andrew's here now, he's getting these drugs. What are the chances that they'll run their course and he'll get better and be able to come home in a week or two?"

Dr. Simpson nodded slowly. This was not a question he wanted to answer, but it was an answer they needed to hear.

"I'd put the chances of that at about two or three percent," he said firmly.

Now it was Dad's turn to be devastated and he melted back into his chair. Dr. Simpson stood to leave, and that's when Mom found her voice.

"We're Catholic," she said, barely above a whisper. "I want Andrew to have the Sacrament of the Sick."

Simpson nodded, satisfied that he had communicated the seriousness of the situation.

"I'll send the chaplain up immediately."

Then he left my parents alone in the room and went out to put me on a ventilator.

My parents met in the 1970s, when they were attending law school in the Twin Cities. As Mom tells it, she saw Dad walking into class one day and was struck by how handsome he was but figured that handsome guys were conceited jerks.

As the semester went on and the two got to know each other, though, Mom found that Dad was not conceited. He seemed aloof at first, but really he was just one of the last of an increasingly rare breed: the strong, silent type. They started dating before the year was over.

It was not an obvious match, except to those who subscribe to the theory that opposites attract. She was a city girl, born and raised in the Minneapolis-St. Paul area. He was a country boy, born on a farm and raised in Springfield, a rural village in southern Minnesota. She was outgoing, ebullient, never afraid to speak her mind. He was quiet, reserved, generally loath to make waves. She was a bleeding-heart liberal, stridently anti-Vietnam War, though not quite a flower child. He was a conservative traditionalist and an Army veteran who, though never gung-ho about Vietnam, hadn't fled the country or looked for an exemption when his draft number was called. He reported for duty on time, then parlayed his math degree into a safe spot at a military testing facility in Arizona.

As different as they were, Mom and Dad shared core principles. Both were hard-working people from meager means who pushed themselves into college and then held down several jobs to pay their own way once they were there. Both loved children and hoped to have some of their own sooner rather than later. Both were intellectuals with a strong sense of morality who were repulsed by the greed and deceitfulness of some of their law-school classmates. Both were Catholic. The more they got to know each other, the stronger their bond grew.

Ironically, as much as my mother opposed the Vietnam War, it was my Dad's short stint in the Army after getting drafted that ultimately brought them together. After he finished his commitment, Dad decided he didn't want to go back to the job he had before, teaching high school math. He wasn't sure he was really interested in studying law either, but he had free tuition from the GI Bill, so he figured he'd give it a shot. He didn't finish — dropping out after almost three years — but it wasn't a total loss because of that girl he'd met in a freshman lecture. He and Mom got married in a bare-bones church ceremony shortly after Mom passed the bar. They were both approaching 30 and basically penniless, but they were educated, hopeful and happy.

My brother Josh was born in April, about a year after the wedding. I came two years later in July and Dan came three years after me in September. My Dad, confident he could keep producing boys, jokingly suggested they try to have a winter baby so they could have "A Man for All Seasons." Mom, coming off a particularly difficult labor with Dan, said he would have to find another woman for that. With three boys under age 6 they had their hands full anyway, even with Grandma — Mom's mother — providing free day care.

Mom became St. Cloud's first female attorney and Dad got a steady, solid job at Fingerhut. They sent my brothers and me to Catholic school and, though we bickered among ourselves almost constantly, we were generally good students and good kids.

Mom and Dad had a real marriage, not a fairytale one. There were fights over money, politics and in-laws and there were rough patches. But though their differences sometimes strained the marriage, their similarities made sure the bond never snapped. Chief among those similarities was the love for their children. Now they were watching one of those children fight for his life.

They sat at my bedside for hours that first night, clutching each other's hands and staring at the lights and dials of all the machines. As the clock passed midnight and went into the early hours of the next day, Nurse Rebecca finally convinced them to check into a nearby hotel. She promised she would call them immediately if anything happened. They went to the hotel but stayed for only a few hours and did not sleep. They just lay in bed, holding each other.

Before dawn they were in a cab, headed back to the hospital.

CHAPTER 4

THE LOST DAYS

As I lay in the intensive care unit, feverish, twitching and unconscious, news of my illness spread. The director of Watkins made her visit to Pearson and then made another to the Kansan newsroom later that night. Friends that I lived with and worked with were being told I had been hospitalized with a very serious illness and that it was contagious. They were being advised to take an antibiotic — Cipro — and monitor themselves for flu-like symptoms.

Several students at the *Kansan* also worked part-time for the local newspaper, the *Lawrence Journal-World.* Soon the *Journal-World* was contacting Watkins, which did not release my name initially, but confirmed that there was a meningitis case on campus and the university was working to contain it. Before my first night at KU Med was over, the paper posted a brief report online. Meningitis is media gold — contagious, frighteningly fast and potentially deadly — and the *Journal-World* editors decided not to wait until the morning print edition.

"Kansas University officials say that a 22-year-old senior in journalism who lives in KU's Pearson Scholarship Hall has been diagnosed with bacterial meningitis and is being treated tonight at the University of Kansas Hospital...," the report began.

It went on to say Watkins officials were working to identify those who had been in close contact with the unnamed student and were offering preventive medicine. It said nothing of my condition. That night and into the next day, only a select few knew just how sick I was — among them my brothers and grandma.

My younger brother, Dan, was finishing his freshman year at St. Cloud State University. As I was arriving at KU Med, he was in a meeting with his adviser, planning out his next semester. His cell phone kept vibrating and he sneaked glances at it, noticing the calls were coming from home each time. As soon as he was out of the adviser's office, he called back.

Mom answered, sounding frantic and rushed. She told him I was in the hospital with meningitis and that she and Dad were heading to Kansas City immediately. Dan had a million questions, but Mom said she didn't have time to answer them. They had to leave, but they would call when they got to KC.

Dan didn't know what meningitis was. He thought it sounded like "laryngitis" and wondered why Mom was so frantic. She was emotional and prone to overreaction, so he hoped she was just being smotheringly overprotective, as usual. Still, he drove home immediately. Mom and Dad were already gone, but Grandma was there. She had arrived just as the others left and knew little more than Dan: Mom and Dad were frantic. Andrew was in the hospital. It was serious.

Just as Dad had done an hour earlier, Dan went to the computer room. He Googled "meningitis" and got some of the same medical websites with the same frightening words. Sepsis, organ failure, hearing loss, brain damage, amputations, death.

By the time Mom and Dad called from KU Med, Dan was trying to persuade Grandma that the two of them should drive though the night to Kansas City. Dad told him to wait. He'd already booked them a flight the next morning.

Dad also called my older brother, Josh, who was living in Chicago and working for Motorola, to tell him he had a plane ticket, too. Josh also made the trip to the computer to find out exactly what was this mysterious illness that was threatening his brother's life. Then he called his girlfriend, Lori, and asked her to come over and spend the night. He didn't want to be alone.

Malcolm Gibson, my journalism instructor, had met my parents at the hospital the night before. He asked whether there was anything they needed. Mom said they had no car and no way to pick up her mother and their other two sons, who were flying in the next day.

So it was that Malcolm, Grandma, Dan and Josh ended up in a car, heading from the airport to KU Med together. Malcolm quickly learned that my brothers dealt with anxiety differently. After introducing himself, Josh sat in the backseat and hardly said a word. Dan, on the other hand, was a constant stream of nervous chatter, relentlessly quizzing Malcolm about his family, his work history, his college years. Dan was fascinated by Africa and African-American culture and when Malcolm told him he had an undergraduate degree in African studies, Dan only got more chatty. He was trying to distract himself, but Josh thought it was inappropriate, given the gravity of the situation. He and Dan had a long history of not getting along, and it was all Josh could do to contain himself until the 30-minute drive was over. Grandma, a full-blooded Swede with the usual Scandinavian temperament, quietly blended in.

The intensive-care unit waiting room was just outside the heavy, metal doors that led into the sterile environment of the unit itself. It was an open room, with a horseshoe of chairs and a television bolted to the wall and, as Malcolm led Dan and Josh past it, they stopped and stared in. The small room was full of young guys, some sprawled in chairs, others on blankets on the floor, some paging through thick textbooks, others talking quietly on cell phones. It was like an orderly, well-behaved frat house.

"Oh yeah," Malcolm said. "These are your brother's friends from Pearson."

I was in my fourth year at Pearson Hall, as were 20-some other guys who had come in at the same time as me in an unusually large freshman class. Most students moved off campus after their freshman year, but many of us stayed. We'd found a cocoon of acceptance and support that was helping us transition from home life to the real world.

While we certainly had our disagreements, we were as brotherly as any fraternity. Usually with this many of them gathered in one place there would be a din of conversation. But the waiting room was quiet.

Mom and Dad emerged from the intensive-care unit and the whole family exchanged hugs.

"How is he?" Josh asked.

Dad sighed. His hair was disheveled and he had dark circles under his eyes.

"He's all swollen," he said. "But they say he hasn't gotten any worse since yesterday."

I could only have two visitors at a time and Dan and Josh wanted to go in and see me immediately, so Grandma agreed she would wait. They donned paper gowns and masks, walked down the hallway and entered my room. Their shock was equal to what my parents felt the day before.

Josh was struck by the swelling. My arms, up in their trays, were like two purple, bulbous sausages packed in a skin casing. For a moment, Josh found himself thinking I reminded him of the Stay Puft marshmallow man or the Michelin tire guy.

Dr. Southwell came in and introduced himself and Dan began peppering him with questions.

"Is he asleep?" he asked.

"He's in a medically-induced coma," Dr. Southwell said. "We've got him heavily sedated so his body can rest and fight this infection."

"His chest is just heaving — isn't there something you can do about that?" Dan asked.

"His breathing is labored," Dr. Southwell acknowledged, nodding patiently. "And we have him on a respirator to get him as much oxygen as possible. We've got to give the antibiotics time to do their job."

A nurse in a gown and mask much like my brothers' came in and placed a blood-pressure cuff gently around one of my bloated arms. A broad-shouldered, middle-aged blonde, she introduced herself as Candace. Dan immediately went back to his questions.

"My mom said Andrew might lose some fingers," he said. "Why?"

"Well, it's a complicated process going on in his body right now," the doctor replied. "He's got a lot of damage to the blood vessels and his body is instinctively pulling blood back into his trunk to protect his organs. That compromises his extremities."

"So, what can we do?" Dan asked. "I mean, there's got to be something we can do."

"I know you want to help him," Dr. Southwell said, putting a hand on Dan's shoulder. "We all do. But we just have to give it time at this point."

"There's got to be something...," Dan started.

Josh snapped.

"Don't you get it?" he snarled at Dan. "Don't you see what's going on?"

Dan immediately got defensive.

"Yeah, I know what's going on," he said, getting up in Josh's face with his voice barely below a yell. "Our brother's dying and you don't seem to care."

At this, Candace frowned and hustled around the bed. She grabbed my brothers by their gowns and gently but firmly pushed them out of the room with a strong hand on each of their backs. Once they were in the hall and the automatic glass doors had shut behind them, she spun my shocked brothers around again and confronted them face-to-face.

"Look, I understand you're upset and I can see why," she told them. "But you can't be saying stuff like that in there. We don't know how much he can hear or how much he can just ... well ... sense, OK? We've got to keep that a positive environment in there, so he has every reason to keep fighting."

My brothers nodded, chastened.

"OK," Candace said, her voice softening. "Why don't you two go cool off somewhere and let someone else visit him?"

When Dan returned to the room an hour later, Josh was back too, sitting at the side of the bed. Dan noticed large, angry-looking blisters forming on my arms and legs. Blisters that hadn't been there when he last saw me.

"What's happening to him?" he asked quietly.

Josh looked up.

"They said he's got fluid building up underneath the skin," he said. "Some of it's blood, some of it's other stuff."

Josh shook his head and reached out to gently touch my arm.

Dan sat down in the chair next to him and didn't say a word. Until then, he had believed that, if the whole family just got to the hospital and supported me, I would get better — that the Marsos could somehow heal me almost through sheer force of will. But now he saw those purple, bulging blisters, some the size of softballs. They had appeared so quickly. Now he realized how little control he had over this situation. Now he understood a little bit of what Josh was feeling.

The two of them sat there together in silence.

For the rest of my stay in the Medical Intensive Care Unit, my brothers were a team. When they were together in my room, they took turns whispering encouragement.

"Keep fighting, Andrew," Josh said.

"Try and move your hands," Dan said.

"Pretend you're playing basketball," Josh added.

A bedside vigil began. Mom, Dad, Dan, Josh and Grandma took turns watching over me and regiments of friends from Pearson and the school paper rolled in to reinforce them. Josh's girlfriend soon flew in from Chicago, too. A quiet, brown-haired Midwesterner with a cheerful spirit, Lori was already basically a member of the family.

Everyone wanted to help, but soon found there was little they could do. They talked to me, but there was no way to know how much was getting through the drug-induced coma. I could be roused into a semi-responsive state with much effort, but I would later remember none of it because of a drug called Ativan that essentially caused amnesia.

So the visitors spent much time with a small, glossy notebook adorned with the Jayhawk logo. Malcolm had provided it, with the understanding that I would be able to read the notes when I got better. And so they sat in the padded chairs and wrote to me while I lay there, just a few feet away. My journalism friends from the *Kansan*, unsurprisingly, took to the notebook rather quickly.

Andy,

Michelle, Neeley and I came to see you on May 1. Everyone was talking to you but it didn't seem like you could hear us, even though we were told otherwise. We could get a reaction out of you by yelling, "Andy!" but it seemed perverse. I heard you reply, "I'm tired, and I can't talk to you anyway 'cause I've got a tube down my throat" — subconsciously, of course. I hope to come see you again when you're doing better, because you are going to get better.

— Ehren

Andy —

Visiting you has given me a whole new way to procrastinate — and it's valid, so when I don't get my 8-page paper done, I'm calling you to help write it. You like writing more than me anyway, right? Anyway, I'm praying for you, so get well soon. We miss you.

—Neeley

Andy —

I'm so glad I had the opportunity to come visit you. I love you bunches and can't wait to be able to talk to you. I will come back often. Don't ever lose hope about "Reset Day." It will happen eventually! See you soon, dancing partner!

(heart) Always,
Michelle

"Reset Day" was an idea I'd told Michelle about during a night of drinking and dancing at the end of another long week of school work. It seemed like all the girls I was interested in were already taken, so I proposed one day out of the year when the relationships "reset" and everyone was single. Just one day when we could all make our moves and tell people how we felt, knowing that they were all unfettered. Michelle thought it was hilarious, but I was half-serious.

The notes from the *Kansan* folks were short and witty in the best traditions of journalism. The notes from the Pearson guys were different. Longer. More emotional.

ANDY,

Wow. Not many times in my life have I not really known what to say, but this is one of them. You've been one of my best friends in the hall the last 4 years. Even though we're not always hanging out, it seems like when we do we don't miss a beat. Times like these really put the important things in perspective, like your friendship. I hope you don't think it's something I've taken for granted. I know how you're a fighter and I know that you'll beat this. But know that if there is anything — ANYTHING — you need along the way I will always be there for you. I lost my only brother before I even knew him; you all are like the brothers I never got to have and I'll do anything for family. Whatever you need, just ask.

Always,
Brandon Tobias

Andy —

In the grand scheme of things, I've always felt blessed in that my family hasn't had much tragedy or many troubling times. I always wondered what would happen if something happened to one of my brothers. I found out last Wednesday. One of my brothers, you, got sick, and unfortunately it took that for me to really realize what the fraternity in Pearson really means to me, and to everyone. I just want you to know that is the main sentiment in the hall right now: we aren't praying for a fellow resident, or a friend, but for a brother. One of the hardest things, for me at least, has been seeing someone so tough, so invincible, in such a vulnerable state. But in the end it gave me some consolation, because you are tough, and you will get through this. But keep in mind, no man is an island and I want you to know that, whatever you need, you got it from me.

Get well, brother,
Josh Wunderlich

Andy —

Here's the update: Twins killing in the Central, T-Wolves on the way to meeting my Spurs in the playoffs and Bands in the Sand went off well despite the adversity of the weather. It's really tough, man. Any of us could be here right now. We are all pulling for you. We just want you back at the hall to watch a little Smallville and play a little basketball, all those simple things that mean so much. It's been four great years and there's many more to come. I'll see you and Randy and Clay a lot this summer. You're always in my mind and my prayers. Love ya man.
Mike Zybko

Many of the Pearson guys had lived with me for our entire college careers. We'd cooked together, eaten together, competed in intramural sports together, and sat up talking and laughing in the dining room into the small hours of the morning when we should have been studying. It was a special group.

Kenny, a Pearsonite from Texas who was a year younger than me, was known as one of the hall's best cooks. He insisted on preparing my family a home-cooked meal of whatever traditional Minnesota fare they requested. They set the menu and he'd figure out how to make it, he told them.

My parents suggested a tater-tot hot dish and a Jell-O salad with carrot shavings in it. Simple, cheap reminders of home. After figuring out that "hot dish" was the same as "casserole," Kenny had little trouble with the entree. But the side dish gave him pause. He couldn't fathom people actually wanting vegetables in their Jell-O, and figured my parents must have been pulling his leg. Just in case, he shaved a few slices of carrot onto the top of the Jell-O mold, where they could be easily picked off. Then he presented it to my parents sheepishly and they laughed.

Matt Unger, a tall, skinny, goofy guy, was in many ways the heart of Pearson. He went to a hobby shop and bought bags and bags of beads, some just solid colors and some with the letters of the alphabet. Then he picked out all the A's and M's and started stringing them together into eye-catching bracelets with my initials. Soon almost all the Pearson guys were wearing them.

"Just to show that we're pulling for him, big-time," Matt told my parents.

Watery-eyed, they asked whether he could make some more. My parents, brothers and Grandma put them on, and then started passing them out to doctors, nurses, visitors and anybody else they could find.

CHAPTER 5

BETWEEN LIFE AND DEATH

With the arrival of the rest of the family, staying in hotels became too expensive. My parents were still holding out slim hope that I would get better soon and we'd all be able to go home, but they also started looking for long-term lodging.

They ended up at Friendship Inn, a house just a few blocks away that rented to families with ailing loved ones. My family took up nearly every room in the place, except for the upper floor that belonged to the middle-aged caretaker, Sharon.

In those first few days, when the Marsos weren't at the hospital, they spent much of their time on the phone, updating friends and family on my condition. Too much time, really. They were emotionally exhausted and needed rest.

When a family friend introduced them to an online journaling site called CaringBridge, it became a clearinghouse for Andy information.

Mom always enjoyed an opportunity to write something besides legal briefs. Her first entry, which came two days after I was hospitalized, was characteristically optimistic and upbeat:

Just about an hour ago, Andy's doctors came through on rounds. To quote Dr. Simpson, "He's not out of the woods yet, but he's been through the darkest part." He will continue to be on the ventilator for the next few days, at least, but Dr. Simpson will be lightening his sedation and, hopefully, he'll be a bit more alert. Brain damage seems to have been avoided, thank God, but he is still at risk for the loss of fingers/toes. A vascular surgeon will be looking in on him today to give an opinion about the viability of those tissues. According to "Jim", the resident we like the most, it may be a week or so before we know whether he'll lose some extremities.

Grandma, Josh and Dan are all here with us. Andy's friends from school (staff and students) have been wonderful. The doctors at KU are fantastic! If this had to happen, this is a good place to be.

PLEASE continue to remember Andy (and us) in your prayers. While the medicine is great, it's been statistically proven that patients who have people praying for them (even if they don't know it) do better than people without prayer.

We'll keep you updated.
Ginny Marso

With the start of the online journal, news of my illness spread, both in Minnesota and Kansas. The link flew from one e-mail inbox to another and soon my closest friends and people I hadn't seen since high school were signing the guest book.

Mom's call to prayer was answered. Prayers came in from as far north as Alaska, where I had cousins I hadn't seen since I was a toddler, and from as far south as Rio de Janeiro, where Gustavo's parents lived in a cramped apartment with a spectacular view of a hillside covered in tropical plants. I had an entire rectory of Catholic priests, an entire convent of nuns, and various Protestant congregations that my relatives belonged to praying for me. A Jewish family friend left a prayer note at the Wailing Wall in Jerusalem and a Pearson buddy studying in China lit candles for me at several Buddhist temples. My former roommate Bharath, who was from India, had his parents praying to various Hindu deities. It was an interfaith effort, as Mom pointed out in one of her journal entries.

The prayer circle spread beyond friends and family after my name was released to the media. My parents soon found that the "meningitis kid" was of great interest to newspapers and television stations, which had been contacting the hospital public relations staff looking for more information. Mom and Dad authorized Malcolm to act as the family spokesperson.

He told the local reporters that I was about to graduate at the top of my journalism class. He told them I was well-liked at the school newspaper, where the other students were busy preparing a "Get Well," video for me to watch when I woke up. He told them about the ever-present crowd of Pearson guys in the hospital waiting room. As his words went out in print, on TV, radio and online, people I had never met began leaving notes in the online guestbook, saying they were praying for me as well.

It was not always easy for Malcolm. His emotions sneaked out during a clip that was played on the evening news two days after my hospitalization.

"We need to get him better," he said, his voice cracking. "It's scary. This is very serious."

Malcolm was used to seeing me as an active college student. He was still thinking of my condition in measures such as whether I was smiling, cracking jokes, busily tapping away at a computer or rushing across campus from an assignment. But those were the old measures. The new measures were things like heart rate, respiration and urine output — numbers that determined whether my organs were working properly. By those measures, I was actually doing better than expected.

Dr. Simpson and Dr. Jim had told my parents what sort of range those numbers should be in. As Dan, Josh, Grandma, Mom and Dad sat in my room they watched my monitors for hours, to the point where the numbers started playing tricks on them. Every time they moved even one or two digits closer to the "good" range, their spirits lifted disproportionately high. Every time they ticked farther into the "critical" range, their hearts fell into unwarranted despair.

In reality, the numbers were holding fairly steady. Dr. Simpson had expected my organs to deteriorate some before they got better, but for whatever reason they were hanging in, even if they still weren't operating at 100 percent — or even at a capacity that could sustain life without a respirator. My kidneys, especially, baffled the doctors. The nurses watched my urine output closely, waiting for it to slow to a trickle as my kidneys failed.

But the yellow stuff kept flowing, to the point where one day Nurse Candace came in to change my catheter bag and happily announced, "He's a peein' machine."

Candace and the rest of the nursing staff had become fiercely protective of me and my family. As Nurse Rebecca and Mom sat talking at my bedside one day, Mom tearfully confided that she was hoping I would be well enough by May 21 to go to graduation. Barring a miracle, Rebecca knew the only way I was getting out of the hospital that soon was in a body bag. But she kept that to herself.

"If there's any way we can get him out of the hospital by then, I'll take a day off and go with him as his personal nurse," she said.

Candace, a hard-crusted Harley chick, told my parents she usually tried to keep emotional distance between herself and her patients.

"But with Andy, when I see you guys in here every day, and I see all those boys sleeping out in the waiting room, I can't help it," she said. "He's special."

Candace deemed my room a "positive-vibes-only" zone. A few days into my hospitalization, two female friends from school came to see me for the first time. They were shocked by all the tubes running in and out of me, and by the sight of my arms and legs, which were now wrapped in bandages stained red and yellow from the bloody fluid weeping out of those gigantic blisters. The girls started sobbing almost immediately.

"Oh, this is so horrible," they cried. "Oh, I can't believe this is happening."

Candace shuttled them out of the room with her strong arms, much as she had done with my brothers days earlier.

"Stop all that caterwauling!" she said with a frown. "You guys can't be doin' that in there. If you gotta do it, do it somewhere else. Nobody needs that right now. The family doesn't need that. Andy doesn't need that."

Candace also clucked with disapproval when Mom flipped on a Timberwolves playoff game and cranked up the TV volume. Candace thought it was too much yelling and whistles and sneaker-squeaking and it might distress me. But Mom insisted. She figured that hearing the T-Wolves dominate Denver would only make me fight harder.

As much as Candace tried to shield my subconscious, she couldn't be there all the time. The day the vascular surgeon came into my room, he was trailed by several notepad-toting medical students. After unwrapping my bandages, he calmly and matter-of-factly began to show the students where the damage to my circulation had caused irreversible harm to my hands and feet.

"He's going to lose this," he said, running his gloved index finger along the base of one of my dark purple digits. "And this, and this, and this."

This particular teaching moment might have passed drama-free, except that Mom was in the room watching all of it with increasing distress. She had been keeping a close eye on my arms and legs every day, often feeling them for warmth. She thought they were looking better, and now this Johnny-come-lately doctor was telling a bunch of people what parts of her son were definitely going to be amputated. It did not sit well with her.

She stormed out looking for Dr. Jim, and dragged him into the room.

The surgeon and his students were already gone. Dr. Jim assured her that he, too, thought my extremities were looking better. Then he went and got Dr. Simpson, who agreed, and stressed that it was far too early for anyone, even a vascular surgeon, to know how much of my limbs would recover.

"Don't put too much stock in what he says," Dr. Simpson said, even though he was one of the doctors who'd told Mom what a hotshot the vascular surgeon was in the first place.

It was one of the first times my family was caught in the middle of a difference of opinion between medical professionals. It wouldn't be the last.

One day in the intensive care unit stretched to two, then three, then four, then five. My temperature fluctuated wildly, occasionally hitting 105. My organs strained. My heart sometimes beat so hard and so fast Dan could see the bed rails shaking. But all anyone could do was wait and hope until the nasty Neisseria meningitidis bugs were flushed from my system.

The day I was admitted I was put on an all-out blitz of antibiotics, a regimen that included Vancomycin, Rocephin and Doxycycline. There was also a steroid, Decadron, and of course, the "wonder drug," Xigris. Approved by the FDA less than three years earlier, it was the first drug in human history developed to treat severe sepsis, the condition that was now damaging my blood vessels at a potentially deadly rate. It was not often used because one of its possible side effects was severe internal bleeding. But in my case Dr. Simpson didn't hesitate – he thought I would die without it anyway.

So those drugs worked their way through my system, killing off the bacteria while mitigating the damage it did to my tissues as much as possible. Every day that I did not get worse, the drugs had more time to work, increasing the chances that I would get better. I just had to hold on and as Dr. Simpson came by on rounds day after day, his notes began to reveal cautious optimism.

> *April 29:*
>
> *I personally evaluated Mr. Marso and agree with Dr. Southwell. Hands continue to grow darker, though feet are warm and there seems to be adequate circulation. I remain concerned for the possibility that hands will necrose.*

"Necrose" meant "die off for lack of blood." It would become a new word in my family's vocabulary.

April 30:

I personally evaluated Mr. Marso and agree with Dr. Southwell's excellent note. It appears that fingertips on the left hand are beginning to necrose — though toes and some right fingers are actually more perfused than yesterday.

"Perfused" was another new word, but a much more pleasant one. It meant alive and flowing with blood.

So it went those first five days, with my family riding the emotional roller coaster while I lay in bed, blissfully unconscious. By the end of the first week, the antibiotics had done their job and I was Neisseria meningitidis-free. There was still a chance my organs would not recover, but every reason to be optimistic that I had reached the bottom and would only get better.

Or, as Dr. Simpson started saying nearly every day, "He's not out of the woods yet, but he's doing about as well as we could have hoped."

At this point, the staff had to make a decision: keep me intubated in the drug-induced coma a little longer or try to ease the sedation and see whether I could start breathing on my own. It was not a clear call. My organs were still laboring — my respiration and heart rate still irregular — and there was no guarantee my heart and lungs would be able to handle the strain of operating on their own. On the other hand, there were mounds of statistical data suggesting that the longer patients were on the ventilator, the worse their final outcomes tended to be. The longer patients went without breathing on their own, the more their diaphragms weakened and the less likely they were to be able to take over their own breathing eventually.

My parents, though eager to see me wake up, didn't want to rush it if I wasn't ready. Ultimately the decision fell to Dr. William Barkman, the hospital's chief of staff. He had been following my case closely, consulting occasionally with Dr. Simpson and Dr. Jim. In his opinion, I was young and in relatively good shape, and my lungs needed to start working on their own if they were ever going to recover properly. He wanted me off the vent as soon as possible,

So, on Monday, May 3, five days into my hospitalization, Dr. Barkman ordered my sedation cut back in preparation for the removal of the respirator and my family awaited my return to consciousness.

Despite Candace's worries, I hadn't heard a thing during those five days — at least nothing that left a permanent memory. I was in a deep and dreamless sleep, and when I started to wake up six days later, it seemed as if no time had passed since I got off that helicopter.

I didn't remember the helicopter right away, or even that I had been sick. Things were hazy. There was a window to my right and I could tell it was dark outside. There were beeping machines, a white room and possibly someone calling my name. I couldn't be sure. I knew, instinctively, that I was in a hospital. There was something in my mouth. Something unpleasant. I didn't want to deal with it. I fell back asleep.

I woke up again. It was brighter in the room. There was blue sky out the window. The thing was still in my mouth. God, I hurt. Everywhere. It felt as if someone had put me in a burlap sack and pushed me down a rocky hill. My hands and feet felt weird. Cold. Stiff. I couldn't move them. My arms were covered with bandages. Maybe they tied the bandages too tight. Maybe that was why I couldn't move. With all my might, I tried to budge. I thought I felt my fingers and toes wiggle. Good enough. I fell back asleep.

The next time I woke up, I was in a different room. I had been moved down one floor, to the burn intensive care unit. Those large blisters had begun to burst and ooze and I had open wounds all over the place. The Medical Intensive Care Unit staff did the best they could to stave off infection, slathering on a silver-based cream and changing my bandages regularly. But the burn unit was a sterile environment where the staff was more accustomed to handling massive tissue damage.

So I woke up in an unfamiliar room. It seemed larger. It was dark again. Nighttime. I realized that the thing was out of my mouth. My throat hurt. Bad. After seven days on the ventilator , seven days without swallowing, it had reached a level of dryness I had never known.

There was a short woman in light blue scrubs at my bedside. She'd noticed I was awake and was looking down at me, smiling a huge, toothy grin.

I tried to ask for water, but couldn't talk. Nothing came out but raspy air. I kept mouthing it, though, and she understood.

"I can't give you water, yet," she said, patting me on the shoulder. "Would you like some ice chips?"

I nodded vigorously, frustrated. *No water? What kind of Nazi hospital is this? These ice chips better be good.*

They were good. The nurse tipped a tiny Dixie cup filled with little round chunks of ice into my mouth. The slow trickle of liquid down my throat was heaven. I was enraptured. Grinning, I looked over to the left. There were two chairs and two familiar faces. One was Josh. He was asleep, but seeing him there made me relax a bit. The other was Michael, who had a book in his lap, but was looking at me, not it.

Michael was one of the younger guys at Pearson. We knew each other, but weren't particularly close. He was smiling at me, but it was a sheepish, slightly unsure grin, as if he didn't feel right being the first one I saw that night. I tried to smile back, to let him know I was grateful he was there. The last drops of ice-chip water drooled out the side of my smile as I fell back asleep.

The first conscious day passed like that, with me waking up usually only long enough to ingest some ice chips and fall back asleep. Being awake was uncomfortable. Besides the all-over soreness, I felt a tugging on my arm from the IVs, and a constant tickle in my nose from the feeding tube that was threaded through there. Then there was the odd sensation of having a catheter inside my penis and another tube jammed up my butt. No, being awake was not fun.

I did enjoy seeing my family members, though, even if my throat was still too hoarse to talk above a barely-intelligible whisper. Mom was brought to tears the first time I woke, smiled at her and mouthed the word "Mommy." Dad, hearing this tale, worked up a plan to test my mental state the first time he caught me awake. One of my parents' greatest worries was whether I would emerge from the coma with my personality intact.

So the first time I woke up in Dad's presence, he leaned over the bed and asked in his soft, deep voice, "Do you know who I am?"

I frowned, put on my best, "Duh!" face and whispered, "Dad."

He smiled.

"OK, that was an easy one," he said. "Do you know who played catcher for the Twins in the '87 World Series?"

My frown deepened. Seemed like an odd question, but I was pretty sure I knew the answer. I could picture one of the guy's baseball cards. Kinda skinny, angular face. Really smooth cheeks and chin, almost like he never had to shave.

"Tim... Laudner," I croaked, with Dad leaning his ear within inches of my mouth so he could catch the words.

Dad straightened up and grinned broadly. He took off his glasses with one hand and wiped a tear away from his eye with the other before replacing them.

"I'm so happy to hear you say that," he said, giving my shoulder a squeeze.

I smiled back. *All right, Pops, whatever makes you happy.* Then I fell back asleep.

Despite the pain and discomfort, there was a simple happiness to that first conscious day. Whenever I woke up, everyone was smiling at me, like they'd never seen someone so wonderful. Nurse Candace and Nurse Rebecca came down to the burn unit to visit and, smiling and crying at the same time, told me I was a miracle.

Dr. Southwell, of course, introduced himself as Jim. He told me that just by waking up, I was answering a lot of prayers. He had a calm about him and I felt safe when he was around. He told me he had been cheering for the Timberwolves along with the rest of the family but he might have to stop now, because they were playing Los Angeles in the conference finals and the Lakers were his team. I shook my head in mock disappointment and everyone laughed as if it were the funniest thing they'd ever seen.

Dr. Jim tried to explain what had happened. There was that word, "meningitis" again, but as he explained to me just how nasty it was, it became much more than just a word. He explained that it was a contagious disease, a bacteria that was passed from throat to throat. Sometimes when there were outbreaks including several different people, doctors could trace it back to a single source, but in my case no one else had gotten it, so there was no way to know where I had picked it up.

That was OK with me. I remembered being at a bar with a bunch of friends from the school newspaper and passing drinks around so other people could try them. I remembered taking dirty cups from the stack in front of the dishwasher at Pearson and reusing them on several occasions. Stupid. I shook my head and decided it was probably better not knowing what preventable exposure put me in this hospital bed.

Dr. Jim also explained that there was a vaccine that prevented four out of the five groups of bacterial meningitis, but I had gotten the one it didn't work against. This, too, was a relief. The idea that a simple shot could have prevented all this seemed like too much to bear. Still, I wondered why no one had told me to get a meningitis vaccine.

I asked Dr. Jim about my hands and feet, which still felt stiff and cold. He did his best to explain the cascade of events that had damaged my blood vessels and that some of the damage might be irreversible. There was a good chance I would lose at least some toes and fingertips. Possibly more.

I fixated on the word "chance," which to me meant there was also a chance everything was going to be fine. I didn't want to consider those other possibilities. After all, I'd come this far and Dr. Jim made it clear that my making it had not been a given.

"How...bad...was...it?" I asked, and he had to lean in to catch each whispered word.

His eyes widened and he nodded gravely.

"It was quite serious," he said. "If it had taken another hour or two for you to get here...."

He shook his head and his meaning was clear.

The memories of that day came rushing back. I shivered at the thought of getting off the helicopter and blacking out. I imagined that being my last living moment on earth, and life suddenly seemed frighteningly fragile. But there was also a rush of relief that I'd survived. There were so many people I loved, so many things I still wanted to do and see. There was a spiritual sense of security — that I had come so close to the end, but God had more for me to do in this life and so had carried me through it. He had put the right people in my path.

There was someone I needed to see.

Clay arrived from Lawrence about an hour later, summoned by Mom at my insistence. I had to fight to keep my eyes open until he arrived, but I was determined. Clay walked in the room and broke into a big grin when I turned my head and tried to wave him over to the bed with my bandaged left arm.

"Hey buddy," he whispered, gripping my bicep. "It's great to see you awake."

I nodded, but didn't waste any words. I would need all the voice I had left.

"Thank you," I croaked, and Clay leaned his ear down closer to my mouth. "For...saving...my...life."

Clay straightened up and shook his head slightly, tears forming at the sides of his eyes. It was the type of thing people only said in movies, yet there he was, hearing it in person.

I smiled and shut my eyes. My work, at least for that day, was done.

The happiness of that first conscious day did not last. My body was free of meningitis, but it was still torn up inside and struggling to recover. Over the next several days, my waking moments remained fleeting and my respiration and heart rate often rose to dangerous levels. I spiked fevers, thrashed about and, during brief moments of wakefulness was alternately burning hot and freezing cold. Suspecting another infection, new doctors came in and took cultures of all my orifices. The cultures came back negative. The doctors were perplexed. I was not as bad off as I'd been when I arrived at the hospital, but I was not recovering at an encouraging rate either.

Friends from Pearson and the *Kansan*, excited about reports that I was awake and able to talk, stopped by the hospital between final exams. Most left disappointed. I either slept through their visit or woke up half-delirious with drugs and fever, raving in hoarse whispers about a disco or a softball game. I had hallucinatory dreams, including one in which I watched a group of my closest friends get into my white minivan and start driving away. The van hit the curb, flew impossibly high in the air and slammed to the ground, exploding into a ball of fire on impact. I knew my friends were in there burning, but when I tried to run to them, my legs wouldn't work. A storefront suddenly appeared next to me and I tried to open the door, to go in and scream for help, but my hands couldn't turn the knob.

I woke up thrashing and struggling and one of the nurses shot something into my IV to calm me down.

My lucid moments were brief. They were usually just long enough for me to remember where I was — *Oh, yeah, hospital* — and why I was there — *Meningitis, meningitis, meningitis*. Increasingly, those lucid moments were also filled with nurses placing a plastic oxygen mask over my face and telling me: "Breathe deeper, Andy. You've got to breathe deeper."

I could tell by the urgency in their voices that this was important to them, but I couldn't do it. When I tried to suck air deep into my chest it always seemed to get caught halfway there. So I breathed more, huffing and puffing in quick, shallow gasps until I passed into darkness again.

My family members could tell that I was not breathing normally, but they could not tell how dangerous this was. Until Nurse Nancy entered the picture.

Nurse Nancy was a "float" nurse, not regularly assigned to the burn unit. She was not happy with what she saw the first night she cared for me. She pulled Dan aside into the hallway and expressed her concern.

"I've been here more than 10 years," she said. "And I've never seen someone survive taking that many breaths per minute."

This was not what Dan wanted to hear. He asked whether she shouldn't do something about it.

"Well, if it were up to me, I'd put him back on the vent," she said.

"Well, I don't know, you're the nurse, do what you've got to do," he implored.

She explained that it wasn't her decision. Dan then rushed to the waiting room, where Mom was sleeping, woke her up and quickly relayed Nurse Nancy's news.

Mom entered the burn unit just in time to hear Nurse Nancy tell someone what she thought sounded like, "I don't want him dying on my shift."

This sent her instantly into full-on Psycho-Mom mode, screaming something about "attitude" and "selfishness" at Nurse Nancy. Mom had been told that it was extremely risky to put someone back on the vent so soon after it had been taken out. Although it might help in the short term, it made it much more likely the patient would never make it off the vent. In Mom's mind, Nurse Nancy wasn't concerned about my safety so much as her own job and was willing to sacrifice my long-term prospects if it would ensure that I wouldn't die on her watch.

Mom was used to being proactive, rather than simply reacting to the world as it came. At home she planned nearly all the dinners. At her law firm she was the boss. In the courtroom, she always had a hand in the outcome. But since that first day Dad had called her and told her I was sick, she felt control slipping away, at the mercy of events she could not change. Her rage looked unstoppable as she unloaded a week's worth of intense stress on Nurse Nancy.

Dan, not knowing what else to do, rushed out of the hospital and sprinted the two blocks to Friendship House to fetch Dad. Dad was awakened by his frantic son, who informed him that his wife was cursing out a nurse who seemed convinced that his other son was dying. A few minutes later Dad was at the hospital, trying to explain the situation to the resident on call.

Nurse Nancy was replaced and never returned to my bedside.

But, in between Mom's curses, Nurse Nancy had let slip that she wasn't the only one who felt I should be back on the vent. She said that she'd talked to several other nurses who felt the same way. Mom went to Dr. Barkman the next day, demanding answers.

Dr. Barkman acknowledged that my breathing was not improving as quickly as he had hoped. He also acknowledged that several of the nurses who were with me for hours each day were concerned about how long my lungs could keep up their pace. But he remained convinced that I would be better off without the vent.

"He can do this," Dr. Barkman said, looking down at me in bed. "He's young, he's strong, he's in good shape. If he were my age, I wouldn't be so optimistic. But he can do this."

His faith in me was not necessarily misplaced. I survived several more days with my respiration rate somewhere in the neighborhood of an Olympic sprinter. All those hours of lung-searing pick-up basketball apparently were paying off.

But my breathing did not get better. It remained labored, strained and shallow. And then, two weeks into my hospitalization, the doctors found out why. I had pneumonia in my left lung, a devastating complication for someone coming off an infection as intense as the one I'd just fought. Dr. Barkman's hand was forced. My lungs were failing. I had to go back on the vent, or I might die.

It was a somber day for my family:

Monday, May 10, 2004 3:00 PM CDT

I will be writing today's journal because my mother is too upset. We received a bit of a setback this morning. Andy is in respiratory failure and will need to be put back on the ventilator. Not only does this lengthen his recovery but also arises other risks. However, being on the ventilator will allow him to rest easier and exert less energy breathing and more on healing. He has developed some pneumonia in his left lung and being on the respirator makes it easier for the doctors to monitor. Although Andy was disappointed when we told him he'd have to go back on the vent, he understood that it was for his benefit. We will need everyone to pray that he will not need breathing assistance for a prolonged time and that no more complications arise. Thank you to everyone who has been supporting Andy through prayers and this website.

—Daniel Marso

I wasn't just disappointed, I was scared, in part because I wasn't quite sure what was going on. The pneumonia diagnosis came after a bronchoscopy, in which a long tube with a video camera on one end was inserted into my throat. Dad was with me as they wheeled me back up to the Medical Intensive Care Unit to do the test. Wearing the oxygen mask that was becoming my permanent fashion fixture, I was having one of my rare waking moments, but because of the drugs I was only somewhat lucid. I understood Dad when he told me they were going to put another tube down my throat, but I didn't understand why. I was convinced that I'd hurt myself playing football. But wait, that didn't make sense. Why was I playing football when I was supposed to be in the hospital? I remembered that I had been very sick. I had just had meningitis.

I was very confused, but one thing I was sure of was that I did not want another tube down my throat. I looked at Dad imploringly, shook my head, tried to tell him through the oxygen mask.

I didn't need to tell him. He knew. His lips trembled and his brown eyes watered as he looked down at me, smoothing back my hair with one of his hands.

"I know Andrew, I know," he whispered "But they have to."

Then he bent down and kissed my forehead.

I was the lucky one. I got to go to sleep when they put the tube in, knocked out on sedatives once again. Dad was the one who had to examine the video screen with Dr. Barkman. He was the one who had to hear the unsettling news that I would once again need a machine to breathe for me. He was the one who had to listen, appalled, as a young medical resident shrugged and said, "It's too bad, but some people's diaphragms just can't handle all that strain."

I was sedated again later that day when they put me back on the ventilator. So I also didn't have to hear a young resident in plain clothes look at my chart and tell Dan, matter-of-factly, "He's taken a turn for the worse."

CHAPTER 6

BACK TO REALITY

Into this uncertain time stepped Greg Koetter and Rick Reisdorf, two of my oldest friends. They had been stuck in Minnesota as their own college semesters wrapped up, logging on to the CaringBridge site several times a day. As I was being sedated and re-intubated, they were finally on their way to Kansas, excited about recent reports that I was awake and talking.

By the time they arrived, I was not. They stood at my bedside silently, absorbing the same initial shock most visitors had — the tubes, the bandages, the swelling that had gone down but was still quite noticeable. The haunting thing was the fingers. My fingers had started to dry up and the staff often no longer bothered bandaging them. They just hung there, stiff and black, like a rotting corpse.

Rick and Greg had things to tell me — things that go along with friendships that span more than a decade and countless shared triumphs and defeats. They could only hope they'd get that chance later.

None of us could quite remember why we'd become so close in grade school. Maybe it was because we all loved sports, but weren't incredibly gifted athletically. Maybe it was because we didn't fit neatly into the traditional social groups; we weren't quite jocks, we weren't quite nerds and we definitely weren't Goths or socialite rich kids. We were just three guys who liked hanging out together. We spent a lot of our time shooting hoops or playing Nintendo at Greg's house. We also helped each other with math homework.

There was no doubt that we complemented each other well. Rick was the entertainer of the group, Greg was the voice of reason and I was a combination of the two, providing just enough goofiness to egg Rick on while helping Greg make sure we rarely did anything too stupid.

Tall, brown-haired Rick provided life and laughter to any room he entered. His wide smile split his face, scrunching his eyes and wrinkling his cheeks. He was affable, self-deprecating and pretended he didn't notice the trail of fawning girls he left in his wake. He was named homecoming king our senior year of high school.

Greg, blond and blue-eyed, had been pudgy when we were younger but had grown to 6 feet tall and lost most of his baby fat by the time we went to college. That was about the only thing that had changed about him. Since fifth grade, he had always been quiet, intelligent and mature. Greg was like a rock that Rick and I knew we could always lean on when life's storms rolled in.

Greg had recently accepted a job at one of Minnesota's largest insurance firms. Rick would start grad school at Syracuse in July. I was graduating at the top of my journalism class and starting my sportswriting career. A few weeks earlier the future had seemed bright for "The Three Musketeers." Now one of them lay in a hospital bed on a breathing machine and the other two were staring down at him.

Rick and Greg were at the hospital for about a week. They tried to talk to me, but I usually didn't respond. I was not lucid enough to know what was going on and I had the tube down my throat, which made it impossible to talk, anyway. The nursing staff had given me a small board with letters and several common words and phrases on it that I could point to if I wanted to communicate, but it was of little use.

Rick and Greg were disappointed, but they didn't show it. They knew my family needed them. My friends from KU were supportive, but there was something even more reassuring about seeing these familiar faces from home.

So Rick and Greg played marathon games of Risk with Dan in the waiting room, distracting him for a few hours at a time. Greg frequently went off by himself to answer his phone. Rick knew he was usually fielding calls from friends back home who wanted the latest on my condition, but he told Dan that it was probably Greg's girlfriend on the line each time, keeping tabs on him.

"Was that Kristine, Greg?" he'd ask when Greg returned, making an exaggerated "whipping" motion.

When Rick suggested racing wheeled office chairs down the burn-unit hallway, Greg at first expressed his usual reasonable reluctance. Then he decided this was a special occasion and went along with it.

At night, as they slept on the floor of Dan's room at Friendship House, they let each other worry. They were haunted by those blackened fingers, wondering just what kind of pain I was in and what the future would hold for me. Rick was so affected that a few days after he returned to Minnesota, he was rushed to the hospital, suddenly unable to move his own fingers. The doctors said there was nothing wrong with them; it was a psychosomatic response to my trauma, and it would pass.

That was days later. When they were at the hospital, Rick and Greg lived out Candace's "good vibes" philosophy, and I seemed to respond to it.

Over the course of their stay, I improved at a rate that surprised the doctors again. By the end of their visit, my lungs were nearly clear and Dr. Barkman was easing my sedation and preparing to remove the vent again. I started to have more lucid moments and during one of them, I used the letter board to try to ask the nurse something.

As I slowly placed my bandaged hand over first the "p" and then the "n" the nurse frowned.

"Are you sure that's the one you want?" she asked me.

As I went for an "e" next, she looked up at Rick and Greg for help.

"Do you know what he's asking?" she said. "I can't think of anything that starts 'p-n-e.'"

Greg knew. He remembered when I won the school district spelling bee in eighth grade. To him, this was a great sign. Not only was I awake and aware of what was going on around me — I could still spell.

"I think he's trying to ask about his pneumonia," Greg told the nurse, giving me a knowing grin.

I nodded. She said I was doing much better.

The next day, after Mom told me that Greg and Rick were going back to Minnesota, I gestured for the phrase board again. Rick read out loud as I tried to isolate the right words and phrases.

"I want..." he said eagerly, then followed my bandaged hand down a long list of nouns. "I want.... I want... I want... wife?"

"I want wife?" he said, looking at me for confirmation, his trademark smile beginning to creep across his face.

I nodded solemnly, and both he and Greg burst out laughing.

"OK, buddy," Greg said. "We'll see what we can do."

As I progressed post-pneumonia and my stretches of consciousness increased, Dr. Jim informed us that I was no longer in critical condition and he would be handing me off to the plastic surgeons to focus on other patients. I did not really know how to express the gratitude I felt toward him. He said he'd still try to come check in on me once in awhile, but I knew I would miss his calm, reassuring daily visits. All I could think to do was raise one wounded arm in his direction.

"Oh, do you want to watch TV?" he said, thinking I was pointing up at the screen bolted into the wall behind him.

"I think he wants to shake your hand," Mom said.

I nodded.

I was sad to see Dr. Jim go, but his absence was eased by one of my new burn unit nurses. Michelle seemed to be about my age and was stunningly pretty. The first time she walked into the room I noticed the thick, reddish-brown hair that swung behind her, brushing her shoulders, and the way her scrubs hung off her slim frame. But it was the nose-piercing that really got me. It was a small diamond stud, barely noticeable at first glance. But it hinted at something just a little wild and dangerous.

Male instincts took over when I first saw her and I tried to grin around the horrid tube in my mouth. She noticed and immediately broke into a smile herself, stifling a giggle.

"Well, hi, there," she said. "Nice to see you awake."

My first thought, of course, was "Oh, yeah, she likes me!"

But even in a half-drugged stupor, I realized how ridiculous that was.

"Sure," my more practical side thought sarcastically. "She's obviously got a weakness for guys in hospital gowns with bandages all over their arms and legs. Oh, yeah, and those tubes coming out of every hole in your body are making her swoon. What's she going to do, kiss your respirator?"

Still, I looked forward to Michelle's shifts. There's an inescapable truth about being a guy: having a pretty girl around makes nearly any situation better.

Michelle seemed to sense that her presence brightened up my conscious moments. I often emerged from long naps to find her sitting in a chair next to my bed, doing paperwork on her lap rather than on the desk outside the room. She'd ask whether I wanted some Chapstick, because my lips were dried and cracking after weeks of intubation. I would nod and she would grab the tube she had brought in just for me and carefully apply it like my own personal make-up artist. Chapped lips was one pain she could soothe.

One night I was having a nightmare about firefighters going into a building that was about to explode. It was one of the vivid, almost hallucinatory dreams that were a side effect of one of the many drugs I was on. I woke up convinced that I had to warn the firemen before they were horribly burned, thrashing around as much as the tubes would allow, my eyes wide with terror.

Dan was in the room, as well as two female friends from Minnesota. None of them had any idea what was wrong. They looked at me and then back at each other, wanting to help but not knowing how. Dan left the room and came back with Michelle, who figured out what was going on instantly. She rushed to my side and began slowly stroking my hair.

"It was just a dream," she cooed. "Everything's all right now."

My racing heart began to slow and I realized where I was and that there was no building about to explode.

Michelle was not the only good nurse in the burn unit. They were all good, with just a few exceptions. One night a float nurse was called in to sub for someone else and she spent most of her shift outside the room on the phone. After getting used to doting care from the regular staff, her lack of attention stressed me out.

This did not go unnoticed by Mom. Unable to do much for me herself, she watched my medical caregivers like a hawk. After that night, she demanded that the float nurse never be put in charge of me again.

Mom was a sweet, outgoing little lady at first blush. But she had a hard side tempered in Catholic schools full of knuckle-rapping nuns and long nights working part-time jobs to get through college. She went toe-to-toe with men on the other side of each case and at the judge's bench. They called her "The Bulldog" behind her back, as well as some less flattering things. Just weeks into my hospitalization, my mother was already developing a reputation at KU Med as someone you didn't want to cross.

But I could not rely on her to fight the battles I had ahead of me.

As I was slowly weaned off the sedatives again, I spent my few waking hours staring at my bandaged hands and trying to push aside any thought of losing my fingers. It would not happen. It could not happen. I didn't deserve it. I desperately wanted something else to think about and Mom provided it when she arrived on a Friday afternoon.

"You're going to get more visitors from home this weekend," she said. "Chris Markman is coming Sunday morning and Marie and Ali are coming Sunday night. They all just got done with school. Isn't that nice?"

I nodded slightly and smiled around the breathing tube. It would be great to see Chris and Marie — two gentle and quiet people who always put others above themselves. But it was Ali's name that gave me a warm feeling.

She and I met as freshmen in high school and dated briefly that year. It was the usual 15-year-old romance — an awkward, one-month courtship that I was not the least bit ready for. On the phone I was great — charming, funny, self-assured. But when we were together, face-to-face, I locked up. My tongue got tied, I didn't know how to put my arm around her without it seeming awkward. Hell, I could hardly look her in the eye. Quite simply, I had no game.

At the time, breaking up was almost a relief. I had only known Ali for a couple of months and my attraction to her was pretty superficial. Her long golden-blond hair glowed when the sun hit it and she had high cheekbones and delicate features like something out of a Disney movie.

She was gorgeous but I was 15, and I figured that I would meet many more gorgeous girls who would be interested in me.

I had second thoughts as the high school years flew on, though. We went to a small school, had several classes together and got to know each other. The more I got to know her, the more I liked her on a much deeper level than her looks. As former "Boyfriend/Girlfriend," we were supposed to play it cool though and avoid each other, at least by the social rules that most high-schoolers follow.

After graduation, Ali stayed in Minnesota for college. I left and was pleasantly distracted by the 10,000-plus girls at KU — most of whom I was afraid to talk to. Then I came home for the summer after my sophomore year and things got complicated.

Ali had just been dumped by her boyfriend and she was lonely. She reached out to a mutual friend, and soon she was welcomed into the group of people I hung out with in St. Cloud. She was back in my life.

Summers were for socializing back then. Most of us had part-time jobs, but didn't work mornings, so we stayed out late almost every night. There were trips to Twins games, a Gin Blossoms concert at the Minneapolis Basilica and countless evenings just sitting around in someone's house. This being Minnesota, there also was a small lake nearby that had a sandy beach where we spent many afternoons lounging and splashing in the water. Alcohol was occasionally involved, but we were a pretty straight-laced group.

All the while I found myself growing closer to Ali. We laughed at things no one else thought were funny and shared little looks and glances that communicated things without words.

As the summer went by, old feelings started to stir. Finally, three weeks before I was to go back to KU, I couldn't take it anymore, so I wrote her a poem. It was the usual lovestruck teenage stuff — rhymey and stuffed with one metaphor after another. But at the time, I thought it was good.

After hemming and hawing some in my mind, I sent the poem to her just before I left for a camping weekend with the guys. Out in a tent, with no phones and no email, there was no way to know how she would react when she read it. But I wasn't worried or anxious. I was relieved.

The day after I got back, she came over to my house. As soon as I opened the front door, she was in my arms, squeezing me in an embrace that pushed her silky hair up against my chin.

"What was that for?" I stammered, shocked.

She loosened her grasp a little and looked up at me with her green eyes shining.

"That poem," she said. "It was amazing."

My parents had left me alone in the house that night and Ali and I sat on the living room couch in each other's arms. I told her that I wanted to give "us" another try even if it meant being in a long-distance relationship. I loved KU and was too practical — or scared — to think about transferring, even for Ali. But I told her I would call every day and come home as often as I could.

I must have come on a bit too strong.

She told me wasn't sure. She wasn't far removed from a difficult break-up, after all.

I understood, but still believed we would end up together. She went home to sleep on it and I lay awake that night with cheesy love songs running through my head.

Ali called the next morning. She just wanted to be friends. That was that.

So I went back to school and tried to forget her. I met a lot of different girls, had a few first dates and even fewer second dates. My overactive imagination began to construct a story where Ali really was the girl I was meant to be with and that's why I could never find a serious girlfriend.

Now Ali was coming to see me in the hospital, all the way from Minnesota. My brain was addled with drugs and pain, but it immediately went to work on a fairy tale. One in which my brush with death made her realize how devastated she would have been if I hadn't made it. One in which she stayed by my side to nurse me back to health and, through her gentle touch, my arms and legs healed and I made a miraculous recovery.

Ali had a life back in Minnesota that included her family, a job and, yes, a boyfriend. I knew all this, but the daydream was just too good to dismiss.

I latched on to it, as a wonderful answer to the question I was beginning to ask: "Why did this happen to me?"

Using the daydream as a pleasant distraction turned out to be harder than I thought. As long as the breathing tube was in, I still had to be fairly heavily sedated. I was awake for very little of each day, and spent even less of that time conscious and coherent. Often it took most of that time just to remember where I was. Each time I woke up I felt a fresh wave of panic and anxiety and was glad to see whatever member of my family happened to be present.

I was also having some trouble discerning reality from the vivid, drug-induced dreams. I seemed to remember something about Ali coming to visit, but I didn't always know whether it was true or I had just dreamed that short conversation with Mom.

So when I pushed through the semi-conscious haze on a Sunday and found myself back in the hospital room with Ali and Marie sitting in chairs near the foot of the bed, it was still a surprise.

They had been talking, but when they noticed I was awake, their eyes lit up and they rushed to the side of the bed. Time was meaningless in that room, but I could tell it was night because their faces were framed by the soft lights of Kansas City blinking through the dark window behind them.

Ali and Marie took turns leaning in to gingerly give me a hug. I could feel the brush of Ali's soft hair against my face, but the moment wasn't like I imagined. Watching them maneuver carefully around the equipment surrounding the bed, it suddenly hit me how I must look to them: Pale, half-stupored with drugs, tubes running in and out of nearly every hole in my body, including one in my nose feeding me liquid nutrients and another in my ass sucking out liquid waste and depositing it in a bag attached to the side of the bed. For the first time, I was keenly aware of that bag and glad that it was mostly obscured by blankets.

Ali and Marie did their best to convince me they weren't freaked out. They chatted about our many mutual friends, telling me how much they all missed me and were thinking about me. I fought to follow the conversation but felt my eyes droop.

At some point, I groggily came back to consciousness. Marie was stroking my hair and murmuring gently.

"Oh Andy," she was saying, her eyes damp. "This is so hard. You're being so brave."

Ali stood behind her looking vaguely uncomfortable. I wasn't particularly at ease, either. This was out of the comfort zone of my relationship with Marie. I was one of the guys that she and the other girls came to watch play basketball or softball. I was supposed to be vibrant and active, a smartass who made her laugh. I wasn't supposed to make her cry.

She felt sorry for me and I didn't like it. Inside I was still that sarcastic guy who loved sports, but now I couldn't talk or run. I felt embarrassed and weak, but only for a few moments. Then I let sleep take me again.

There was some pressure on my upper right arm. That was all I knew as I cracked my eyes open to find myself in the hospital bed again. It was dark outside, nighttime again, but there were always some lights on in the room.

A nurse was at the side of the bed, one I didn't recognize. The squeezing on my arm came from the blood pressure cuff she was deflating. She detached the cuff's Velcro with a loud rip and hung it back on the bedside railing.

Ali and Marie were standing at the foot of the bed, watching the nurse and talking quietly. I couldn't hear what they were saying and I didn't think either of them knew I was awake. I was about to raise my hand to give them some sign that I was coherent when I realized what the nurse was going to do next.

She had moved to the foot of the bed and was lifting up the covers on the right side.

My God, she's going for the poop bag! Doesn't she realize there are people in the room? What the hell!

A wave of panic swept over me. There was nothing I could do. She had an empty bag sitting on the bed and was already detaching the full one, ready to switch it out. Anything I did would draw more attention to it, so I did the easiest thing I could think of — I pretended to be asleep.

I let my eyelids drop until there was just a sliver of light coming in. The nurse unhooked the full bag of crap and I saw it in all its sloshy-brown glory.

God, why do they have to use clear bags? Is it that important to monitor my stool?

With the feeding tube up my nose, I couldn't smell anything other than plastic, but I imagined the odor emanating from the small hole at the top of the bag.

I hoped fervently that Ali and Marie would somehow not notice all of this. But it was the only activity in the room and they were watching the whole thing. Ali wrinkled her nose and turned to whisper something to Marie.

I was mortified. For the first time since I regained consciousness, I felt the helplessness of my situation. Some people say there's no greater humiliation than needing someone to wipe your ass for you. Those people should try pooping in a bag and then having someone hold it up for their closest friends to see.

I wanted to cry, but I was still feigning sleep and knew that would blow my cover. For an instant, I let myself wish I was dead — that my heart had stopped the day I flew in on the helicopter. But something inside me recoiled at that thought and, in a flash, my humiliation was replaced by a sudden sense of reality.

That bag of shit was real. Those blackened fingers poking out of the bandages were real. Ali may have been standing there, but this was no romance novel, no episode of General Hospital. She couldn't reach down and place her hands on my face and suddenly make everything OK. There was nothing magical about her. She was just a girl and I was just a guy. A guy who had a lot more to worry about than his minimal love life.

The pedestal I had been building up for Ali over years and years crumbled in that moment. I realized that I had used her as an excuse for my own dating failures. This idea that she and I were meant to be together — that was a nice, soft way to mask the truth whenever my own fears and insecurities kept me from pursuing the kind of long-term relationship I thought I was entitled to.

My next emotion was an odd one: anger. I was angry with Ali for not being everything I'd built her up to be. I was angry at her for being there and seeing the bag of my shit, I was angry at her for not being able to fix me, and I was angry at myself for buying into all of that.

It was irrational, but I didn't care. I was tired of being afraid, tired of waking up to anxiety or even panic. I wanted to feel something different. Anger would have to do.

CHAPTER 7
MOVING DAY

My anger didn't last long. The next morning a young, bespectacled pulmonary doctor with neatly parted brown hair decided it was time for my breathing tube to come out again.

Mom and Grandma were obviously excited by the news. I was a bit apprehensive. I remembered the previous time the tube came out, and gasping vainly for air while nurses crouched at my bedside, pleading, "Breathe deeper, Andrew, you've got to breathe deeper."

I shuddered, and the doctor noticed.

"Don't worry, Andrew," he said, giving a little smile as he patted me on the shoulder. "You're breathing much better than you were a few weeks ago. You'll do fine."

Before I knew it, I was sedated again, watching drowsily as a fuzzy figure removed the tube. I was vaguely aware of an unpleasant tugging in my throat and wanted to gag, but didn't have the energy. Instead, I drifted off.

When I woke up, the tube was out and my throat was feeling raw again, though not quite as bad as last time. I turned to see Mom sitting in a chair to my left, smiling up at me from her crossword puzzle.

"Water," I croaked.

"OK, Andy-Panda, I'll go find a nurse," she said, pausing first to kiss me on the forehead.

Ice chips again trickled delicious coolness down my burning throat.

With the tube out, I was less sedated than I'd been at any time since I entered the hospital. For the first time in weeks I spent hours at a time awake, even sitting up in bed. Chris had already gone, unfortunately, but Ali and Marie came to see me one last time and were delighted that I was awake and able to talk, albeit only in hoarse whispers.

Everything seemed a little more normal. I sat up and mostly listened as they chattered back and forth about our friends — who was dating whom, who had already found a post-college job, who hadn't been seen in a while. I interjected once in a while with snide comments when I could come up with them and, though I often had to repeat them to be heard, they usually drew a laugh. It felt good and I enjoyed the fact that I could finally look at Ali without getting that familiar twinge in my stomach. We were friends.

The removal of the breathing tube signaled a new phase in my hospitalization. I was still in one of the burn unit's intensive care rooms, but the doctors were confident I was going to make it, and it was time to think about recovery rather than survival.

I was turned over to Dr. Thomas Lawrence, a plastic surgeon who worked with burn patients. Dr. Lawrence was a middle-aged man whose slicked-back black hair had strands of gray creeping in around the ears. He was unfailingly cheerful and his eyes often seemed big behind his glasses, as if he were trying hard not to blink. Staff members consistently called him "one of the best around."

Dr. Lawrence explained to Mom and Dad that he would be the one doing whatever amputations were necessary after my tissues stabilized. He said he would wait until the "line of demarcation" between healthy tissue and dead tissue was clearly defined. Some surgeons, he said, wouldn't hesitate to lop off my legs below the knees and my arms below the elbows, just to be on the safe side. But his aim was to save as much tissue as possible, even if it was damaged.

"Then you can always cut higher later on," he said, matter-of-factly.

Dr. Lawrence also told my parents he could save more of my hands by encasing them in "full-thickness" tissue grafts taken from my abdomen. He explained that this meant sewing my hands inside my abdomen for three weeks to provide enough soft tissue between bone and skin for the graft to take.

I accepted the idea of the full-tissue graft without really thinking about what it would mean to have my hands sewn into my abdomen. I was still convinced that my fingers were going to come back — or at least mostly come back. If it turned out that I had to lose some fingertips, well, then, I would do what it took to retain as much as I could. If that meant trying this full-tissue graft, that's what we would do.

On May 21, 2004, three days after my breathing tube was removed and 24 days after I was first hospitalized, I was deemed "stable" and moved out of intensive care.

The whole family came to celebrate my going about 25 yards down the hall to one of the burn unit's "regular" rooms, 5211. There was much more space in the new room. The high-tech, air-circulating bed jutting out near the far wall dominated it, but there were fewer big machines around the bed. The far wall consisted of three side-by-side plate-glass windows. Outside I could see the flat roofs of a few nearby businesses, part of a parking ramp and the residential neighborhood south of the Med Center.

There was a bathroom just inside the door on the left and I wondered immediately if I'd be able to use it. My catheter was still in, but now that I wasn't sedated, the butt tube had thankfully been removed. The last couple days in intensive care I had been using a bedpan, but I figured I would soon be mobile enough to get in this new bathroom and actually sit on the toilet. Now that would be a treat.

By the time the nurses and techs rolled me from the gurney onto my new bed, I was feeling tuckered out from doing two transfers in quick succession. I drifted off into another nap and, when I awoke, found Mom bustling around the room, putting the finishing touches on her decorating.

She had hung little religious items with inspirational messages on several walls. One, from the Book of Jeremiah, read, "For I know the plans I have for you," declares the LORD, "plans to prosper you and not to harm you, plans to give you a future and a hope." That was nice, though it made me wonder why what seemed to be pretty considerable harm had already come to me.

Across the room, she hung a small stitching of a beach scene with footprints in the sand and the famous Christian quote, "When you saw only one set of footprints, it was then that I carried you." That made me chuckle.

"What's so funny?" Mom asked, cocking her head to the side and grinning along with me.

"Oh, nothing," I said.

That quote always reminded me of one of my favorite articles from *The Onion*. At one time the satirical newspaper did a lot of fake point/counterpoint editorials. One of them featured a picture of Jesus on one side saying his famous line about footprints in the sand. The counterpoint was a picture of a sour-faced, middle-aged guy with the headline, "Bullshit Jesus, those are my footprints." Blasphemous? Possibly. But still pretty funny.

Besides the religious paraphernalia, Mom was also displaying cards from friends and family to lift my spirits. My bed faced the TV, of course, but that hung just below the ceiling, which left room underneath for one of my favorite cards. It was a huge piece of white poster board signed by a bunch of the kids from the scholarship halls at KU. Some of it wasn't visible under the foot of the bed, but during my first day in the new room I scanned time and again the signatures and messages on the top half.

Many of those people, my classmates and friends, would be walking the next day through the campanile, down the hill and into the football stadium for KU's annual graduation ceremony.

I would not be among them. Though I was out of intensive care, I was in no condition to leave the hospital. I still had my catheter and my feeding tube in, I still had the IV opening in my neck, though it had tape over it now because I was getting most of my pain meds from a 24-hour morphine patch on my back. My limbs were still numb and blackened and it hurt to move. I had open sores and infection was a huge danger. I'd still be in Room 5211. Despite Nurse Rebecca's generous offer, there was no way I was going to make it to graduation, even if she were at my side.

I was one of those kids who actually enjoyed school, a kid who read a lot, knew a lot and raised his hand a lot. I tried not to be too insufferably smug about it, but academics came easy to me and I knew it. My classroom mentality hewed closely to a poetic verse that sprang from Big Daddy Kane's rap career: "I hate to brag, but damn I'm good."

The honor of leading the journalism class of 2004 onto the football field as the grad with the school's highest GPA seemed more my right than a privilege. Now the guy with the second-highest GPA would get that spot.

That wasn't the most gut-wrenching part of missing graduation, though. Friends I lived with at Pearson or worked with at the school paper would be strolling down that hill. They'd be footloose and carefree, cracking jokes and taking pictures as they went. Some of them would likely be naked under their robes. I would miss out on making those memories with them and, even if I suddenly recovered miraculously the next day, that would still be something precious that meningitis stole from me.

As a consolation prize, I was supposed to watch the ceremony unfold on a live Internet feed in the burn unit's staff workroom. I felt like I was entitled to more, but for the sake of my parents, I tried to act excited about it.

CHAPTER 8

TWO GRADUATIONS

The staff workroom was about what I expected: a narrow, windowless space with a big wooden table in the middle. There was a computer on one end of the table attached to a projector. The large, white screen dominated the other side of the room.

I was rolled into the room on an inclined chair with inflatable pads that circulated air similar to my bed. I was positioned at one end of the table while Mom, Dad, Grandma and Josh all took chairs around it. Dan, with the university's blessing, was taking my place at the graduation ceremony.

"He printed out a picture of you and he's going to tape it to the front of his gown so everyone knows why he's there," Mom had told me earlier in the day.

I leaned back in the chair as one of the nurses fired up the computer. He started telling us about how to access the Internet on this particular PC, but Mom stopped him, letting him know that her first-born son was an electrical engineer and could probably figure it out. Josh took over from there and soon found the website for KUJH, the university's student-run television station.

KUJH's website was supposed to be showing the graduation live. But when Josh accessed the feed, we instead got footage of an old football game between KU and Colorado. Mom checked the clock, noting that the ceremony should have started.

"I don't know," Josh said. "Maybe it's on a slight delay."

But, after watching about 20 minutes of former KU quarterback Bill Whittemore scrambling for dear life and winging passes, it became clear that the graduation ceremony wasn't going to air. At least not live.

"Well, this is just ridiculous," Mom said, shaking her head.

I didn't really mind. I was just glad to be out of my room, doing something that felt normal — watching football.

"We could show Andy the CaringBridge site," Dad suggested.

Mom brightened up immediately.

"Yeah, go there, Josh," she said.

I had been hearing about this site for days. Members of the family regularly brought in little notes they had copied from people wishing me well on the site's guestbook. Now I finally got to see the originals for myself as Josh scrolled down through dozens and dozens of letters from the outside world. One of the most recent ones was from my seventh-grade science teacher. I was shocked he even remembered me:

Hello Marso family!

I just learned of Andy's situation from the Carpenters last night, and they passed on the website information. I am relieved to hear that Andy's condition is on the upswing. Andy, hang in there and know that you will be in my prayers!

Sincerely,
Bob Ellenbecker

Then there was an old note from Dr. Jim, whose kind words even made up for his being a Laker fan:

We have come a LONG way in the care of Andy, and I am confident he will continue to do well. He has made truly amazing progress. There are few patients that come along in one's career who impact us personally, but Andy has been one of those for me. It has been a real honor and privilege for me to be Andy's primary doctor, and he is a testament that prayer and science can come together for the greater good and have a profound impact on one's life. I hope that we remember all of the others sick and ill in the hospital at this time, and lift them in our prayers as well. It may not be scientifically provable that prayer works, but Andy is testament that faith has a powerful impact in medicine. Therefore, let none of us ever forget that no matter how good our medicine is or how cutting edge our treatment modalities may be, it is God who heals and that we as physicians are merely His instruments.

Jim Southwell Jr. D.O.

Josh scrolled on and on through the messages and I read them hungrily, my heart filling up with the love that was flowing to me from all directions. There was a note from Marie, telling everyone to send me videos so I wouldn't get bored, a note from our parish priest back in St. Cloud, letting me know that all of St. Peter's was praying for my family, and countless other notes from people who just wanted me to know they were thinking of me. Some were hospital staffers, some were friends from KU, some were people I hadn't seen since high school.

My eyes welled up and a few tears rolled down my cheeks. I always knew I wasn't fighting alone because my family had been there every minute. But at that point I began to realize just how many people I had in my corner.

"Andy, a lot of people have been asking for an entry from you," Mom said. "Is there something you want us to post on here right now?"

I wanted to say something deep and meaningful or at least something witty to let everyone know that I was still the same sarcastic jackass, and that wasn't going to change.

But nothing like that came to mind.

"Just tell them I can't express the gratitude I feel to all of them," I said huskily through the catch in my throat. "Tell them I'm getting better."

I rolled back to my room a little later, exhausted physically and emotionally.

Two days later, I had my own personal graduation.

My hospitalization was still making news on campus and KU Chancellor Robert Hemenway was following it. When he heard that I wouldn't be able to come to graduation, he called Malcolm Gibson and offered to present my diploma in person at the hospital.

I had met the Chancellor briefly at a couple honors functions and found him to be a likable, down-to-earth guy; almost grandfatherly — if your grandfather happened to be a published author considered an expert on American literature. It would be good to see him, but I was more eager to get a look at that diploma. It was proof that I had actually been allowed to graduate even though I missed my last three weeks.

Rick and Greg drove back down for the event and they brought another old friend of ours, Tim. After going to grade school with us, Tim had gone to a different high school, but we had stayed close through Boy Scouts. In fact, he and I were frequent tent-mates on camping trips. At one point, we calculated that by the end of high school we'd spent close to 100 nights together, a figure we were somewhat reluctant to share with others. It was far more than either of us had ever spent with a girl.

Even with me confined to a bed and still scratchy in the throat, the four of us easily fell back into boyish banter. We sat in my room one night watching the hockey film "Miracle" (we were Minnesota boys, after all, even if none of us were particularly skilled skaters). Drowsy from drugs, I was dozing off for stretches of the movie and fighting to stay awake the rest of the time.

"I think he's asleep," I heard Tim whisper as my eyes drooped once again. "Maybe we should turn it off and leave so he can rest."

I definitely didn't want them to leave and I didn't want them to have to turn off the movie. I felt like they were my guests and I should be making sure they were having a good time, even if that was somewhat ridiculous given the situation. Luckily, a team shower scene popped up on screen, giving me the perfect opportunity for a sarcasm surprise attack.

"Oh-h-h-h-h, yeah," I said as several bare-chested young males appeared on screen. Tim, Greg and Rick busted out laughing. My half-asleep state and the hoarseness of my voice had made it sound even sleazier than I hoped.

The graduation ceremony at the hospital quickly became something bigger than just Chancellor Hemenway handing me a diploma. Malcolm had gamely handled media requests for weeks to give my family some private time, but the reporters were eager for an appearance from "The Meningitis Kid" himself. As a budding journalist, I understood the power I suddenly had. People all over Kansas City were following my story, and the emotional impact I could have just by getting in front of a camera and saying a few words was tremendous. I could thank all the strangers that had been praying for me, I could get the word out about meningitis, and I could tell everyone how supportive the staff at KU Med had been. I also just thought it would be kind of cool to be on TV.

Malcolm suggested that the Chancellor's visit would be a good time to hold a press conference and take care of all the media requests at once. I agreed.

So two days after KU had its university-wide graduation, the hospital's public relations staff turned the burn unit break room into a makeshift briefing room. The long dining table in the center was replaced with several rows of folding chairs and a podium appeared in front of the microwave and fridge.

Jeny, a redheaded, ever-smiling burn tech about my age, prepared me for my close-up. In just a few days, she had become one of my favorites. She called me "Andy-man," which coming from someone else might have annoyed me. Coming from her, it made me smile.

Jeny did the best she could to make me presentable. She changed the bandages covering my arms and legs and helped me into a fresh hospital gown after washing my face and shampooing my hair with a special shower cap. Then she combed my hair and parted it down the middle, which was a serious project. At Gustavo's suggestion, I had let it grow into thick, wavy locks during my last semester.

I was still pale and I had a feeding tube up my nose but, all in all, I looked as good as I could.

By that point, I was a little nervous about the press conference, but almost everyone I loved most in the world was there to support me. The whole family, of course, along with three of my oldest friends from St. Cloud. Clay and Randy had promised to show up as well.

When Dan wheeled me down the hall to the break room, I was expecting a big crowd, but I wasn't nearly prepared for what I got. As soon as we entered the room, cameras clicked and flashed. The metal folding chairs were full. Hospital staff stood along both walls and in the back next to several TV cameramen. Chancellor Hemenway was at the podium, which was clustered with microphones. A low table had been set next to the podium and Dan wheeled me over to it. Mom and Dad were already seated there, behind another bank of microphones.

When Chancellor Hemenway first started talking, I didn't register a word — I was too busy absorbing all the faces looking back at me. The front chairs were full of reporters in slacks, button-down shirts and dresses, press credentials hanging from their necks and notebooks in their laps. Along the left wall in front of the windows stood Tim, Rick and Greg, together in a row. Clay and Randy were also there, a little farther back.

Then something Hemenway said caught my ear.

"... His struggle, his bravery, his courage are very much on people's minds these days at KU," he said. "He's a true Jayhawk in every sense of the word."

That put a lump in my throat. I came to KU from Minnesota not knowing anyone. I found a home with the Pearson guys, but I always felt like a bit of an outsider on the campus at large. Most of the other students came from eastern Kansas and it wasn't unusual for them to run into old high school friends on the way to or from class. I would eavesdrop, a bit enviously, as they reminisced about a certain teacher or football game, aware that I would never fit into that particular world.

But now I felt the power of what the chancellor was saying, the power of being part of that larger KU community. I had 20,000-some peers pulling for me simply because I went to class in the same giant buildings and cheered for the same basketball team. I had never been prouder to be a Jayhawk.

Someone handed the chancellor my diploma, a piece of paper inside a folder with the university's seal on it. He opened the folder and read the inscription:

"The University of Kansas, by the authority of the Board of Regents of the State of Kansas and upon the recommendation of the Faculty of the School of Journalism, confers upon Andrew Joseph Marso the degree of Bachelor of Science in Journalism, with all its rights, privileges and responsibilities. Given under the seal of the University of Kansas this 23rd day of May, 2004."

He bent down and set it in front of me with a familiar smile, the one where his nose crinkled up and his glasses shifted ever-so-slightly on his bald head. The room broke into applause. As I looked at the diploma, the words began to blur. I didn't want to cry, not with all those TV cameras around, but the emotional train was steaming out of control. I turned to the windows on my left, staring through the Venetian blinds to try to compose myself. I saw Rick, Greg, Tim, Clay and Randy, clapping along with the other people in the room. Rick was giving me an unsure grin — trying to reassure me — and a great warmth washed over me. The five of them were my best friends in the world — three from Minnesota, two from KU. I had wanted to bring them together so many times and now here they all were. And yet the circumstances were so far from what I had imagined. There would be no games of Ultimate Frisbee in front of Fraser Hall or nights out at The Wheel, sipping beers and stealing glances at pretty girls. I wanted to laugh with them, but instead there I was, desperately trying to keep from crying. It wasn't right. It wasn't fair. I deserved better.

The clapping subsided and it became obvious that everyone was staring at me, waiting for me to say something. I tried to whisper a tiny "Thank you" into the microphone, but my voice was so hoarse that even I couldn't hear it. I sat there, frustrated, touched, scared and angry all at the same time.

Finally, my chest heaved with sobs and the tears began to roll down my cheeks. The photographers clicked their shutters one after another and I only cried harder as I realized that I was breaking down in front of a large portion of the greater Kansas City area. This was the emotional "money shot" the photographers were looking for and I had given it to them at the expense of whatever tiny bit of machismo I still possessed. This was me, broken down to my most vulnerable.

Mom put her arm around me and rubbed my shoulder, but I just blubbered with my chin on my chest, large teardrops staining the front of my hospital gown.

"He just wants to say, 'Thank you,'" Mom said, and I nodded helplessly.

Actually I just wanted to get out of there. I wanted to go some place where I could cry in peace. Dan seemed to sense it. Suddenly he was behind me, turning me away from the table and wheeling me back into the hallway. Jeny and three other nurses were on his heels and followed us into my room. One of the photographers came after us, still frantically clicking pictures. Dan turned around and flew into a rage when he saw him. He left my side to shove the man out and I could hear him yelling at him out in the hall.

I wasn't alone. Jeny had her arm around me and soon the other three nurses were crouched next to the wheelchair, sobbing along with me. They hugged me, but I was afraid to hug them back with my bandaged arms.

After a few minutes like that, the sobs began to subside. The nurses straightened up, but stayed in contact with me, rubbing my shoulders and stroking my hair. Slowly I began to relax.

Jeny stood up and sighed, wiping her eyes with the back of her hand.

"Well, Andy-Man," she said. "Bet you've never had four girls cry with you before."

I smiled, even with tears still stinging my eyes.

Eventually the media was herded out of the burn unit and I rejoined my friends in the break room. We ate cake, talked and watched TV, and for an hour or so I was able to forget the wheelchair I was in and the hospital bed that awaited me. Clay and Randy told stories about Pearson, including how I had unofficially been voted "Most Normal" in a scholarship hall full of varying degrees of social awkwardness. Rick and Greg filled them in on some of my less normal exploits, like when I used to strip down to my boxer shorts while playing basketball on the driveway behind Greg's house on hot days. There were plenty of laughs and for the moment their friendship refueled my will to get better so I could join them outside the hospital.

I would need that fuel desperately.

I missed a few things at the press conference while I was in my room crying. I missed Dr. Barkman taking the podium and deflecting the credit for saving my life from KU Med to Clay, whom he called "the real hero." I also missed Dr. Lawrence briefing the reporters on what lay ahead for me.

"He will almost certainly have amputations of some parts of most of his digits," the doctor told them. "It may take another month or so to really have that completely defined. We're hoping that maybe it can be in a little less time. The key point is that we don't want to sacrifice any tissue that has any chance of being salvaged."

Saving as much tissue as possible meant that I was about to become acquainted with one of the parts of my recovery that would give me nightmares for years: the "tank room."

CHAPTER 9

FLOATING FLESH

The damage to my blood vessels was so severe that my limbs had turned black as the outer layers of skin and fatty tissue died from loss of circulation. When I was transferred to the burn unit I was told that my skin damage was equal to third-degree burns over 30 percent of my body. To save my arms and legs, all that dead tissue would have to be removed. The process of removing it is called "debridement," probably because that sounds nicer than "slicing off dead skin." It is the standard procedure for treating severe burns, but something I had never heard of before my hospitalization, nor could I have imagined such an ordeal being part of the healing process.

The only enjoyable part of debridement was the shot of Fentanyl I got beforehand. A nurse named Bob came in one day several weeks into the process and administered the opioid, 80 to100 times more potent than morphine, to hedge against the pain.

Nothing could hedge against the trauma of what I was about to see.

Bob injected the Fentanyl straight into my bloodstream, through the IV port in my neck. Immediately a wave of pleasant warmth rushed over me and my muscles relaxed and went limp. My mind was still fuzzy when a short, cute wound tech named Linda entered the room a few minutes later.

"Ready to go Andy?" she asked, her voice muffled by her surgical mask.

"Ready as I'll ever be," I mumbled. It was my stock response.

She and Bob helped me slide from my inflatable bed onto a gurney. Then we began wheeling down the hallway. It was a short trip, but my sense of dread grew with each turn of the squeaky wheels. Linda backed through the door and pulled me into the tank room in one motion. It was windowless and dominated by two shallow metal tables separated by a shower curtain. It was oppressively hot and humid in there, by design. Patients with large open wounds have trouble regulating their body temperatures. The nurses and wound techs always came out of the tank with soaked hair and beads of sweat under their eyes.

With assistance I scooted from the gurney onto one of the metal tables, where only a thin foam pad separated my body from the stainless steel. Then four low walls were swung up from the bottom of the table and snapped into place around me, forming a shallow tub. We were ready to begin.

First the techs removed my hospital gown, carefully pulling out my arms until I was naked except for my bandages.

"Here, let's cover up your private area," Linda said, placing a tiny washcloth over my groin.

Nice try, I thought. Linda always referred to that as my "private area," but in truth, it hadn't been private for some time. Since I arrived at the hospital it had been viewed by countless doctors, nurses and probably even a few custodians and unwitting visitors who caught a free show when I got careless with the backless gown. I was starting to forget that I was supposed to be embarrassed by nakedness.

Besides, I was much more anxious about what I would see when the bandages were removed. That took much longer than shedding the hospital gown. The outer layers of gauze unrolled easily, but the lower layers — tinged red and black with a combination of blood and scabby dead tissue — tugged painfully on my wounds. Two movable shower heads dangled from the ceiling and Linda and the other techs used them to wet the bandages so they wouldn't stick so much as they peeled off.

Then I got a look at my arms and legs. No matter how many times I saw them, it always made my stomach turn. Around mid-thigh and near my shoulders the skin was red and raw. Lower on my arms and legs it was just pitch black, like the worst burn I could imagine. My fingers were beginning to curl into shriveled, lifeless claws. I desperately wanted to flex them, but there was no feeling left. No matter how much I focused and strained, I couldn't move them.

After absorbing the initial shock, I rested my head back and stared at the ceiling. I couldn't bear to look at those limbs very long. If I didn't look, I could pretend those weren't my arms and legs. They just couldn't be. I couldn't feel them, after all, so those hideous things must be attached to someone else's body.

But once the debridement started there was no denying it was my body they were working on. After a gentle spray of water, the techs began to slowly remove the black flesh. Sometimes they were able to just pull it off with forceps, exposing healthy layers of pink and red underneath. Other times they had to slice carefully inward with scalpels, removing layer after layer until I began to bleed. That was the signal that they had reached living, viable tissue.

There was nothing to do in the tank room but lie still and try to occupy my mind with something other than what they were doing to me. The only distraction was a CD player and the burn techs were always willing to bring my music in there and play it. It would have been the right place for something dark like Marilyn Manson or Korn, but I had never been into that. I tried some guitar-heavy rock like Van Halen and the Scorpions, but it was never intense enough to pull me out of the pain. Sometimes I went for lighter, vocal-driven fare like John Mayer and David Gray, hoping it would be soothing. But it just seemed to annoy or depress me. As Mayer droned on about his "quarter-life crisis" and struggling to find meaning in his life, all I could think was, "Yeah, John, I wish that was my biggest problem right now." The tank was where I had many of my "Why-me?" moments.

The wound techs did their utmost to be gentle, sacrificing speed by giving me a short break if I cried out in pain. I gritted my teeth through the tugging as the black flesh pulled away. I squirmed at the sting of the scalpels drawing blood. And all the while I kept those claw-like fingers raised up away from the rest of me so I wouldn't feel their icy, dead touch against a part of my body that still had sensation.

Sometimes Dr. Lawrence came into the tank room to assist with the debriding. Unlike the burn techs, he cut deep, quick swaths into my skin. He was like a spelunker, doggedly digging into my body and exploring it for living, bleeding tissue. He would not stop until I was crying and begging for another shot of Fentanyl, which was so strong it could only be administered once an hour.

The tank room walls were mostly bare, but on the ceiling and the wall opposite my head there were two hard-to-read sentences printed on a label maker. One said, "We care," and the other said, "We are here to help." That could be hard to remember in the tank room.

The final 20 minutes of each session were the worst. The table sloped slightly toward my feet to drain the water, which by then was topped with floating bits of dead flesh. Over the hour-and-a-half or so I was usually in the tank, my body gradually slid down the incline, a millimeter at a time. Eventually the balls of my feet, which had been debrided down to the bone in some places, would graze the hard steel of the bottom wall, sending electric jolts of pain through my legs.

Then the burn techs would take a moment to drag me back up higher on the table and, for the first time in my basketball-loving life, I would thank God I wasn't taller. Dragging me up the foam pad just to have me slowly slide down again also caused problems. The skin on my butt, while not quite as bad off as my arms and legs, had also been damaged. It was paper-thin and fragile and kept tearing open no matter how many different wound dressings the nurses and techs tried. The layer of foam was only about an inch thick, and my raw, bleeding bum stung more and more fiercely with each passing moment. Near the end of the session that pain often overwhelmed all the rest and I begged for someone to help me turn over on my side and take the pressure off that throbbing area. When they finally complied I let out a groan of relief as sweet, cooling air caressed my burning backside like the finest liniment. It would have been funny — if it hadn't hurt so damn much.

Mike Nolte knew all about the tank. A middle-aged father of three girls, Mike was burned in a horrible car accident in Missouri a year before I got sick. He had been pulled over on the highway by a state trooper for driving too slowly in the passing lane. He was ordered into the back seat of the patrol car while the trooper wrote the ticket because it was supposed to be safer in there.

On that day, it wasn't safer. A driver in a one-ton pickup truck drifted onto the shoulder and plowed into the trooper's Crown Victoria, which burst into flames as the gas tank ruptured. Trapped in the car, Mike watched the trooper burn to death and was near death himself when two Good Samaritans came upon the accident and risked their lives to drag him out of the inferno.

Mike spent months at the University of Missouri hospital, going through the same torturous treatments to remove the burnt skin that covered nearly half his body. He had been back home in Kansas City for only a few months, recuperating and getting back to work at the bridal store he owned, when he saw the first news reports about the University of Kansas student stricken with a rare bacterial infection.

He followed my case from then on and decided to reach out to me and my family.

When Mike first came to visit I was struck by how well-groomed he was. Nice slacks, a stylish, long-sleeved shirt and dusty blond hair in the carefully-messy spike style that was trendy right about then. At first I couldn't see any of his injuries. But then, as he greeted me with a slight smile and sat down next to the bed, I started to make them out. One side of his face was a bit shinier than the other, almost waxy. It was faint, though — the kind of difference you'd only notice if you were looking for it.

Mike was quiet and there was a nervousness about him initially. He glanced around the room, his eyes slightly watery behind his glasses. It occurred to me that this was all still very familiar for him — the bandages, the beeping of machines and that indescribable but distinct hospital smell. Visiting me forced him to confront memories that were recent and vivid.

We chatted for awhile, making small talk about my mom's hyper-protective tendencies and the hot weather. Then I decided to just ask the question that was really on my mind.

"So," I started, "did you hate the tank as much as I do?"

At first he just nodded, a haunted look in his eyes. Then he opened his mouth to respond, leaning forward.

"Of course," he said. "It was by far the worst thing I've ever had to go through. I always wanted them to give me as much notice as possible before they took me in there so I could get my mind ready."

"I know what you mean," I said. "It's so hard to get your head around. I mean, there's times in there when they're pulling skin off and I'm watching it go down the drain when I just want to shout, 'Hey, I'm a real person, not a mannequin, and that's a real foot,' but I can't even talk 'cause of the pain."

"I couldn't even think," Mike replied, nodding vigorously. "I remember when my pastor came up to visit me and I told him about how hard it was for me to go in there. I told him I couldn't even pray, the pain was so bad. It just overwhelmed everything."

Now it was my turn to nod. Even the familiar words of the "Our Father" or the "Hail Mary" often slipped from my mind's grasp when the sting of the scalpel shot through me.

"He told me something that helped some," Mike said, still talking about his pastor. "He said, 'Mike, you can offer up that pain as a prayer. God will understand.'"

That made sense. God was experiencing the pain right along with me, so I could talk to him without actually saying or thinking a coherent word, which was reassuring. I was just glad to know that I didn't have to be ashamed when tears squeezed out of my eyes in the morning at the thought of my impending trip to the tank. It wasn't just me; it wasn't all in my head. It really was as bad as I thought.

But seeing Mike reminded me that others had faced it, too, and made it out the other side. Intellectually, I knew this. Hell, there were rooms full of other people up and down the burn unit hallway who were enduring the same treatments. But we were pretty isolated from each other, both for privacy and because we were all prone to infection. Even surrounded by family it was easy to feel alone, because they couldn't take that painful part of the journey.

When I got back from the tank one day, I rolled into bed and tried to rest my still-stinging body. I had gotten used to lying in bed and having people take care of me. I didn't want the rest of my life to be like that, but I had it in my head that this would all go away at some point and I would get better. At that point I would pick up my old life where it left off. In the meantime, though, I figured I would just wait it out and let people feed me and dress me.

I had two physical therapists who had other plans, though. Rachel, a young, athletic blonde, was in charge of my lower body and Mylene, a slim, middle-aged brunette, was looking after the upper half. They would come in my room a few hours after I got back from the tank and ask whether I wanted to go to the rehab room down the hall and put in some work. By then my aching butt was lying comfortably on the pressure-relieving airbed, so I was in no hurry to go anywhere. Besides, I usually reasoned, how much can I really do until my hands and feet come back?

"I don't really feel like it today," I'd usually say.

Then I would absorb their frustrated looks and usually allow Rachel to at least stretch my legs while I stayed in bed or try out some new wrist strap that Mylene had made to help me hold a cup or fork.

This went on for a week or two while, behind the scenes, Rachel and Mylene were planning an intervention of sorts. One afternoon when Mom was there they entered my room along with the burn unit's care coordinator.

"Rachel and Mylene are worried about your recovery," the coordinator began, looking slightly uncomfortable. "They say you've been reluctant to set goals or pursue independence."

Pursue independence? I was confused.

"I'm just waiting until I get better," I said. "I'm tired when I get back from the tank room and it takes so much effort just to get out of bed. What's the rush?"

The coordinator opened her mouth, but Rachel broke in impatiently.

"The longer you stay in bed, the more muscle you'll lose and the harder it will be to get it back," she said.

"You need to start considering what you'll do when you leave the hospital," Mylene added.

"What do you mean, 'What I'll do?'" I said. "I've got an apartment with my friends lined up. I've got a job waiting for me. I'll go back to doing what I used to do. You told me I'd be able to do everything I used to."

At this point Rachel, Mylene and the coordinator all looked at each other, something unspoken passing among them. I looked from one to the other, wondering what the hell was going on.

"You'll be able to do everything, but maybe not in the same way you used to," Mylene said slowly.

"What do you mean?" I asked.

"You need to start working with them on adapting to your body so you can be independent," the coordinator said. "Otherwise we'll have to discharge you to a nursing home after your treatments are complete."

That sentence hit me like a freight train. I had a sudden flash of myself in a nursing home, a 22-year-old in a crowd of gray-haired octogenarians, having my food spooned into my mouth and spending the day staring out the window from my bed.

I felt my eyes welling up and I could only stifle the first couple sobs. Soon my chest was heaving and the tears were pouring down. Mom jumped out of her chair like an angry bear ready to defend her cub.

"How dare you," she said. "My son will never be in a nursing home. His father and I will take care of him as long as he needs us."

"Mom, be quiet," I mumbled thickly through my tears.

"No, Andrew," she said, glancing back at me just for an instant. "This isn't fair. You're going through something they could never understand, and...."

"SHUT UP, MOM," I yelled, bringing everything, including my tears, to a screeching halt. "They're right. I need to work harder. I don't want to live with you and Dad for the rest of my life. I want to get back to my life. I need to work harder."

With that I began another painful ordeal: daily visits to the rehab room, a large space dominated by a bank of windows on the far wall. The room was just a few dozen feet down the hall, but it was a process getting me there. My legs were already covered by several layers of gauze, but Rachel and Mylene rolled Ace bandages around them tightly while I was in bed for greater protection, and to keep any swelling down. Then they called in one of the nurses to deflate my bed so it would be low enough for me to get out of it and into a wheelchair.

The mattress flattened down to nothing and for a moment my butt burned as I sat on little more than a slab of steel and a couple sheets. Then I did my best to stand up, turn and plop down in the chair. I put one arm around the nurse and the other around Rachel, so only the slightest bit of weight was on my feet when I stood, but it still felt as if I was being stabbed all the way up through my legs. It was just the beginning.

When we got to the rehab room I was taken to a platform walker. It had four legs like the standard walkers that old people use, but it also had padded troughs extended from the top that I could strap my forearms into because I couldn't use my hands. Rachel and Mylene stood on either side of the wheelchair, ready to help me up and into the walker.

It always took time for me to work up the courage to try to stand. They coaxed and prodded, gently telling me that this was what was necessary to walk again — that I had to maintain as much strength and flexibility in my feet, ankles and legs as possible. I sat, taking slow, deep breaths, and then tried to get up. Rachel and Mylene hoisted me toward the arm troughs, but I balked as the daggers began stabbing into my ravaged feet. I collapsed back into the chair with a grimace. False start.

We started over and this time in their coaxing and prodding I detected the slightest note of impatience. *This isn't a lot of fun for me either*, I thought bitterly. Finally, I took a few more deep breaths and went for it, determined to go all the way this time.

The daggers stabbed into my legs again, but I pushed through and pressed my arms into the troughs to take as much pressure off my feet as possible.

"OK Andy, now let's try and take a few steps," Rachel said. She was stationed next to me with one hand on my back and the other on the walker.

I shuffled forward, feeling like I was in some kind of "Twilight Zone" nightmare. The bottom of my feet were stripped down to the bone in some places and oozing and dripping blood. Putting them down on the hard linoleum was like walking on knives, even with all the gauze and Ace bandages providing padding. I alternated between gasping and gritting my teeth, tears slowly squeezing out my eyes. But I inched forward, one tiny bit at a time, with Rachel always exhorting me to "just go a little bit farther."

Finally I could stand it no longer and collapsed back into the chair, which Mylene had been pushing behind me. I held my legs up as the burning in my feet slowly subsided. The tears flowed freely as Rachel and Mylene patted me on the back and told me what a great job I'd done and how brave I'd been. I didn't feel very brave as I thanked God it was over.

It wasn't over for long. A few minutes later Rachel said, "OK, ready to try it again?"

The process was repeated, with me even more reluctant and difficult to persuade. After two or three walks — they covered a total of about 15 feet - I was usually spent physically and emotionally and let them know that I would not be leaving the wheelchair again unless it was to get back into that glorious airbed.

Then Mylene took over with the upper body, which wasn't nearly as painful, but was just as frustrating. After she stretched out my elbows and shoulders we'd try out whatever new contraption she had for the day. Usually it was something to help me eat on my own. She made a cuff that held a spoon or fork and wrapped around my wrist with Velcro. After attaching it she'd give me something to eat.

It had never occurred to me before just how much force it took to stab something like a slice of apple with a fork. I thrust my arm up and down, but the apple just slid around the plate. Finally I trapped it against the rim, but when I stabbed at it the prongs of the fork still wouldn't pierce it easily. When I finally seemed to have it, I lifted it toward my mouth, but I had to twist my arm around to get the fork in the right position, and in twisting it the barely pierced apple slice came free and dropped in my lap. I wanted to scream. But there was nothing I could do except start over. After a few deep breaths I went at it again, shaking my head. *All this for one damn bite of apple?*

Sometimes Mylene switched to a spoon and tried to get me to eat soup or watery oatmeal. I could get it in the spoon OK, but by the time I had twisted it up to my mouth, most of it had slopped out onto my hospital gown. By the end of lunch I looked like a baby in need of a fresh bib.

The sessions in the tank room and in physical therapy were tortuous, but the alternative was to amputate both legs below the knee and both arms below the elbow. That was not an option that I or my family were willing to contemplate. There was still hope that enough blood vessels would be able to repair themselves and that the burn techs would find some healthy tissue next time they cut into my hands and feet.

During the early days of my hospitalization Mom and Dad had spoken with a young female resident who had contracted meningitis in college. Like them, her parents had been told she might not survive the first night. Like me, her limbs turned black, her feet in particular. But much of her circulation returned and she lost only one toe, though she did have scarring on her arms and legs.

With that in mind, the whole family was trying to find some way to help coax my extremities back to life. Sharon, the caretaker from Friendship House who used to be a respiratory technician, suggested they look into the hyperbaric chamber.

The hyperbaric chamber is a cylindrical tube made of glass that can be adjusted to any air pressure. It is often used to simulate underwater pressure, or help scuba divers recover from the bends. The chamber can be pumped full of a high-oxygen mix of air to essentially help force more oxygen into a person's bloodstream in a procedure known as hyperbaric oxygen therapy. A session in the hyperbaric chamber may be used to treat anything from slow-healing wounds to carbon monoxide poisoning.

After reading up on hyperbaric oxygen therapy, Mom and Dad were hopeful that infusing my blood with extra oxygen might somehow help heal the ravaged vessels in my hands and feet. My doctors were skeptical, but the hospital had a chamber and the prevailing sentiment seemed to be, "Can't hurt, might help, so we might as well give it a try."

So one day, after I'd had tubes inserted in my ears to accommodate the pressure, a man named Louis came to take me to my first hyperbaric session.

Louis was a tall, wiry man who looked younger than he probably was. He wore glasses and always sported colorful surgical caps rather than the dull scrub-matching ones most other people on the burn unit wore. I wasn't sure what exactly his job was — he wasn't a doctor as far as I could tell, but the nurses and techs seemed to defer to him. Without exception, they also seemed to love him.

"Hey buddy," Louis said in a deep, soft voice. "You ready to do this?"

I nodded. I had heard that some people felt extremely claustrophobic in the hyperbaric chamber and I was a little nervous about it. I was also a little nervous because I was hoping so desperately it would work — that it would cause some quick and dramatic improvement in my limbs. I knew there was little evidence to suggest that would be the case, but that didn't stop me from imagining it.

Louis helped me onto a gurney as I slid my butt across the bed with my bandaged arms up in the air. Then he put some blankets over me and I settled in for a long ride. Mom was coming along and she and Louis chatted quietly about the other folks on the unit as he pushed me down the hall. He hit a button on the wall and the double doors at the end of the hallway swung open automatically. Just like that, I was out of the burn unit for the first time in several weeks.

The rest of the hospital was pretty much what I expected. White walls on all sides with heavy wooden doors here and there, most of them labeled with names that meant nothing to me. People in white coats and blue scrubs moved out of the way of the gurney without looking at it, often carrying on conversations or sipping coffee as they went. Some of them looked as young as me, or even younger. Then there were the "civilians," visitors in street clothes carefully making their way to see loved ones. Some of them looked down at me as they passed, then glanced away quickly.

I knew what they were thinking: *Wonder what he's got?*

I pushed my arms farther under the sheets, even though they were covered in bandages, anyway. Soon we were in an elevator, riding down, down, down, all the way to the basement where the chamber was. Compared to the hustle and bustle of the upper floors, this level was fairly deserted. Just a few white coats passed, their eyes on the charts held in front of them.

We entered one of the doors and there it was, the hyperbaric chamber. It was a long cylinder with glass around it that looked a little like the old iron lung the guy had in his living room in the movie "The Big Lebowski."

Louis introduced me to Lynette, the tiny, black-haired woman who was in charge of this enormous machine.

"We'll just slide you in there and I'll increase the pressure gradually so it stays comfortable," she said. "You probably won't even be able to feel any difference. You can watch a movie if you want. Here's a list of what we've got."

I nodded, chose "Star Wars," and then said I was ready. Louis took my blankets and they gave me new ones, special ones that didn't build up static electricity. With all that concentrated oxygen in the tube, Lynette explained, we had to be careful about making sparks. Then Louis helped me slide onto a pallet at the mouth of the chamber. They gave it a push and soon my entire body was inside, with my head at the mouth.

"Are you comfortable?" Lynette asked.

I nodded tentatively, knowing she was asking whether I was ready to be shut up in there for a couple hours.

"OK, I'm going to close the door now," she said.

With that, she swung the circular portal closed and there was a hiss of air as it sealed. The glass seemed incredibly close on all sides and I wondered how they could get a truly fat man inside this thing. But at least I could see out. There was Mom, looking at me anxiously. I gave her a little grin, just to let her know I was all right. The TV was above the chamber and to the right, a small 20-inch model like the one in my room back in the burn unit. The yellow opening text of Star Wars was rolling up the screen and the film's audio was being pumped in through a speaker somewhere near my head.

For a moment the audio stopped and Lynette's voice came on instead. Apparently the speaker was also an intercom.

"I'm going to start raising the pressure now," she said.

I nodded anxiously. *Do what you gotta do. I'm not going anywhere.*

As she anticipated, I didn't feel a thing. After 15 minutes or so she broke in to tell me that the pressure was at the prescribed therapeutic level, and she was going to maintain it there for a couple hours. I nodded and asked her to turn up the volume on the TV a bit.

Being in the chamber turned out to be no problem. It was a little annoying being so confined that I couldn't raise my arm to scratch my nose, but I had no overwhelming feelings of panic or claustrophobia. Worn out from being in the tank room, I relaxed and watched a movie I had seen a hundred times. By the time Luke met Obi-Wan Kenobi I was starting to doze off. By the time two of them entered the Mos Isley space cantina I was fully asleep, with the weird music of the alien band serenading me.

I woke up two hours later when Lynette swung open the portal and let me know I was done. I had slept through the de-pressurization process completely.

"I hope this helps," I said to Mom and Louis on the way back to the burn unit. "Because it's so easy to do."

CHAPTER 10

THE SEARCH FOR LIVING TISSUE

As May moved on and I passed the one-month anniversary of my hospitalization, burn-unit life became my new normal: Get poked and prodded awake about 8 a.m. (much earlier than I preferred), force down a mouthful of pills with breakfast, steel myself for the trip to the tank, then a brief rest while watching the end of "The Price is Right" with Grandma.

Someone from the custodial staff generally came down about that time. Many of them would chat with me or the family while emptying the trash or wiping down the counters. One of my favorites was Mary, a soft-spoken older woman who always gave me a big smile and asked, "And how is Andy today?" She was sweet and grandmotherly and always assured me I was looking better, even on days when I was sure I wasn't.

Javier, a small, balding man who spoke almost no English, was another favorite. I noticed that he would say "Hi," very softly and shyly when he came in and one day I decided to try some of my old high school Spanish.

"Hola," I said. "Como estas?"

It was a pitiful attempt, but his face lit up. He went on and on in Spanish as he did his work and I smiled and nodded politely, catching a stray word here and there. After that he finished every visit by taking the hand of whoever was in the room and praying the "Our Father" over me in his native tongue.

After the custodians left, most days there was more torture in physical therapy before I got to crash back into the airbed and struggle through lunch. Then I'd head down to the hyperbaric chamber in the afternoon, by which time I was exhausted and needed a nap. I still spent much of my "free time" sleeping. I was off most of the sedative drugs, but the combination of going to the tank and physical therapy left my eyes heavy and my body weak.

There were signs I was getting better, though. All of my tubes were out, except for my IV and the catheter expelling my urine. After the feeding tube came out, the burn unit nutritionist recommended I consume at least 2,900 calories a day, and as much protein as possible. She pointed out that I had lost a considerable amount of weight during my drug-induced coma and my body was working hard on healing every minute, even when I was asleep.

For the first time in my life, I wasn't too keen on eating. The hospital cafeteria had the uncanny ability to consistently produce a combination of dry meat and soggy vegetables. I wondered why they couldn't borrow a little moisture from the veggies and pass it over to the meat. But achieving that balance was somehow impossible and it became hard to choke down dry hamburgers, even though Mom and Grandma were constantly trying to get me to eat more.

Mom took the calorie-counting mission to heart. She and Grandma fixed me Swedish meatballs, mashed potatoes, green beans, sourdough bread and strawberry shortcake one day when I absolutely couldn't find anything on the menu to choke down. Another time my hunger got the best of me and I ate nearly all of a hospital cheeseburger. Mom held it for me as I took each bite, beaming with pride. For days after, she insisted on telling every nurse, custodian and visitor about how well I had eaten.

"Ah, the frickin' cheeseburger," I finally said after hearing the story for the fourth time. "It's becoming a legend."

Soon the entire burn unit was trying to feed me. Brandi, a nurse, had heard how much I liked the CreamSlush at Sonic, and, not knowing what flavor I preferred, brought me three kinds one day. After I recounted a few stories from the semester I spent in Italy the year before, Nurse Bob made up a big batch of tiramisu. Mom spooned me out portions for a week, placing the carefully labeled leftovers in the break room refrigerator each day. Doran, a wound tech, told me he was taking a trip to Milwaukee and I jokingly asked him to bring me back some bratwurst. He returned with a dozen, which he grilled and brought in on his day off.

Though most every day in the burn unit included a considerable amount of pain, I was feeling the love — and tasting it too.

After a couple of easy first sessions in the hyperbaric chamber, we ran into complications. I began spiking regular fevers — miserable heat waves that swept over my body without warning and left me drenched in sweat. In my room there were at least a few steps that could be taken to relieve the misery.

Whatever family member happened to be at my bedside would fling off my blankets, crank the air conditioning down to 60 degrees, and place washcloths drenched in cold water on my forehead, neck and chest. Eventually, after I'd left big, dark, sweat marks on my hospital gown and bedsheets, the internal inferno would subside and I'd be able to relax. But there was no such relief in the hyperbaric chamber.

I was in there one afternoon, dozing off and watching "Groundhog Day." It had become my go-to movie, perhaps because I also felt I was living the same day over and over. Suddenly, a fever hit and jarred me awake.

Fire was pushing through my trunk and radiating out into my arms, which were pressed against my sides under a suddenly unbearable wool blanket. Beads of sweat gathered on my forehead and in my armpits and I began to breathe heavier. I turned my head from side to side repeatedly.

Lynette was sitting next to the tube looking over some papers when she looked up and noticed me wriggling about.

"Is something wrong?" she asked, cutting off the "Groundhog Day" audio as she pushed the button to activate the intercom.

"I feel really hot," I gasped.

Her brow furrowed as she squinted through her thick glasses into my chamber. I had been in the tube for a little more than an hour, which meant that it had been brought up to the ideal therapeutic pressure, but not for very long. There was no way she could reach in and adjust the blankets herself, and to get me out she'd need to gradually dial back the pressure, which took about 15 to 20 minutes.

"Can you wiggle free of the blanket at all?" she asked. "Push it down under your feet?"

I started to give it a go, but was skeptical. I could sort of bunch the blanket up around my chest by rolling my shoulders, but with my blackened, useless fingers there was no easy way to pull it down any farther, especially with my movement restricted. I ended up just gathering the blanket over my midsection, which made my trunk even warmer. By that point, the exertion had me dripping sweat, and starting to pant. Lynette noticed that things were not going well.

"I'm going to cut this session short," she said, getting up from her chair. "I'll get you out of there, but it's just going to take a little time to get you back to a safe pressure, OK?"

I nodded again, this time more vigorously. *The sooner the better.*

I lay there helplessly, at times panting and fogging up the glass above my head. Heat filled my head, my chest, my arms and legs — what I could feel of them — and my groin. Sweat slid down my armpits and inner thighs and all I could think was *hot, hot, hot.* I felt myself beginning to shake, which often happened when the fevers took hold. It seemed like forever until Lynette finally opened the hatch and slid me out of the tube. The blankets were stripped off and Louis wheeled me back up to my room, woozy and disoriented in just my gown and bandages.

The usual treatments were applied: air conditioning cranked up, cold washcloths placed on head and chest, two Tylenol quickly swallowed. Eventually my internal temp began to normalize and I fell into a restless nap.

That was the end of my trips to the hyperbaric chamber — none of the doctors wanted me going in there while those fevers and sweats persisted. Besides, they told my parents, it had been more than a month since I was admitted and there was little hope of any of the blood vessels repairing themselves at this point, hyperbaric chamber or no.

That was one of the few things the doctors agreed on regarding the fevers. As for the cause of them, there was much debate.

An infection was the most likely culprit, though I had been on all sorts of antibiotics and my wounds had been monitored closely for signs of foulness. I was cultured in every orifice and in every tube going in or out of my body. Everything came back negative. No discernible infection.

A multidisciplinary tug-of-war followed. The infectious-disease doctors surmised that the fevers had to be my body reacting to all the dead tissue still attached to it. It just wasn't normal, and therefore my internal thermometer was periodically going haywire, they insisted. They recommended speeding up the debridement process and getting rid of the black and shriveled portions of my extremities as quickly as possible.

Meanwhile, Dr. Lawrence insisted he had treated many patients with skin damage even worse than mine and had rarely run into this problem. He was still reluctant to start cutting aggressively until he was sure the "line of demarcation" between dead tissue and viable tissue was clearly drawn, lest he cut off something that could be saved. The small legion of plastic surgery students who followed at his heels nodded in agreement.

I had no idea what to do and my parents, caught in the middle, used their free time to probe the Internet looking for independent answers. Mom found a couple of anecdotes about such fevers occurring in other meningitis survivors, but none of them provided any hints for effective treatment. In fact, one hypothesized that the patient's hypothalamus gland or thyroid was permanently damaged by the initial soaring fevers of the meningitis. The patient still suffered episodes like mine 15 years later. Mom decided not to share that particular outcome with me right away.

In the end, Dr. Lawrence more or less won out. We decided that the fevers, while uncomfortable and disconcerting, were not dangerous enough to spur any rash decisions about my limbs — decisions that would be quite permanent. We'd remain on Dr. Lawrence's timetable, patiently waiting for the line of demarcation, and save as much of my arms and legs as we could.

We didn't have to wait long.

A week later, I was scheduled for what amounted to exploratory surgery, to be done June 2. Dr. Lawrence had decided that the line of demarcation was showing itself in the parts of my hands and feet that were starting to shrivel and look dried out. The skin farther up my arms and legs was also black, but still fairly smooth and taut, suggesting that underlying tissues were still living and blood-filled.

Finding out for sure where that blood flow ended would take some aggressive debridement — likely down to the bone in some places. It was the kind of cutting that Dr. Lawrence figured I wouldn't be able to handle without full anesthetic, and I wasn't about to try to talk him out of it.

I did have my reservations, though. The only time I had been under was when I got gassed to get my wisdom teeth out and this would be a more serious drugging. I knew that there were cases when people went under and never woke up. I tried to ask Dr. Lawrence about this the day before the surgery, but he brushed it off.

"I really think the risks will be fairly minimal," he said, his eyes popping out in that weird way of his. "Your breathing and heart rate have been very stable for the past couple weeks and we'll be monitoring them the whole time, of course, to make sure nothing goes wrong."

That wasn't my only concern, though. I was also afraid of waking up with one or more of my limbs unexpectedly missing.

"Now, this is just going be skin you're taking off, right?" I asked. "No matter what you find once you get in there, you're going to tell me before you start cutting off... anything else?"

"That's right, just skin," he said, then took my right hand to illustrate.

"I'll start here on the side of your hand," he said, running his finger along the bandage just below the base of my right pinky. "I'll cut in there and a little bit higher on these fingers."

Now he was pointing out my ring finger and middle finger, indicating he would slice into them just above the first knuckle.

"And nothing on the thumb right?" I asked.

My right thumb was still plump and some shallow debriding had revealed healthy, pink skin underneath. Only the nail and the skin right around the nail was still black. I still couldn't move the thumb much, but there was feeling there — actually too much feeling. The raw layers of new skin were hypersensitive and it felt like little electric shocks every time I ran the tip of the thumb over something even as soft as a towel. But I had been told that was normal and that it would wear off. All in all, the entire medical staff seemed pretty encouraged by that little pink appendage.

"Right, I'm not going to touch the thumb," Dr. Lawrence confirmed.

We went on like that, with him pointing out each spot on my hands and feet where he was going to slice deeper and deeper until, we hoped, he hit something still living.

"You'll probably need a couple of blood transfusions, but that's a good thing," he added. "The more you bleed, the more viable tissue you've got in there."

I nodded, but I knew that bleeding always came with a price.

"Um, how much is it going to hurt, you know, when I wake up?" I asked.

Dr. Lawrence paused.

"That's hard to say," he said. "It's different for everybody. But we're going to do everything we can to mitigate your pain. You'll have your Fentanyl patch. Just be sure to ask for more meds if you have breakthrough pain."

So that was it. I was left to contemplate my first trip to the operating room. I didn't want to do it, but then again, it had to be better than the tank room.

While I was anxiously awaiting my first surgery, I got a piece of unrelated bad news. I noticed that Dan hadn't been by to see me in a couple days and, when I asked about his absence, Mom reluctantly told me he had driven back to Minnesota.

"I didn't want to tell you right now," she said. "But Shaggy's very sick."

Shaggy was our beloved dog, a scruffy, brown-haired mutt I picked out at the Humane Society some 16 years earlier because she reminded me of Benji from the movies. She had been our family pet since I was 6 years old, always bounding up to greet me when I came home, the most timid and gentle dog a person could ask for. It's a cliché, but she was, in some ways, my best friend. There were many times when we'd sit together on the stairs just inside the front door, when I'd pet her head and slowly work through my emotions.

Shaggy's hearing and eyesight had both started going bad and she wasn't quite as quick to jump up and wag her tail when you shook her leash and asked about going for a walk. For months I had been preparing myself for her death and just hoped that I was at home when it happened so I could say goodbye.

"Jan called last week to say that Shaggy has pneumonia," Mom continued. "She's stopped eating and just wants to lay down. The vet says there's nothing he can do, so Dan went home to be with her when they put her to sleep."

I nodded, but my chest felt like it was squeezing up inside. A few tears escaped and rolled down my cheeks.

"I'm so sorry, Andrew," Mom said, leaning over the bed to give me a hug. "I know you loved her. Jan and Mark took great care of her, but I just don't think she could handle adjusting to a new place at that age."

There were a number of different thoughts I could have used to comfort myself at that moment. I could have dwelt on the fact that Shaggy had lived a long, comfortable life. I could have considered her torment and confusion at being suddenly abandoned by the only family she had ever known and been glad that she wouldn't have to suffer that any longer. I could have been proud of the continued maturation of my little brother, who, without hesitation, agreed to drive more than 1,000 miles in a few days, just so Shaggy would have someone who loved her there in her final moments.

But I was immersed in my own misery, and didn't want any of those thoughts mucking it up. When I thought of my beautiful dog's impending death, all that came to mind was, "Well, that's about the way things are going right now."

Two days later I woke up from my first surgery without any memory of actually having gone to the operating room. The anesthesiologist had come into my hospital room to start the IV and I was knocked out before we even left.

I groggily emerged from my drug-induced slumber back in my room. *Ouch. Ouch. Ouch.*

"Oh-h-h-h-h," I moaned, and instantly Mom was there by my side, stroking my hair.

"Hey, Andy-Panda," she said, her voice barely above a whisper. "How are you feeling?"

"My right hand," I mumbled, vision still hazy. "It's burning. Oh-h-h-h-h, it hurts. It hurts."

"I'll go get a nurse," Mom said. "We'll see if we can get you some more pain meds."

When Mom left I craned my neck and blinked my eyes a couple times, trying to focus on my hand. It was a bulge of white, bandaged even more heavily than usual. There appeared to be a couple of red spots on it, but it was impossible to tell what had gone on underneath.

In my groggy state, I felt sure that Dr. Lawrence had gone back on his word. It hurt so much I thought he must have cut off part of my hand. Mom returned with the nurse and I choked down two pain pills. Soon I was drifting back into a haze of semi-consciousness, but I was still convinced something had gone wrong.

"He said he was just going to take skin," I said.

"He did Andy, that's all he took," Mom insisted.

"He said he was just going to take skin," I repeated, before forgetting what I was talking about and passing out.

I spent much of the next day and a half drifting in and out, drugged on pain meds and Ativan. When I was awake, all I was really aware of was pain cutting into my right hand or burning in my knees. Dr. Lawrence had done some serious debriding on them, too, to the point that a sizable portion of both kneecaps was exposed and would have to be grafted over with new skin.

Meanwhile, unbeknownst to me, Mom and Dad were scouring the hospital, looking for any kind of advice on how to help me accept emotionally what Dr. Lawrence had found in his journey into my tissues. They listened to an occupational therapist, a rehab doctor and even solicited opinions from the pain management specialist and dietitian — anyone who might have treated other people with serious, life-changing injuries.

In the end the best advice they got was just to be there and be sensitive to how I would react to the news. So when Dr. Lawrence came in to give me his report, Mom, Dad, Dan, Josh and Grandma were all there.

It's normal practice in the business world to deliver bad news on a Friday, so perhaps I should have been a little more prepared for what was to come, but the days kind of ran together and it didn't even register that's where we were on the calendar.

"When I got in there it pretty much confirmed what I thought," Dr. Lawrence said. "Your toes are necrotic all the way through and all of the digits on your hands have at least partial damage, except your right thumb. I'd like to amputate the toes as soon as possible — early next week, if you're up to it."

My head was swimming. I felt dizzy and warm.

"All the toes?" I asked.

"Yes, all the toes," Dr. Lawrence said. "We'll need to do some grafting to close up the feet afterwards. I'll take donor skin from your thighs for that. I'll also remove the rest of the necrotic tissue from your lower legs and graft over that. Your heels have been debrided fairly deep and I'm not sure that an autograft would take, so we're planning to cover that with Integra, which is an artificial skin...."

He kept talking, but I stopped listening. I turned my head and stared out the window, trying to imagine life without toes. The dumb things came to mind first. There'd be no more wearing flip-flops or experiencing the thrill of cutting a toenail that had grown seriously long. Then I thought of the feeling of sand between the toes, curling them luxuriously in bed when I first woke up from a long sleep, or dipping them gingerly into a pool to test the water. All gone. That made the tears come.

Later that day I met with Mylene and the care coordinator, who wanted to talk about plans for my rehab after the surgery. I wouldn't be able to bear weight. My feet would be too tender and it was imperative to give them time to heal and give the grafts every opportunity to take. We'd continue to work on leg flexibility, so I'd be doing stretching exercises in bed. We'd also focus more on the upper body and try to get me to eat on my own more effectively and maybe even start using the computer.

That was all well and good, but I couldn't get my mind off the surgery.

"Will I be able to walk?" I asked.

"Yes, I guarantee that if you put in the work, you will walk again," Mylene said.

"What about sports?" I said. "Will I be able to run and play sports again?"

Mylene sat down on the edge of the bed and grasped my upper arm. She held my gaze for a moment before answering.

"Andy, you will be able to do whatever you want to do," she said. "You may not do it in exactly the same way, but you will be able to do it."

I spent the rest of the day in a silent funk, brooding and depressed. I wanted someone to blame, but the only person I could possibly pin this on was God. So I told him, silently, how unfair he was being. I had been told time and again that he would never force me to endure more than I could handle, but this was more. This was way more.

That night he sent help.

Mom came into the room for one of her usual afternoon shifts, beaming with a smile I hadn't seen much of lately. She could barely wait until she'd gotten in the door to tell me what was up.

"I talked to the most amazing man on the phone last night," she said. "He's an accountant nearby here and he got meningitis when he was 17. He lost both of his feet and some fingertips, I think."

"Really?" I asked. "How old is he now?"

"I don't know," she said, frowning slightly. "I think in his 30s. He's married and he said he's got a kid on the way."

"Anyway," she continued. "He called me out of the blue last night and said that he saw something about you on the news and just felt like he should try and get in touch with you. He gave me his number and said if you ever want to talk, you should give him a call."

"What's his name?"

"Matt Bellomo."

"Can we call him now?"

"Sure."

Within moments, Mom was holding the phone up to my ear. I found myself talking to a man with a deep voice and a slight, almost imperceptible accent. Even over the phone he exuded energy and positivity.

"What's up, brother?" he said.

I immediately liked his familiarity. He was cool, at ease, as if he'd known me forever even though we'd never met.

"Not much," I said with a chuckle.

We made small talk for a while. He was a Yankee fan, so I chided him about the "Evil Empire." We talked KU basketball. He told me about his wife, his voice rising with excitement when he talked about her pregnancy. He was ready to be a dad.

Eventually we got down to the more serious topics. I told him about the upcoming surgery, and about how the uncertainty scared me more than anything.

"I'm not going to sugar-coat it for you," he said, his voice turning appropriately somber. "It's going to hurt. It's not going to be easy.... And your life's going to be different."

I nodded, feeling the beginnings of tears start to push at my eyes.

"But let me tell you something else," he said. "And make sure you remember this: this is not the end. Life isn't over. It doesn't stop now, I promise. It will be hard, but you've got to stay positive, OK?"

"OK," I said, holding back the tears.

"Take one step at a time, OK?" he said.

"OK," I replied.

"And I'm here for you any time you need to talk, OK?" he said. "Any time, night or day, you can call me, all right?"

"All right," I said, forcing my voice to hold strong. "Thanks, man."

"Hey, it's no problem," he said.

Before Mom hung up the phone he promised to come visit me after the surgery.

The weekend before the amputations turned out to be rather busy. A group of Pearson guys, those who lived near Kansas City, brought dinner over for the family Saturday night. It was a ground beef casserole, salad and fruit, a simple meal but a definite step up from the usual hospital fare. I was moved into the cardiac chair and we ate together in the break room down the hall.

There was plenty of small talk as they filled me in on the last few days of life in the hall. I had missed the Senior Dinner, which was a big affair that year because my class of 20-plus seniors made up almost half the hall. The guys brought a video of it and we watched as each person I came into Pearson with was honored. Afterward they filled me in on who was leaving for what job in what city, who was still with what girlfriend and was feeling pressure to propose, etc.

I smiled and laughed at the appropriate times, but a significant portion of my mind was occupied by the 800-pound gorilla in the room — the upcoming amputations. No one wanted to discuss them and it was clear why:

they had no idea what to say. They wanted to talk about happy things, and so did I.

"Remember that time when me, you and Caleb won the three-on-three tournament?" Matt Unger said, giving me a big, toothy grin that split his scraggly goatee and mustache. "That was awesome, huh?"

"Yeah man," I said. "We dominated."

That tournament was a scholarship hall event, so it wasn't as if there were a lot of world-class athletes in it. But it had been awhile since three Pearson guys won it and Matt, Caleb and I had a lot of fun doing it. We played five games on a single Saturday on the concrete court nearby in 90-degree-plus heat, coming in between games to suck down ice water while sitting in front of an air conditioner.

Caleb was probably Pearson's best athlete. He was a former high school quarterback, pitcher and point guard whose strong, stocky frame belied above-average quickness and coordination. Matt was the kind of guy every basketball team needs — tall, tireless and unselfish. He wasn't a great shooter, but he rebounded and defended ferociously and was outstanding on the pick-and-roll.

It was a pick-and-roll that won the tournament championship for us, in fact. Matt screened my defender on the right side, knowing I was much better dribbling that direction. As I went right, my defender decided to switch and Matt's defender decided to stay with him. Matt rolled to the basket, taking them with him, and I was left open. I rose up for a jumper, the one basketball gift that I provided to complete our trio. One of the defenders sprinted out at me, trying to recover, but it was too late. I had already released the ball, feeling its hundreds of tiny bumps roll off my fingertips. The basketball hoop was one of those industrial-strength outdoor models with a double-thick orange rim that was rigid and unforgiving. It didn't matter though. The shot was pure from the moment it left my hand and it ripped through the chain net without even touching the rim for the winning point.

That feeling: marvelous.

I enjoyed the lighthearted laughs with my Pearson boys, but the next day I met with a girl who forced me to talk about the impending life-changing surgery. A reporter from the *Kansan*, Julie Jones, came to interview me for a story for one of the summer issues.

I had seen Julie around the campus journalism haunts but knew her only vaguely. She was upfront about her discomfort with the assignment.

"I'm nervous, 'cause I know you're a way better reporter than me," she said, and my chest swelled up even as I shook my head in false modesty.

Watching her fiddle nervously with her small, spiral notepad, I found myself feeling sorry for her. It was an odd feeling given my situation, but I knew a little bit about what this was like for her. Once, while working on a feature story about a graduate student who had just returned from a tour of duty in Iraq, I gulped hard and asked what he thought about the people protesting the war.

Uncomfortable questions and uncomfortable moments are part of journalism. To do it well, you have to ask them. Julie was going to have to ask me some, and I resolved to make it as comfortable as possible for her.

She started off the right way, easing into the interview with some light questions about hospital food and how tough it was to force down 3,000 calories every day. She asked about my stack of videos, many of which were old Minnesota Twins baseball games that Josh had taped for me. Poor Julie was probably trying to lob a softball when she asked about the picture of Shaggy that was set up near the bed. Her face registered shock and sympathy when Mom, who was sitting with us, told her that Shaggy had just been put down. After that she apparently decided she might as well jump into the hard questions.

"So, what are you feeling right now, about this upcoming surgery?" she said slowly, as if wading into deep water.

I was silent for a moment, taking the time to form an honest answer to a question that I hadn't really been willing to ask myself.

"The next step is pretty scary to me," I said finally. "There's a lot of uncertainty with me about how it's going to look and how much pain there will be afterward."

I went on to explain that, because it was the toes I'd be losing in this round of surgery, I wasn't quite as worried. I'd be able to hide my feet most of the time. I was more afraid of losing fingers, and it was wearing on me not knowing how many I'd lose.

"Yeah, it just seems like one trial after another for you," she said, shaking her head. "How are you holding up emotionally?"

"It's up and down," I said. "Whenever they tell me what the next procedure is, it's tough. It's like, 'Why do I have to go through this?'"

I didn't want her to think it was all doom and gloom all the time. I rambled on about the privilege of being alive, I told her to make sure to mention the tiny miracles of Clay coming to get me when he did and insisting I see a doctor, of Dr. Luckeroth giving an immediate, spot-on diagnosis, and of the helicopter arriving at Lawrence Memorial when it initially looked like I'd have to take an ambulance.

Then I told her about my family and friends. About how hardly a minute went by when Mom or Dad, Josh, Dan or Grandma weren't by my side. About how my friends kept visiting, both from Kansas and from Minnesota, almost daily. About how all of their love was keeping me going through all of the uncertainty and fears about the future.

"Honestly, I would have had a nervous breakdown if they weren't here," I said. "I've had a lot of support."

After about a half-hour Julie said she had enough material for her story, which was good because I had been in the tank before she arrived and was worn out, physically and emotionally. It was difficult to confront what I was about to go through, but she helped me get a lot of things off my chest and I felt a little more ready.

CHAPTER 11

THE TOES COME OFF

A day later, I returned to the operating room for the first procedure that would fundamentally change the shape of my body. It was a Monday and with no formal physical therapy or occupational therapy on weekends I had had plenty of hours to rest and prepare. Still, the pain from the last surgery remained — reduced to a dull ache, but hinting at what lay ahead.

Mom and Dad, Josh, Dan and Grandma were all there to squeeze my shoulders and give me hugs before I went under anesthesia. Mom and Grandma sniffed back tears and the Marso men were somber. I did my best to lighten the mood.

"At least I won't have to worry about them torturing me in PT with that walker for awhile, right?" I said, trying to smile.

They smiled back and, after we all exchanged "Love-yous'" they left the room. Once again I was off to dreamland, wondering anxiously what I'd wake up to.

Three or four hours later, Dr. Lawrence came out of the operating room to brief my parents. After a month of uncertainty, they would finally get an answer to at least one of their questions: how much of my feet would I lose? The news was not good.

"Once we got in there, we had to cut farther and farther back to find tissue that was still viable," Dr. Lawrence said.

All my toes were gone, and he also had to cut back all the way to the balls of my feet. Basically, about the front half of both feet were amputated. He told my parents this was only a little worse than he had expected going in, but to them it seemed like a big difference.

Dr. Lawrence added that in debriding and grafting my legs he'd had to remove a section of my right calf muscle, which had also become necrotic. He quickly added, though, that he didn't expect this to prevent me from walking in the long term, because I'd already been able to bear some weight on the leg in physical therapy with the dead muscle in there. What was left of the muscle would likely be able to compensate.

All in all, he thought, the grafts that he took from my thighs and applied to my knees and lower legs looked good. But it would be about a week before he would be able to tell whether they would truly take. The heels were more dicey. They were debrided down to bare tendon and bone and even with the high-tech artificial Integra skin it might be difficult to get those areas to close permanently.

Still, that was a future consideration.

I would be brought up to speed on this conversation later. At the time I was back in my room, still zonked out on anesthetic. When I started to come to later that night, I was in no mood to hear how the surgery went. All I wanted was more sedatives.

The pain after the first surgery was nothing compared to the amputations. Everything below my waist screamed. My feet felt as if they were being crushed in a vise, my calves burned and my thighs, where they had taken the top layer of skin for the grafts, stung as if I had scraped them across asphalt. Any movement made the pain ten times worse.

I lay as still as I could and moaned. I could barely form a coherent thought, much less vocalize it, so I just kept moaning out of habit. Dad stayed in the chair by my side all night, not sleeping. The only time he left was to ask the nurse whether she could give me another dose of painkillers. I was maxed out, but still could hardly bear it.

I got through that night and the next morning with the nurses giving me IV Fentanyl as if the whole thing was one continuous tank-room session. Every hour I'd get the shot of warmth, feel my jaw muscles unclench and grab 30 to 45 minutes of feverish, twitching sleep. Then the pain would break through and I'd wake up and go through 15 minutes or so of moaning and crying before the nurses would dose me again.

Mom and Grandma took Dad's place at the hospital come morning and sat there, tears running down their cheeks to match mine. They had begun moving from the Friendship House into an apartment near the hospital, a more permanent solution now that it was apparent I wouldn't be able to return to Minnesota for quite some time. They were exhausted, but they couldn't sleep any more than I could.

Assessing the damage to my feet during my few minutes of relatively drug-free consciousness was impossible. I was bandaged from the groin on down, and my lower legs were wrapped in several other things over the bandages. There was a thick layer of foam meant to cushion the wounds and a Saran Wrap-like layer over that meant to compress the foam and hold down swelling. It was all cinched tight with an outer layer of cloth that had several Velcro straps. A plastic tube was wedged in underneath the dressings on each leg and attached to a motor that sucked air out from under the dressings. I was told they were called "wound vacs," and they were meant to draw the ragged edges of the wounds together.

By the next afternoon the stinging in my thighs had diminished to an annoying itch. I was able to stay conscious without moaning, but my lower legs still felt as if they were being continually crushed. I thought back to the opening scene of "Dances with Wolves," the one set in a field hospital a few hundred yards from a Civil War battleground. In the movie, surgeons go from one wounded soldier to the next, amputating legs without anesthesia like an assembly line — or disassembly line. That just didn't seem possible to me. I was getting the best painkillers money could buy and still I could barely take it.

After three days and the help of a drug called neurontin, which the pain management specialist prescribed when I told her about the crushing feeling, I finally woke up one morning with only a persistent ache in my feet and the ever-present itching of the donor skin sites. Given what I had been through in the preceding days, it felt nearly divine — as if I had died and gone to manageable-pain heaven.

Grandma was sitting next to Mom, who was munching on a muffin.

"That smells good," I said. "What kind is it?"

Mom smiled, obviously thrilled that I was taking an interest in food for the first time in days.

"It's banana nut," she said "but this is the last one. I think your father's been eating them while you're asleep."

I sighed, and put on my best sarcastic voice.

"My own father holding out on me. Doesn't he know I'm on a high-calorie diet?"

Mom and Grandma laughed as if it were the funniest thing they'd heard in years. The worst was over, at least for awhile.

Mom decided I was in good enough shape at that point to have visitors again. That night Matt Bellomo stopped by on his way home from work, fulfilling the promise he made before I went under the knife.

I watched his legs carefully when he came in and when I saw how well he walked — an easy, natural stride —a big grin split my face. If he could do that without any feet at all, surely I'd be OK.

"What's going on, brother?" he said, grasping my shoulder. He was grinning, too, and again seemed completely at ease, though I suspected the hospital probably brought back bad memories for him.

In many ways Matt was completely unremarkable physically, the kind of guy you wouldn't glance at twice if you saw him in the supermarket. Average height, average build, dark hair and glasses. He was missing a few fingertips, but no one would be able to tell unless they studied his hands fairly closely.

I liked the fact that he seemed so ordinary, so "normal." I mentioned this to him.

"Yeah, most of the people I work with have no idea," he said. "I mean, they've only seen me wearing pants, so they'd be shocked if I told them I had no feet."

"So you can walk all right?" I asked. "I mean, you looked great walking in, but how far can you go?"

"I can go pretty much as far as anybody else," he said. "Shoot, two years ago I went back to the motherland, you know, Italy, and I climbed all the steps to the top of St. Peter's at the Vatican. You know how far that is?"

I nodded. It was a hike. I had climbed those steps myself the year before during my semester abroad. Matt and I spent the rest of his visit talking about Italy before he decided he should probably go home to his wife.

"Hey, don't hesitate to call, brother," he said before he left. "Your mom has my number. Anything you need, or if you just want to talk, you give me a ring."

Matt's visit put me in good spirits and later Randy and Clay came over to watch the Timberwolves. After helping me recover while in intensive care, the T-Wolves had apparently decided their work was done. They were in the midst of losing to Dr. Jim's Lakers in the Western Conference finals. But I didn't care. It was an excuse for some of my buddies to visit.

"Phew, it's hot out there," Randy said, sweeping his hand across his brow in an exaggerated gesture as he walked in.

"Your mom's hot out there," I quickly replied, then added, for emphasis, "O-o-o-o-o-oh, snap."

"Gawd," Clay said, rolling his eyes.

"Don't worry, Clay," I said. "Your mom's hot out there, too."

Randy chuckled and shook his head.

"Same old Andy," he said.

It was nearly a week before I got to see Dr. Lawrence's handiwork. I was taken to the tank room drugged on Fentanyl, but not completely knocked out. There the burn unit staff began the arduous process of removing all the dressings on my legs.

Peeling off the outer layers took long enough, but when they moved to the bandages that were up against my skin, things slowed to a crawl. No matter how much they sprayed down the gauze with water, everything seemed to stick to my bloody lower legs. I gasped and hissed through my teeth as the gauze tugged free, one square centimeter at a time. The nurses and burn techs went as slowly as possible to make sure none of the raw or grafted tissue tore off with it.

By the time they finally got down to my bare legs I was stinging all over and vainly trying to keep tears from squeezing out of my eyes. Then, as they started to wipe my legs gently with soapy washcloths, I crunched my abdominal muscles together and craned my head forward so I could get a look at what I was working with.

It wasn't pretty.

The healthy skin taken from my thighs had been put over a machine that punched holes in it and stretched it out so it would cover a larger area before it was grafted on. That skin was now plastered over my lower legs and blood oozed from the hundreds of little holes struggling to heal over. Some were red and dripping, others were dark with dried blood. The light blue pillows my legs were resting on were soon streaked with trails of crimson.

The edges of the grafts were actually stapled on to my legs to keep them secure, giving them a jarring, Halloweenish effect. I felt as if Dr. Lawrence had patched me together like Frankenstein's monster. But at least the black, dead tissue was gone.

I glanced down the length of my legs to my feet, which were barely recognizable. They were two bulbous, swollen blobs that seemed as wide as they were long. Their color was a mix of bright reds, slightly less-swollen pinks and yellowish heels where the artificial Integra skin was peeling off in some places. There were dark, heavily bruised grafts in the front of the feet where the toes used to be. The staples holding those on glinted under the tank room's bright lights.

"I'm a little concerned about the heels, and your right knee is still trying to close up, but we can always re-graft those areas if they don't take," Dr. Lawrence said, the surgical mask over his mouth shifting up and down. "Overall, I think the grafts look pretty good."

I decided to take his word for it, hoping it would look better down the road. I laid my head back and didn't look again until the nurses had wound the Saran Wrap stuff over my legs again.

CHAPTER 12

THE ADVOCATES

As I moved into the middle of June and my second full month of hospitalization, the experience seemed to be wearing on everyone. The burn unit staff was doing a tremendous job keeping me comfortable under the circumstances, but a couple of oversights drove my parents into a fury.

The first came courtesy of the cooling blanket meant to help bring down my frequent fevers. It was hollow so it could be filled with cold water and then put underneath me to regulate my temperature quickly.

Very early one morning, as Dad snored in the chair next to me, I was awakened by one of the night nurses who came in to check my temp and blood pressure. It was something they did every few hours. I was feverish again, so the nurse placed the cooling blanket under me before she left. I fell back asleep and neither Dad nor I awoke until Mom arrived to relieve him a few hours later.

When I groggily came to, Mom was in the middle of yelling at someone and the cooling blanket was hanging from her right hand and dripping onto the floor. Apparently there was a small puncture in it and the icy water had been slowly leaking under my legs for hours. Mom arrived to find me lying on soaked sheets, with a small puddle between what was left of my feet. She did not take it well.

I couldn't feel any moisture because my legs were so heavily wrapped, but I quickly discerned what had happened based on Mom's yelling.

"... Everything Dr. Lawrence has been saying about how good the grafts look and now look at his legs," she said. "Look at them! They're soaked through. After all he's been through, if this ruins it...."

"Mom," I said, as loud as I could. "Can you please quiet down?"

Finally noticing that she had woken me, she rushed over to the bed.

"Don't worry Andrew," she said. "They're going to get you some dry sheets and I've sent your father to get Dr. Lawrence."

"OK, whatever," I replied, wanting nothing more than to go back to sleep. I was not a morning person.

Dr. Lawrence appeared shortly afterwards, looking harried, with Dad on his heels. He ordered my bandages taken down as Mom loudly brought him up to speed. As it turned out, the water had only penetrated the first few layers of cloth and the Saran Wrap stuff underneath was fairly waterproof, anyway.

"Even if the grafts do get a little wet, they should be OK," Dr. Lawrence added, blinking a mile-a-minute. "They're strong enough to endure it."

Finally, after Dr. Lawrence left and I rolled from side to side so the nurses could change the sheets with me still in bed, Mom calmed down. Just as things grew quiet and I began to drift back to sleep, my breakfast arrived and I was shaken awake again.

Dad managed to keep his temper in check during that episode, which wasn't much of a surprise. He had always been the calmer of my parents and he recognized that the leaking of the cooling blanket was a fluke — it couldn't justly be considered anybody's fault.

But one night later Dad's considerable patience stretched to its breaking point.

We were watching television late into the evening, me in the bed and he dozing in the chair, as usual. One of the local meteorologists broke into a "Seinfeld" rerun, briefly apologized for the interruption and then launched into his important business.

"The National Weather Service has issued a tornado watch for most of the Kansas City metro area, including portions of Johnson, Wyandotte and Jackson counties, effective until 2 a.m.," he said. "We're also under a thunderstorm warning right now. Here in the weather center we're tracking a super cell moving northeast towards the Kansas City area with the potential to produce large hail and damaging winds.

"This storm has already resulted in a tornado in northern Sumner county near the town of Mulvane, just outside Wichita, so we'll be monitoring that closely and we'll keep you updated. We've got footage of that tornado near Mulvane, shot by one of our storm chasers. Preliminary indications are that it was at least an F2 or possibly an F3. No word yet on possible damage or injuries."

At that point we were treated to the footage, fairly crisp and steady roadside camera work that started with a jarring peal of thunder. A bank of dark clouds hung low over the prairie and a thin tornado moved slowly behind what appeared to be a grain elevator.

Having lived my entire life in Minnesota and Kansas, I was no stranger to this type of storm. I had never been in a house that was hit by a tornado, but I had ridden out several near-misses in basements. I remembered quite clearly one night in high school when I was sleeping over at Rick's house and a tornado brushed by St. Cloud. His mom and dad herded the entire family of seven downstairs, carrying his toddler brother Robby, who writhed and moaned at being woken in the middle of the night.

As the rest of the family settled in to what was fortunately a spacious basement, Rick, his dad and I gathered around a big bay window on the landing just below the first floor and watched as debris swirled and lightning lit up the sky again and again. At the time it wasn't frightening. It felt like an adventure.

But lying in the hospital, listening to the report of the approaching tornado, I was a little afraid. I was stuck in bed, unable to stand, walk or even shield myself effectively. I was suddenly keenly aware of how helpless I was.

The rain began to pound against the window, first in quiet, pebble-like pings and then in a steady, pounding rumble. Then the wind howled, rustling branches outside and shaking the window. The storm's intensity increased until the lightning flashed so frequently it almost looked like daytime and the thunder seemed to roar right on top of me.

Even Dad couldn't sleep through it. He was up out of the chair, staring out the window.

"What do you think they do here if there's a tornado?" I asked.

"I don't know," he said, glancing back at me. "I guess they probably have some kind of shelter or maybe they just move everybody out into the hallway. They must have some kind of procedures. I mean, we are in Kansas, right?"

Dad gave me a reassuring grin, but I wasn't quite satisfied.

A few minutes later the nurse on duty, Mike, came in for my regular blood-pressure check. He was a hefty guy with a round face and short, spiky hair, very competent and usually good at going about his business without waking me up. But I wasn't feeling much like sleeping, so I asked "Big Mike" what the burn unit procedures were in the event of a tornado.

"We'll roll your bed as far away from the window as possible and then shut the blinds," Mike said.

As Mike began to tighten the blood pressure cuff around my arm I caught Dad's eye and gave him a look that I hoped adequately expressed my skepticism. Moving the bed away from the window was all well and good, but the room was only about 15 feet long and I was pretty sure that if 80- or 90 mile-per-hour winds shattered the window, a few shards of glass might reach me. As for closing the Venetian blinds, was that meant to put one flimsy barrier between me and those shards of glass? Or was it to keep me from seeing what was going on outside and panicking?

"My dad and I were thinking maybe you would wheel everybody out into the hallway," I said.

Mike shook his head and pushed his hand down on the bed.

"These airbeds are plugged into the wall," he said. "The cord won't reach out into the hallway, so we'd have to transfer everybody to chairs or gurneys, cause you don't want to unplug the beds and have them deflate. I wouldn't worry, though. We've never had a problem before."

After Mike left, I remained concerned. Soon there was a deafening peal of thunder and suddenly the lights went out. Not all the lights — the ones in the hall outside were still on. We could see them through the door, which was open a crack. But my room went dark, the TV winked off and even the hum of the air conditioner was silenced.

"Aw-w shit," I muttered, for the moment not worrying about what my straight-laced dad would think of my cursing.

"I'll go find out what's going on," he said.

In only a few minutes the room began to feel stuffy and beads of sweat formed on my forehead. I wondered what the temperature was outside and how hot it would get inside. That fear was soon superseded by another, however. When the hum of the AC disappeared, it was replaced by a strange hissing noise. I turned my head left and right, looking for the source, but I felt it before I saw it. The bed was deflating underneath me.

"Dad," I yelled toward the door. "Hey, Dad!"

He rushed back in, a flashlight in hand and his eyes wide behind his glasses.

"What is it?" he asked.

"I think the bed's deflating," I said.

"Shit," he said. "I'll go get somebody."

I was quickly becoming engulfed in sheets as the remaining air fled from under my body to the edges of the bed. Before long my butt was pressed against the metal bed frame, aggravating the bloody sores in that region.

When Dad returned with Mike I was gritting my teeth to keep from crying, lying on nothing but some sheets, a deflated mattress and a metal bed frame. Mike rooted around the bed, looking for the outlet where it was plugged in.

"I'd have to move the bed to get at it," he said finally, straightening up and wiping sweat from his eyes. "I don't get it. The back-up generator's going, so it shouldn't have deflated."

"Can you just please do something?" I said, forcing the sound out from between my teeth.

First he and Dad pushed the bed toward the door, both to find the outlet and to get the bed away from the windows. Mike already had closed the blinds. After shifting the bed, he unplugged it and tried a different outlet. No luck. Then another. Still nothing.

Fortunately, Mike had a brainstorm. He left the room and came back with an armful of pillows, then enlisted Dad's help rolling me over on my side while he slide the pillows under me. It was instant relief — not quite as nice as an inflated air bed, but a major improvement over where I had just been.

"Better?" he asked.

I nodded.

"OK, I've got to go check on some other patients," he said.

After he left, Dad scoured the room, looking for another outlet. It didn't take long. There was a small night stand just left of the bed on which rested a box of Kleenex and my jug of water. When Dad slid it away from the wall it revealed a circular electrical outlet framed in red. Clearly there was something different about this one.

"Well, what the hell," he said, his voice dripping disgust as he straightened up while holding his lower back. "This is where the bed's supposed to be plugged in. This outlet's hooked up to the generator and there's nothing plugged in there. Unbelievable."

He called Mike back into the room and the plug was jammed into the new, special outlet. Immediately air flowed in and I could feel the odd sensation of being lifted as if by magic. Mike was apologizing profusely, but it barely registered in my mind. I was beyond the point of caring. The bed was inflated and comfortable now. It was late and I was exhausted. I drifted off to sleep to the sound of Dad berating Mike out in the hall:

"... Stupid oversight ....Going through all that pain for no reason...."

I was lucky to have five advocates with me throughout most of my stay in the burn unit — Mom, Dad, Grandma, Josh and Dan. It wasn't that way for all the patients. A tiny toddler in the next room wailed often during the week or two he was there. The staff did its best to keep him company, going so far as to rock him in a little toy wagon with one hand while doing paperwork with the other.

Mom told me that one of the nurses had apologized for all the crying. Apparently the toddler's mother was an unmarried teen who was not particularly attentive. She had accidentally scalded the child in the bathtub, and now she only stopped by to visit for a few hours each day. She was frustrated because the baby didn't want to play when she was there, and so she had more or less handed her child over to the staff.

I could only shake my head, realizing how much support I'd taken for granted. Here I was, surrounded by all this love and a little child — who had to be more scared than me because he had no idea what was happening — had no one. It was unimaginable. I was 22 years old and still felt I needed every bit of support I could get just to make it through each day and night.

My family made sure I had that support every day.

It started at 7:30 a.m., when Grandma would arrive and help the nurses poke me until I convinced them I really was awake. She'd stay through the morning, watching "The Price is Right" and helping me find something palatable to order for lunch. But one of her most important jobs came after I returned from the tank room.

I generally spent more than an hour in the tank with my jaw clenched and my shoulders hunched, trying to steel myself against the pain. I also had my arms raised the whole time because I didn't want those frigid, black fingers touching the rest of my body.

When I got back to my room my upper body was usually sore and Grandma gave me shoulder rubs whenever I asked. It wasn't easy — she couldn't get around behind me because the bed was against the wall, so she had to reach across my head to get to my opposite shoulder. Also, the nearly 80-year-old joints in her hands were swollen and arthritic. But she never complained. Her arthritis made her a better masseuse from my viewpoint, because her grip was light and gentle. It felt feathery after the horror of the tank.

Grandma usually didn't say much. She was, after all, a full-blooded Swede. But one morning, when the nurses had come by to let me know that

I would be going to the tank soon, I just broke down. In the anxiety and anticipation of what was to come I felt panicked, helpless, and began to sob.

"Andy, what's wrong?" Grandma said, leaning over the bed and putting her hand on my head.

"I just.... I just don't want to go," I blubbered. "I just can't do it today."

The tears kept pouring down and soon Grandma's chest began to heave and her tears were mixing with mine on the hospital gown and the bedsheets. I was shaking my head, not knowing what else to do, but Grandma slowly started stroking my hair and whispering to me through her tears.

"It's OK to cry, Andy," she said. "It's OK. You can't be brave all the time. It's OK."

For some reason, hearing her say that made a difference. She had lived through the Depression, lost her husband to cancer when she was 46, stoically survived open-heart surgery and then spent her golden years caring for her father, who lived to 96. She knew a thing or two about suffering, but I had rarely seen her shed a tear. Yet there she was, pouring them out and telling me it was OK to do the same.

Around lunchtime Mom would arrive and Grandma would go back to the apartment. Mom was diligent about making sure I got my calories. I did my best to feed myself, raising the trembling fork to my mouth with the help of the Velcro cuff that secured it to my wrist. But whenever I set my arm down to let it rest she was quick to grab another fork and try to feed me herself. She didn't want my lack of grip to provide any excuse to slack on eating.

In the afternoons I would often drift off for a nap with Mom in the chair next to me, reading the paper or doing the crossword puzzle. Later she'd wake me to order supper and watch "Jeopardy." Ken Jennings was in the middle of his otherworldly run and we marveled at his command of categories that ranged from Astronomy to Zoology.

Moments like that were quiet and homey and I could almost pretend that I was just a kid on summer vacation, watching TV with his mom. But there was something not quite right about that picture. My Mom had always been a working mom. Although she enjoyed spending time with me, I knew that both she and Dad had other responsibilities.

"How are you going to keep the law office going?" I asked one day in mid-June, after she had been away from home for nearly two months tending to me.

"Don't worry about that," she said. "I've postponed some of my cases and I've farmed out some to other attorneys in town."

"What about Dad?" I asked.

"He's got a lot of time off saved up," she said. "And Fingerhut told him to take as much time as he needed after that."

"But he won't get paid," I said. "What are we gonna do about money?"

"Andrew, don't worry about it," she said. "We'll be fine. The most important thing right now is for you to get better."

I shook my head. She wasn't treating me like an adult.

"Look," I said. "I love you guys, and I'm glad you're here. But ... if you need to go home for awhile... well, I'll be OK."

Now it was her turn to shake her head. She got out of the chair and came to stand beside the bed, rubbing my bandaged arm.

"I don't think either of us would be able to go back and work anyway," she said. "We couldn't stand to be away from you with everything that's going on here. This is where we want to be. Besides, we're doing OK, really. It's odd, but a few days ago your Dad and I were talking about what a miracle it was that we had finally saved up a good chunk of money for the first time in our lives and then this happened...."

"Oh, jeez, well, that makes me feel real good," I said, rolling my eyes.

"No, no, that's not the point," she said. "Obviously there's never a good time for this to happen, but I feel like God made sure that it only happened at a time when we could handle it financially, so we could just be by your side and help you through it without worrying about money."

I was still skeptical.

"We don't know how long this is going to take," I said. "Savings can run out."

"We're still pulling in some money," she said. "I have a lot of outstanding accounts, a lot of people who still owe me and have owed me for years. I've got my staff working on those and, now that they've got so much time to spend on collections and not the usual legal stuff, we're actually making as much money as we were when I was in the office, if not more."

That satisfied me. Mom had sometimes complained about how hard it was to get some of her clients to pay up. If the Marso Family had to call in a few of its old debts to get through this, well, so be it.

Like Grandma, Josh also quietly did his best to help. He stayed at the hospital for the first eight weeks straight, taking shifts at my bedside, before he had to return to work in Chicago. Even after he went back, he and his girlfriend, Lori, made regular trips to Kansas City on weekends.

Lori worked for United Cerebral Palsy and was able to bring one of the organization's old laptop computers on one of the weekend visits. Josh, who had been writing computer programs before most people even knew what email was, set out to find a way for me to use the laptop without my fingers.

He installed a program called "Dragonspeak" and brought it by one afternoon to show me how it worked.

With Mom and Lori looking on, he set the laptop on my special hospital tray, the one that swung out over the bed. Even with the computer positioned in front of me, though, I didn't know what to do with it — my bandaged arms still ended in unfeeling fingers. Fortunately, whenever there was a computer in the room Josh couldn't keep his hands off it and he was soon leaning out over my bed, tapping the keys. Then he plugged in a slim, beige microphone.

"See, you can actually give commands and the program will carry them out," he said, then pulled the mic towards his mouth.

"File... New," he said.

A blank, white document opened on the screen.

"There, now you can type whatever you want," he said, putting the mike in front of me.

"Uh, OK. Hi, this is Andrew," I said, feeling a little uncomfortable talking to a computer. "The rain in Spain falls mainly on the plain."

Mom giggled, Lori smiled and Josh leaned over to check the screen. The program had gotten a few things wrong. "Andrew" had become "and rue" and "plain" had become "plane." This exposed some obvious glitches the software had with proper names and homonyms.

"Well, you need to train it to recognize your voice, anyway," Josh said. "Adapt it to your accent and cadence."

He pulled up another program that had sentences the computer wanted to hear me say. I went through them one by one, often repeating myself to make sure my pronunciation was flawless. There was one that had to do with trees in winter that the computer and I had trouble connecting on.

"... snow-covered boughs," I said.

"Snow-covered bo-u-gh-s," I repeated.

"Snow-covered b-o-w-s," I said, stretching my mouth into an

exaggerated "O."

It was no use. I started giggling and soon I was full-on laughing and shaking my head.

"What's going on?" Mom asked.

"It keeps typing 'snow-covered bowels,'" I gasped between guffaws.

Mom and Lori laughed and even Josh cracked a smile. I told him I was done training the computer, but then he pulled up one last program. The computer had a bunch of short stories pre-loaded on it and I could access them simply by saying the title into the mike. I could scroll through the text with voice commands also. I spent the next hour or so reading Mark Twain, which made for a nice break from my usual TV regimen.

Dan wasn't as savvy with computers, but he was just as eager to help.

One day during rounds Dr Lawrence came by and told me he had been talking to Dan earlier in the week.

"He asked me if there was any way I could give you some of his fingers," Lawrence said, grinning. "I told him, 'Oh no, that's not quite how it works.' I mean, there have been a few hand transplants done, I think in Kentucky, but they generally use cadaver hands."

I smiled along with Lawrence but inside I was deeply touched, and filled with a fierce love for my baby brother. He tended to be impulsive and I was sure he hadn't thought through exactly how much pain and sacrifice such an operation would require. But it was powerful that he would even ask.

Having been denied the opportunity to give up some of his digits, Dan had to settle for giving up his time and his comfortable bed. He and Dad split the night shift, staying by my side and sleeping in a chair that didn't look all that inviting even though it folded flat.

One night I woke up slick with sweat, feeling as if the blankets were pushing down on me with unbearable heat. I was having another fever. I got the blankets off my chest by swinging my arms up from my sides, but then they rested heavily on my groin, and I found that I couldn't sit up enough to get rid of them.

"Dan," I said softly, turning to my right to see him curled up in the chair, asleep. "Dan," I repeated, this time much louder.

"Uh-h-h... What... huh?" he said, shifting around.

"I'm really hot," I said.

"OK," he said, blinking himself awake and swinging his legs out so he was sitting up.

He pulled all the blankets off me, then put the back of his hand on my forehead.

"Yeah, you're burning up," he said.

Dan knew the drill. We'd gone away from the cooling blanket after the leak incident, but he went into action on our other fever treatments. First he cranked up the air conditioner as cold as it would go, then he walked over to the sink and ran the water for awhile, checking it every now and then with his hand to make sure it was cold. He wet three washcloths and brought them over, putting one on my forehead and slipping another behind my neck. He helped pull my arms out of the hospital gown and placed the third washcloth on my bare chest. Then he went to find a nurse who could get me some Tylenol.

He came back with Harry, a young guy who was on duty that night. Though he worked the graveyard shift, Harry always seemed to be full of energy. He was one of the many folks on the burn unit that I genuinely enjoyed seeing.

"There you go," he said in a thick Spanish accent as he tipped a Dixie cup with the pills in it up to my mouth. "I might as well take your blood pressure, too, while I'm here, huh? Save me from waking you up later."

I laid my head back and relaxed as he put the cuff on my arm. I could almost feel the fever coming down.

"I feel a lot better now," I said. "But I've soaked the damn sheets again. I'm so tired of lying in my own sweat."

I wrinkled my nose in disgust, but Harry was upbeat, as usual.

"I know what you mean, man," he said. "I sweat all the time at night. My bed is always sweaty."

"Ugh," I said. "I bet your wife loves that."

"Actually, she does," he replied, his face splitting with a devilish grin as he raised his eyebrows suggestively.

Dan and I looked at each other and shook our heads. Then we burst out laughing and Harry joined in on his way out the door.

Many nights Dad and I stayed up talking. I knew I needed rest and I knew I'd regret it in the morning, but I hated the moments of silence when I was lying there trying to go to sleep. That was when all the fears that I had been keeping down would creep in – how would I make it through the morning and another trip to the tank? What if my fingers didn't come back and I was disfigured in a way that was tough to hide? How would I function after leaving the hospital and would life ever be worthwhile again?

I tried to distract myself by talking about other things with Dad. One night I thought back to that graduation ceremony a few weeks earlier. All the cameras, all the reporters, not to mention all the people visiting that CaringBridge website, hungry for any kind of update on my status. Why were they paying such close attention? Why was this all so compelling?

"Dad," I said, "Is what's happening to me really that unusual?"

His brow furrowed.

"What do you mean?" he asked.

"I mean, there's so many people following this story, so many people wondering how I'm doing," I said. "Is what I'm going through really that unique? I mean, people get paralyzed in accidents and stuff every day. They can't use their arms and legs at all. But you hardly ever hear about that stuff."

"That's true," Dad said, his eyes narrowing a little in thought.

This was one of the things I loved about my Dad; he was a really thoughtful guy. He didn't like to jump to conclusions or say the first thing that came to his mind. I could tell he wanted to get to the root of the question, not just give me some B.S. about how people were entranced by how brave I was. Mom, bless her heart, liked to launch into those platitudes. But then, I think that was partly because she actually believed them.

Dad was given to more complicated analysis.

"That's true," he said again. "People are paralyzed every day. But I think this is a little different, don't you?"

"I don't know," I said. "Why is it different?"

"Well, usually when someone's paralyzed, that's the result of a traumatic accident or a stroke or something," he said. "It's a quick event and then it's over. They've got a really tough adjustment to their new life, but there's not a lot of pain. They just lose feeling. What you're going through is a day-by-day thing and there's pain every day. Plus, just the fact that it's drawn out makes it more of a useful news story, right? We might hear about that person who's paralyzed on the day of their accident, but that's kind of where the media leaves it. Right now nobody knows how things are going to turn out for you, so that keeps people interested and keeps the reporters coming around."

"I guess that's true," I said, relishing the opening for a great pun Dad had just given me. "My story does have 'legs' as they say in the business."

I grinned and Dad grinned back, but then something else occurred to me.

"What about people like Uncle Don?" I said. "His battle has been going on for years, and he's a vet. You would think the media would be all over that."

Uncle Don was Dad's older brother, and most of my sensitivities to disabled people had been formed by watching him. He was diagnosed with multiple sclerosis just after I was born and since then, despite trying every mainstream and fringe treatment —including bee stings — he had gradually been losing the use of his limbs.

Don had been in a motorized wheelchair for as long as I'd known him. We saw him once every couple years when we'd visit his home in Colorado or when he would show up at our house in his giant RV. I'd watched his fingers and arms grow more and more limp with each visit.

Uncle Don had been a mechanic during the Vietnam War, fixing helicopters that dropped Agent Orange, a harsh chemical meant to clear jungle foliage. He was also a crop duster in civilian life, which exposed him to pesticides. There was some speculation that Uncle Don's exposure to chemicals might have caused him to contract MS. Whether or not that was true, I had always thought that what happened to him was incredibly unfair — first having to give up flying and then feeling your limbs give out on you a little bit at a time. I was always amazed that he was able to go on, traveling the country in his RV with the help of his nurse attendants, chatting up strangers and putting me and my brothers on his lap for rides in his wheelchair. That seemed like a story worth telling, at least as much as mine.

"Yes, your Uncle Don, he does have a great story," Dad said, as if reading my thoughts. "But he's a pretty private guy. And his story might be unfolding a little too slow for most reporters."

Dad was silent for a moment and I wanted to change the subject. In my attempt to avoid heavy thoughts I had gotten into a conversation that was, well... pretty heavy. But then he continued.

"Maybe that's a story you could write someday," he said. "He asks about you a lot, Uncle Don, when I talk to him on the phone. He's following this thing just like everybody else."

I nodded, wondering how in the world I could ever do a story like that justice. Dad and I lapsed into a companionable silence as we both ruminated on it.

About an hour later I was still awake when he got up and started heading toward the door.

"I've got to go walk around a bit or I'll start snoring away and you'll never get to sleep," he said, pausing at the edge of the room. "Is there anything you want me to bring you?"

Dad asked this question each time he got up to roam the halls at night. It was well-intentioned, but it was starting to strike me as absurd. Sure, there were about a million things I wouldn't mind him bringing me, but I was confident that hardly any of them could be found within the walls of KU Med.

"Yeah Dad," I said, giving him a wry grin. "Dancing girls."

It was the best I could come up with. Dad was a good sport.

"Oh, OK, Mr. Smart-Aleck," he said. "Just get some sleep, all right?"

I nodded and he closed the door behind him, shaking his head in fake exasperation.

Memories of my time in Italy (above), helped sustain me during my hospitalization, which began a few months after I visited Rick in Minnesota (left) during my senior year spring break.

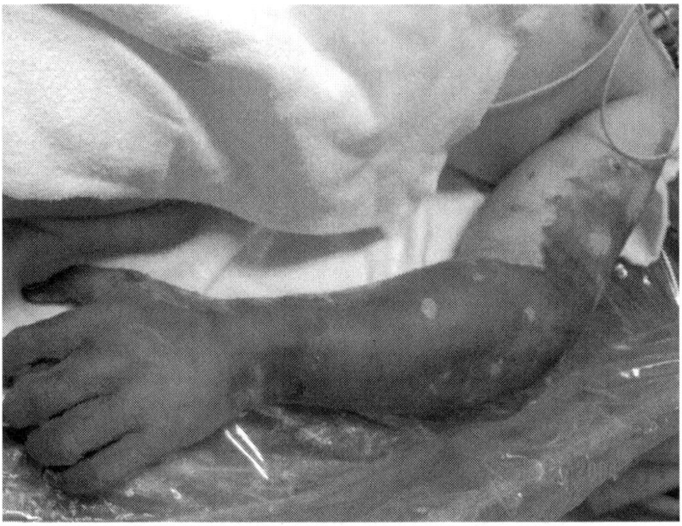

Meningococcal bacteria released toxins that damaged my blood vessels and ravaged my limbs.

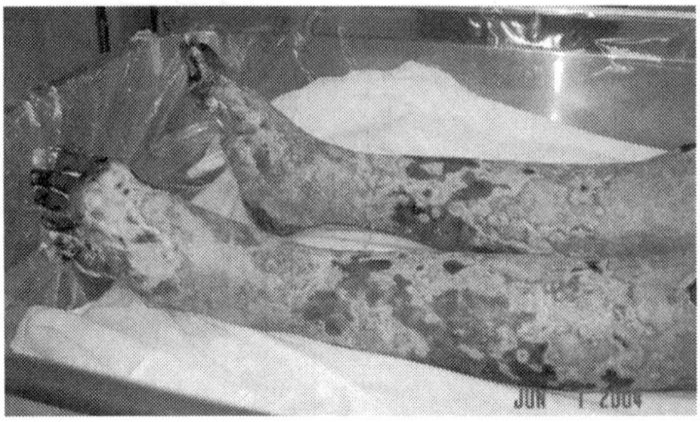

My caregivers in the University of Kansas Medical Center's burn unit became like a second family during three months of excruciating treatments to remove dead tissue.

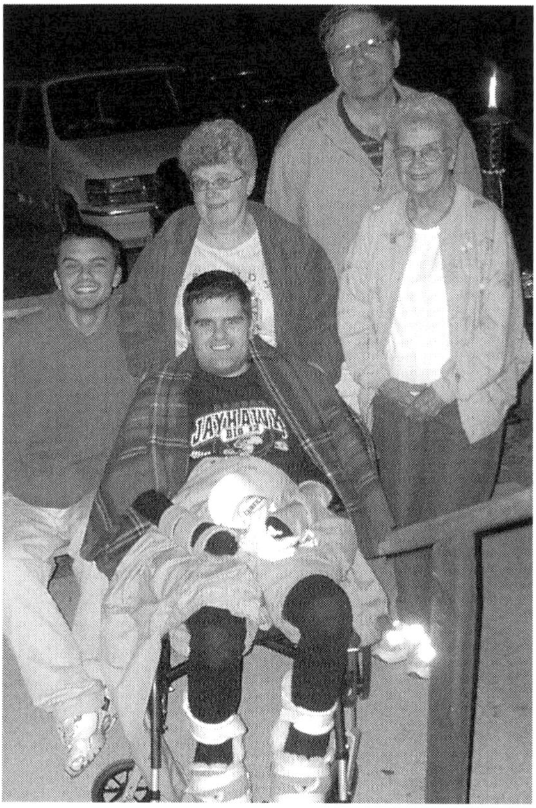

My first family was at my side throughout a year of rehabilitation, helping me transition back into public life. I also got support from strangers, like Minnesota Twins manager Ron Gardenhire (above).

My new life included camping with old friends (above) and visiting Brazil (below).

CHAPTER 13
LET'S MAKE A DEAL

During one of our late-night talks Dad told me he'd formed a new theory on how I might have gotten meningitis. My being Catholic and all, was it possible it spread to me through the communion cup?

I responded with a sarcastic joke about how heretical it was to suggest that the blood of Jesus might be infested with potentially deadly microbes. I was loath to reveal to my rather traditional father that I had only been going to church about once a month. I thought that was still a pretty good ratio for a college kid — there are only so many free hours on the weekend — but I had been brought up on the once-a-week church plan.

I wasn't dropping away from the Church completely. I just felt I was taking a little time to examine my faith. There were things I struggled to reconcile with the Vatican, like the role of women, attitudes toward homosexuality and the relationship between clergy and laity.

But I still believed in the Jesus I read about in the Bible, even if I didn't always recognize him in the Church. Meningitis did not change that.

The way I saw it, if God did not exist, than all of this had happened at random. I had somehow won an absurdly awful reverse-lottery and gotten a disease that afflicted a tiny number of people — a disease threatening to rob me of my limbs.

I couldn't stomach that. I had to believe that there was a God, and that this was part of his plan for me, even if it did not seem fair. Maybe that was delusional, but at the time I felt I would rather live with the delusion than try to survive without it.

On one of the first nights after I regained consciousness, a middle-aged woman came into my ICU room and began emptying the trash. When she saw that I was awake, she laid the trash bag down, came over to the bed and stood over me, smiling.

"You will be OK," she said, softly, her eyes a shade of brown as deep as I'd ever seen.

I nodded stiffly.

She furrowed her brow.

"I know you will be OK," she said softly, but firmly. Then she gestured to my bandaged hands and feet. "You have the wounds of Christ."

To me, being "OK" meant keeping my hands intact. A month after the cleaning lady made that prophecy, it was becoming clear it would take a miracle beyond modern science to make that happen.

Dr. Lawrence was pushing for more amputations, noting that he wasn't seeing any improvement in my fingers and that it might be time to give up on them. It was hard to accept that that was God's plan.

At that point some well-meaning soul decided it was time for me to start seeing the hospital's psychiatric staff.

Dr. Stiers was a soft-spoken older fellow with a bushy mustache and glasses. I hated him immediately and irrationally. Right about then, I took a very dim view of anyone who thought they could help me. Unless you could somehow restore blood flow to my fingers, or magically make the crushing phantom pain in my missing toes go away, I didn't want to see you. I wasn't interested in talking about my feelings, and I wasn't interested in trying to explain what I was going through, especially with someone who still had all his fingers and toes and had not experienced the tank room.

So Dr. Stiers and I began passing an hour together in my room each day, him holding a clipboard and venturing a quiet question every now and then, me seething silently and rarely giving more than a one-word answer. It was less than productive.

Stiers wasn't clueless. He could tell his presence was odious to me. To his credit, he never seemed annoyed or frustrated. He never pushed me, never raised his voice or insisted I give him something to work with. He just kept coming around, sitting next to the bed and absorbing my hateful silence as the minutes slowly ticked away.

If it had been just him coming in, things would have been fine. But KU Med was a teaching hospital and Stiers had several psychology students also assigned to me. They weren't as persistent as he was. Instead they would come in the room after he left, stand awkwardly by the bed with a clipboard, ask me a few questions, make some notes and then jet out of the room as fast as possible.

I had no idea what they were writing on those clipboards. They were obviously all working from the same textbook, though, and one after another came in and asked nearly the same questions. Each time I heard an identical question I gave an identical answer, but I spat it out with more anger and rolled my eyes more emphatically.

Then one day one student decided to go off script. He was trying out the overly cheery approach, giving me a big smile and acting as if we were just two buddies chatting. After the usual series of questions, he put the clipboard under his arm and tried one I hadn't heard before.

"So," he said, "Are you satisfied with your situation?"

A fuse went off in my brain.

I had been staring up at the ceiling, but now my head jerked around to look him in the face. He stood there with that idiotic grin, waiting for an answer. He was serious.

My jaw clenched and I started shaking my head. Then an odd impulse came over me. I started to laugh. It was a hard, caustic laugh that came from deep in my diaphragm like a cough and roughed up my throat on the way out.

"Am I satisfied with my situation?" I yelled. "Am I satisfied with my situation? Are you kidding? Look at me!"

The grin disappeared from the young man's face and he took a step back.

"What if I say, 'Yes'?" I asked. "Then what? Are you gonna put me in a straitjacket and lock me up? Cause I think you'd pretty much have to be crazy to be satisfied with this situation."

Mom and a nurse rushed into the room.

"What's going on?" Mom asked. "Andy, what's wrong?"

"I was just...," the psych student began, but I cut him off.

"Get him out of here," I screamed. "Get him the hell out!"

The nurse grabbed the guy's arm and escorted him from the room.

The therapists couldn't help me deal with the impending amputations to my hands because I still hadn't accepted that they were actually going to happen. Dr. Lawrence was pretty clear about it — he had sliced farther and farther into most of my fingers and hadn't found much promising tissue. His prognosis was that I would keep my right thumb and, if I allowed him to sew my hands into my abdomen and do the full-thickness grafts, I could also retain part of my left thumb and part of my right ring finger and middle finger. All the rest were goners.

A strange sense of relief came with this. For more than a month I lived with the uncertainty of not knowing how damaged my hands would be. I spent hours staring at that one, plump, bandage-free right thumb, watching the blackness slowly recede day by day, wondering what was going on in that thumb that wasn't happening in the rest of my fingers.

Now that Dr. Lawrence had made it clear that there was no hope for the rest of my fingers medically, I knew exactly what was needed: a miracle. No more putting my trust in the doctors and waiting on them to make something happen; my only recourse was to get it from God.

So I set out to do that, praying every night — and several times a day whenever the mood struck — for God to restore my hands. I didn't do it out loud and I didn't ask anyone else to pray for it. I knew from many years of Catholic school that I wasn't supposed to use prayer like that. I was supposed to pray things like, "God, if it be your will, please restore my hands." But that didn't really make sense to me. If it was God's will, then he was probably going to do it anyway, whether I prayed for it or not. So I threw good doctrine out and prayed, unashamed, for a miracle.

I tried to make every bargain with God I could think of, including that if he'd restore my hands I'd never use them for masturbation again. After awhile it occurred to me that that was actually a relatively small price to pay for the kind of miracle I was asking for, so I upped the ante.

"God," I prayed silently one night, "If you give me back one of my hands, just one, then I'll spend the rest of my life feeding poor people. I promise."

That wasn't the only promise I made. I'd join the priesthood, I'd travel across the country singing God's praises, I would never let another curse word slip through my lips. All I was asking in return was that he restore just one of my hands. I had decided that one was enough.

There were times when I was certain he had granted my prayers, but only when I was asleep.

One night I dreamed I was back at KU, in the squatty, concrete liberal arts building, Wescoe Hall. It was a time between classes and the wide hallway was full of students in shorts and T-shirts, backpacks slung over one shoulder as they strode through, many of them yakking into cell phones.

I stood in the middle of the hallway, a rock in the middle of a swirling, rainbow-colored stream of people. I was staring at my hands. I had raised them, palms up, and was looking down with awe at 10 perfect, pink fingers. I carefully flexed them one by one and felt the joy of that old sensation that I used to take for granted — I could move my fingers! God had answered my prayer!

I looked around at the people passing by, oblivious to my presence. I wanted to grab one of them and show them my hands, explain what had happened, share this utter joy with someone else. But who would believe such a miracle? They would think I was crazy.

I ran down the hall, and another rush came over me as I realized that my feet worked again, too, as well as they ever had. It was almost like I was floating. I burst through the doors at the end of the hall and out into the sunlight. I was on a second-floor landing, looking down at the concrete stairway that twisted down to ground level. The stairs were crowded with people, milling about on their way up or down.

Farther down the stairs I spotted someone I knew. It was Eric Duncan, a guy I lived with at Pearson. Eric was a staunch Christian, not shy about talking about Jesus. I could show him my hands. I could tell him about the miracle. He'd believe me.

I started rushing down the stairs, trying to shove my way through people in front of me who were moving too slowly. I could see Eric's light brown hair bobbing way in front of me, but I couldn't quite reach him. I tried to yell his name, but my voice didn't work. Odd. For some reason it was very important that I reach Eric, that I share this with him, but there were just too many people in the way. I thrashed around, trying to make a path and trying to yell at him, but my efforts were in vain.

Then I woke up. The back of Eric's bobbing head was gone, the crowds of other kids were gone, Wescoe's gray concrete exterior was gone. I was back in bed, in my hospital room and I was gasping and shaking, having worked myself into a frenzy. Dad was stretched out in the chair next to me, snoring. I looked down. My hands were still wrapped up, covered in the same bandages. I tried to flex my fingers. Nothing. I strained with all my might, my brain telling all the dead muscles in those digits to do their thing. Not so much as a quiver.

I began to cry.

The sight of my fingers became more distressing every time I went to the tank room and saw them with the bandages off.

The fingers were not simply black, they were withering away, dried out, shrinking and wrinkling up. They were also starting to curl into claws. When I asked why, Dr. Lawrence explained that as the tendons died they contracted, bending the entire finger. Near the base of each finger there were deep crevices where he had cut into the soft tissue looking for blood flow, and exposed the inner workings of my hands. I especially tried not to focus on those parts. It looked like Freddy Krueger.

Part of me was repulsed by these withered, unfeeling, claw-hands and was actually eager to see them amputated. Cut them off and be rid of them, already. No one should ever have to look at such awfulness.

But the bigger part of me, the part that was winning out, was concerned about life after amputations. This was different from my feet. I was confident I'd be able to walk again and, beyond walking, how important were toes really? Sure, my feet would be a little mangled, but I could usually hide them easily and go about my business with no one any the wiser.

This hands thing was different. First of all, I needed my fingers to do all kinds of things. Write, type, drive, dress, shower, etc., etc., etc. How in the hell was I going to do those things if I let them take my fingers off?

And the appearance aspect was weighing on me as heavily as the function aspect. I couldn't hide my hands. I could wear gloves sometimes, maybe, but that would look awfully strange in summer. I could get prosthetics, but people would still notice when I tried to use my hands that something wasn't right. I was going to look different; there was no getting around that. People were going to stare at me.

Dr. Lawrence became more insistent that we were wasting time, that there was no point in delaying any further. The internal medicine doctors agreed. The sooner I got rid of those necrotic fingers, they said, the sooner my mysterious fevers would go away.

But I kept stalling. I told them it had only been a couple weeks since I had my toes amputated and I needed a little longer to recover from that surgery. I told them I wanted another few days to do arm raises and stretching exercises with Mylene so that my upper body would be strong going into the procedure. Dr. Lawrence gave me skeptical looks, but Psycho-Mom had my back and he wasn't about to tangle with her.

This went on for several days, until one night when Harry the nurse was in my room changing my bandages. The bedside changings weren't as bad as the tank because there was no debriding and it was quicker, but it still hurt for them to peel the old bandages off. Harry carefully wet down each strip of gauze so it wouldn't stick and then pulled them off, one little bit at a time. It was just he and I in the room.

As usual, Harry was going about his work cheerfully, chatting me up and trying to distract me.

"The Royals, man, they lost another one tonight, huh?" he said. "They are so-o-o bad, man."

"Yeah, it's pretty rough this year," I answered, sucking in some air as he dripped sterile water from a piece of soaked gauze into an open wound on my right hand.

"Pretty rough every year," he said with a chuckle.

All of a sudden he went quiet. The ever-present grin changed as he pursed his lips and narrowed his eyes in concentration. He was ever-so-gently dabbing away the water and Silvadene cream from a large crater in my hand where the base of my pinky finger used to be. Then he paused and leaned down, studying the area carefully. I wondered what was up, but didn't want to look too closely.

Harry put his hand under my wrist and raised my arm until the shriveled black fingers and raw, debrided flesh were right beneath my eyes.

"Look here, Andy, look at this," he said, as serious as I'd ever seen him. He was pointing into the crater below my pinky with his gloved hand. "See that white thing right there? That's your tendon....You have to let them operate."

CHAPTER 14

A BIRTHDAY POUCH

A week later I was celebrating my 23rd birthday with my right hand stuck in my stomach. After Harry showed me my tendon, he left and I broke down, crying myself to sleep. The next morning, when Dr. Lawrence came on his rounds, I told him I was ready to schedule another surgery. I asked him to start with the right hand because I wanted to get back to using my dominant arm as soon as possible.

So I woke up after surgery with my right hand gone except for the thumb and a few finger segments sewn snugly into the soft tissue of my abdominal wall. Dr. Lawrence warned me that for three weeks after the procedure I would have to keep my arm very still so the full-thickness graft could take. When I first woke up that wasn't too difficult. Recent experience had taught me post-surgical pain was most manageable if I stayed motionless.

By that point I was either getting tougher, or the medical staff was getting better at regulating my pain. Besides chopping off my fingers and slicing my side open to put my hand in there, Dr. Lawrence had also taken a couple more skin grafts from my thighs and applied them to my ravaged heels, placing them over the base of synthetic Integra skin that had been grafted on weeks earlier.

It was not a minor trip to the operating room, but I seemed to recover quickly. There was still the day spent drifting in and out of consciousness and moaning incoherently, but by the next morning the pain had dissipated to the point where it no longer consumed my every waking thought.

Then I was able to focus on the sensation that went along with having my hand in that abdominal pouch. It can only be described as icky. It was warm and moist and I soon started to wonder how difficult it would be to keep my arm still for three weeks when my instinct was to yank my hand out of there.There was a wide cloth strap that wound around me, jamming my arm tight to my torso, which provided a first line of defense.

Within a few days I found that the best course of action for dealing with the pouch was to try not to think about it. Thankfully, my birthday was full of distractions.

Cherie, a young nurse who probably could have made more money as a model, gave me a card that made my face flush.

Dear Andy,

Happy happy birthday! I'm sorry that we've met under these circumstances, and it sucks that you have to be here on your b-day, but by this time next year we'll be celebrating your full recovery. You are such a strong person and I'm so proud of what you have accomplished. Try to take things one day at a time; you've already become so much stronger physically, emotionally and spiritually. I'm glad I have had the opportunity to meet you. You are such a great person.I hope you still have a great b-day regardless of the situation. We'll try to make it an easy-going day for you!

— Cherie

Jeny and a couple of the other burn techs bought me John Mayer's newest album. I didn't deem it necessary to tell them I'd actually grown tired of Mayer's melodrama. It was better than his previous CD, anyway.

Brandi, the nurse who previously brought me the CreamSlushes, marked my birthday by giving me a DVD of a Blue Man Group concert.

"Have you ever seen them before?" she asked timidly.

"No, but I've heard a lot about them," I said. "I had a friend at KU that raved about them."

"I went to their show once," she said. "It was so cool the way they use pipes and barrels and stuff as instruments. Just thought it might give you something new to watch."

"Yeah, it's awesome, thanks," I said, then motioned up to my room's old TV and VCR with a grin. "Now somebody just has to get me a DVD player in here."

"Yeah, sorry about that," Brandi said, her face falling. "I couldn't find it on VHS."

"No, no, it's cool, I was just kidding," I quickly added. "I want it on DVD, you know, for when I get out of here."

After a few more assurances Brandi left. Nurse Bob and Doran then came in with a Minnesota Twins T-shirt.

"Bob wanted to get you a Royals shirt, but I talked him out of it," Doran said.

"We decided you've probably suffered enough," Bob deadpanned.

It was Bob's day off, but he had cooked up a fresh batch of tiramisu and come over personally to wish me a happy birthday. I expressed my thanks as best I could, but found myself in awkward emotional territory for a male. I couldn't help wondering what it would have been like if I had met those guys under different circumstances. I could see us going out for barbecue and beers or wasting away spring afternoons at Kauffman Stadium. Instead they were changing my bandages and emptying my bedpans.

As evening arrived there were more gifts. Malcolm Gibson and his wife, Joyce, came with a boxful. One of the first things Malcolm pulled out of it was a glass jug of beer from Free State, a microbrewery in Lawrence.

"It's Oatmeal Stout," he said, smacking his lips.

"Pour me a glass," I said, motioning with my unpouched hand. "I haven't had a beer in, sheesh, like two months."

"I don't think that's such a good idea," Mom said, shaking her head. "You're on a lot of pain-killers, hon."

"You're probably right," I sighed.

Mom felt bad about depriving me and eventually decided that it couldn't hurt to give me a taste. She poured some in a tiny paper cup and lifted it to my lips. It tasted bitter after all of the burn unit Powerade I'd gotten used to.

Malcolm also brought two KU T-shirts from Bonnie Henrickson. Bonnie had recently been named the women's basketball coach at KU and had read about me in the local papers. Odd coincidences bound us together. I was from St. Cloud, which caught her eye because she had been a star player at St. Cloud State University after growing up in nearby Willmar, Minnesota.

Bonnie also knew more than she ever wanted to know about bacterial meningitis. In her previous job at Virginia Tech, a promising freshman player named Rayna DuBose was stricken with the illness just a few years before it got me. Like me, Rayna went from the picture of health to critical condition overnight. Actually, she started in a more robust state, considering that she was an NCAA Division-I athlete and I was little more than a weekend gym rat.

Even with the advantage of all her conditioning, though, Rayna barely made it. Her kidneys failed, she had a heart attack and her limbs were even more severely damaged than mine. In the end she had to have both arms amputated below the elbow and both legs amputated below the knee. Yet she had recovered and was living independently with the help of prosthetics.

As Malcolm relayed Rayna's story, I shook my head. I couldn't believe that I had never heard any of it. A Division I athlete who lost both arms and legs after getting to live her basketball dream for just one season: it was tragic, yet also inspiring and seemed like something that should have been part of the national consciousness, at least for rabid sports fans like me. The fact that it hadn't drawn more media attention struck me as sexist. Chris Paul was a freshman phenom for Wake Forest's men's basketball team at the time, and I imagined the national headlines if it had happened to him.

I didn't mention any of that to Malcolm, though. I just told him I wanted to hear more about Rayna and he said he would let Bonnie know.

The stream of birthday visitors continued. Clay and Randy showed up with a box full of old videos because they knew my taste in movies as well as anybody.

"Sorry, man, I couldn't find 'The Scarlet Pimpernel,'" Randy said with his usual impish grin.

"That's a shame," I said, shaking my head. "Jane Seymour is so hot in that."

"Dude, she's still hot," Clay said. "Dr. Quinn, Medicine Woman."

"Underrated show, really," I replied.

That night when Dad and I were the only ones still around, Jason from Pearson showed up with his girlfriend, Stephanie, and his mom, Melva. Melva, as usual, came bearing homemade baked goods, including a birthday cake.

Stephanie was carrying a small boombox, which was unusual. Before I could ask what was up, Melva set down the cake and Stephanie flicked on the boombox. Bass-heavy beats of some hip-hop song started thumping and suddenly Melva and Stephanie were jigging about, bent at the waist and twirling their arms in the air.

After a few moments Stephanie flicked off the boombox and she and Melva collapsed in a fit of breathless giggling. Bemused, I glanced over at Jason. He just shrugged, his bespectacled face red.

"OK, so what was that all about?" I asked when the giggles had died down a bit.

"Well, your dad said you were looking for dancing girls," Melva answered. "This was the best we could do on short notice."

The three of them stayed for an hour or so, and we shared laughs and cake. Then Dad and I went into our usual late-night ritual of watching TV until we both fell asleep.

"Good effort on the dancing girls, Dad," I said before I dozed off. "But next time I guess I'd prefer that they all be under 40."

A few days later the entire burn unit was abuzz with the news that Keith Langford was in the building.

Langford was a KU basketball player, a 6-foot-4 shooting guard from Texas with a silky-smooth left-handed jump-shot and an uncanny knack for getting to the basket. KU basketball was a fixture on national television and the players were minor celebrities not only on campus, but throughout the state. Langford, one of the leading scorers, was better-known than most.

Langford was also a student in the journalism school. He was a year behind me and we'd never had classes together. But Malcolm knew I was a basketball fan — like most everyone at KU — and asked Keith to visit me.

When he walked into my hospital room behind Malcolm, Keith was the epitome of cool. He was dressed in the basketball team's unofficial off-court uniform: a T-shirt and baggy, gray sweatpants. A thick, silver chain with a cross at the bottom hung from his neck and he had large diamond, or fake diamond, studs in each ear. His hair was trimmed short and neat, his sideburns forming perfect little rectangles.

Malcolm did the introductions and Keith shook hands with Mom and Dan, who had hurried down to the hospital. A basketball junkie himself, Dan wasn't about to miss this.

Keith pulled up a chair next to my bed and folded his lanky frame into it. It soon became clear neither of us really knew what to say.

"Thanks for coming," I finally said. "I'm a big fan of yours."

Keith seemed a little embarrassed. He glanced around the room, taking in my IV bag, all the bandages, the hospital gown.

"Shoot, man, I'm a fan of *yours*," he said, shaking his head. "I can't imagine going through all this."

That was more than I'd expected to hear from him and it was all I needed. I smiled and shrugged like it was nothing — my own little macho pose. Dan had been quiet until then, but couldn't hold off forever.

"I like your tatts, man," he said to Keith.

"Huh?" Keith said, turning to face him.

"Your tattoos, man, your ink," Dan said. "I like it."

Keith had several tattoos, the best-known being a Superman-style logo with a "K" instead of an "S" on one of his biceps.

"Oh, thanks," Keith said somewhat sheepishly.

"Yeah, I'm thinking of getting some ink, myself," Dan said with a little half-nod.

"I don't know, might not be such a good idea," Keith said, perhaps seeing Mom frown. "You know you can't really undo them or anything if you change your mind."

"Yeah I know, I know," Dan nodded. "But if I find something I really like, something that really speaks to me, then I might get one."

I soon became a silent bystander as a bemused Keith argued the pros and cons of tattooing with Dan. I was still glowing inwardly at the compliment Keith had paid me and for the time being I was glad to have a somewhat goofy little brother to entertain him because I really didn't feel like I had anything interesting to talk about. I'd spent the last two months staring at the same four walls.

Keith stayed for more than an hour and he, Malcolm, Mom and Dan seemed to get along just fine. I was able to just kind of relax and enjoy their conversation. At the same time one nurse after another came in just to "check on" one thing or another, all the while casting surreptitious glances at the college basketball star who was actually in the very same room.

Before Keith left we wished him luck on his senior season, which was still about five months away, and tried to persuade him to sign with the Timberwolves when he got done with school. Coming from the Deep South, he didn't seem to cotton to that idea.

"I'm cold here in Kansas, man," he said with a smile and exaggerated shiver. "I don't think I could handle Minnesota for very long."

"Oh, c'mon," Mom said. "You'd only be outside for as long as it takes to get from your heated limo to the arena."

"Still," Keith said. "We'll just wait and see. Anywhere in the NBA would be pretty good."

Before he left he told me he expected to see me at some games come winter.

CHAPTER 15

FINDING HAPPY PLACES

The day after Langford's visit was the Fourth of July. Dad raised the blinds and we kept an eye out for fireworks, though the burn staff warned us we might not be able to see any.

A little past 10 p.m., they started to appear. Little bursts of color just barely cleared the high buildings on the horizon. It wasn't the greatest view, but it was a welcome change after staring at the same rooftops and street for months.

A week after the pouching surgery, I returned to the tank room with a lot of work left to do. Just removing all the bandages from my legs took 15 minutes because they were wrapped in so many layers. The ones touching the skin had to be wet down and peeled off slowly so the fragile new skin underneath didn't break. I clinched my teeth and hissed in sharp intakes of breath each time I felt the sting of flesh beginning to tear. The nurses and techs took that as a warning and would stop, apply more water, and tug even more slowly. It was painstaking, for them and for me.

There was some worry that the grafts on my heels and knees weren't taking. A healthy person doesn't have much soft tissue over those areas to begin with, and mine had been debrided almost to the bone before the grafts were applied. The grafts were thin, fragile strips of skin. They appeared to be fraying around the edges, with pinkish-red fluid oozing out whenever the bandages were removed.

Dr. Lawrence was on vacation, so a Dr. Monaco came into the tank to check out the trouble spots. She told me the heels would likely need further grafting. The knees she thought would be OK.

"They hurt a lot," I informed her, trying to look in her eyes and not glance down at the tuft of my pubic hair that had emerged from under the washcloth. "They have me trying to bend my knees in PT and sometimes when I do it just burns. Feels like the skin is tearing."

"Hm-m," she said, leaning down for a closer look at the knees, which again made me wish I could shift that washcloth with my mind. "It may just be that the bandages are sticking to the wounds because they're still exudating."

I had been in the hospital long enough to know that "exudating" meant there was blood, pus or some other fluid leaking out of my body. The jury was out on whether this was a good thing. Ideally, of course, the body does not leak fluids, but holds them in. At least, that was my non-medical opinion. But Dr. Lawrence assured me that exudation was often part of the healing process and, therefore, not a bad sign for someone in my condition.

"What do you think?" Dr. Monaco asked Doran, who was in the tank that day.

I was a little shocked. A doctor asking for advice from an underling? Somewhere far below us, was hell freezing over?

"We could try Duoderm," Doran said through his surgical mask. "When we dress wounds with that it tends to give a little more flexibility."

Dr. Monaco agreed and after that I had new, gel-like coverings over each knee, which seemed to help the grafts underneath stay moist.

The grafts on my lower legs were taking fairly well, which meant some of the staples holding them on could be removed. This was also a slow process. I didn't like to watch too closely, but as far as I could tell, the nurses and techs used a pliers-like instrument to grasp and pull them out. Surprisingly, this usually didn't hurt — the staples were small and smooth and slid out fairly easily. But every once in awhile one would catch a nerve or snag a bit of flesh on its way out.

My left arm — now my only free arm — still needed considerable work. There were patches of blackened, shriveled skin that had to be sliced away. Some of them, especially on the forearm and hand, were deep and required slow and careful scalpel work.

About the only thing that wasn't touched in these new tank sessions was that right arm, now firmly secured to my side with the navy blue sling that crossed my chest. With the bandages removed and the hospital gown off, I could see exactly where my hand went into my abdomen. There was my arm, my wrist, my thumb, and then, below it, the rest of my hand plunged into the incision in my stomach. It was disconcerting.

My stomach bulged out at that spot, the skin stretched taut as if a large blister had formed on that side of me. There were lots of stitches holding the hand inside the abdomen — big, thick, black ones. The strip of skin where the hand and stomach met had turned black. It would have to be debrided later.

The stomach incision was ringed with Xeroform, a yellow gauze covered in Vaseline that was meant to stay on until the pouching procedure was finished. A yellowish liquid oozed out from the sides of the Xeroform, dripped down and dried on my hip, forming a crusty brown film that the nurses and techs scrubbed away in the tank. I decided not to ask whether the fluid was yellow on its way out of my body, or the Xeroform made it that way.

With all this work to be done, the tank sessions got chaotic. One day they had me in there with six other people — a nurse, two burn techs, Dr. Lawrence and a couple of his students. One of them was shampooing my hair, two split up leg duties and began peeling off the bandages, while Dr. Lawrence poked around in what was left of my free hand with his scalpel, looking for viable tissue. It was like a full-service car wash that was overstaffed.

Some of what was going on didn't even hurt. The shampooing was actually quite pleasant, as any guy who has had an attractive girl run her fingers through his hair can verify. But it was just too much activity for me. The different sensations all hitting me at once became overwhelming and I started to cry. It was just little whimpers at first, but the feel of those few tears rolling down my cheeks seemed to set me off even more. Then I became ashamed of my tears, which plopped yet another emotion atop a steaming pile of them that was building up inside me.

Soon I was full-on sobbing.

One of the nurses working on my legs stopped and looked up.

"Andy, what's wrong?" she asked.

I could only shake my head, still sobbing. Dr. Lawrence briefly stopped cutting.

"Am I hurting you?" he asked, his bespectacled eyes gazing quizzically over the top of his mask. "This is all dead tissue here. It shouldn't hurt."

Again, I shook my head. It did sting occasionally, but it was nothing compared to what I had been through in earlier tank sessions. It was just too many people working on me at the same time. I understood that it would make the whole process go faster, but at the same time it just freaked me out. I was getting too immersed in what was going on, too aware of the nightmarish state my body was in. One would think that after more than two months I would be used to it, but I had faced much of those first two months with an odd sense of detachment, especially in the tank. I had convinced myself on a subconscious level that this was not really my body, but for some reason that delusion had become harder to keep up.

That particular trip to the tank, though no longer than the rest, seemed interminable, and I'm sure it was no better for the staff. I sobbed and cried, despite all attempts to console me. The nurse and techs took turns stroking my hair and whispering that everything would be OK, but it was no use. I was a mess.

The next morning Dr. Stiers, the psychiatrist, was back to see me.

"I've been told you're having some trouble dealing with your debridement sessions," he said, taking his usual seat next to the bed and resting one leg on his opposite knee.

As usual, I said nothing. The very sight of his thick, walrus mustache and glasses brought the taste of bile to my throat, irrationally.

"Is it possible that you've been through so much pain that now you're starting to anticipate the pain and the dread of it is making it worse than it actually is?" he asked.

"I don't know," I replied. "You're the doctor,".

He seemed to take an actual verbal response — even an acidly sarcastic one — as a good sign.

"Often, when we're anxious about something it heightens our bodies' reception of physical stimuli," he said. "We start to breathe more shallowly, or even hold our breath in some instances. Our muscles tense up and every sensation is magnified."

What he was saying made perfect sense, and I knew that I was tensing myself up in the tank, literally clenching my jaw against pain that I figured could come any moment.

Before he left, Dr. Stiers tried to teach me some breathing exercises that he said would help me relax in the tank. It was pretty simple stuff — just 10 deep breaths, in through the nose and out through the mouth, every time I found myself getting anxious.

But because it was Dr. Stiers, and I had predetermined that this guy could do nothing to help me, I decided I wouldn't do his stupid breathing exercises. I was willing to concede that what he had said about my tensing up in the tank and making things worse was probably true. But it seemed to me that focusing on breathing was not the answer. I needed something to take my mind off what was going on and plant it firmly on something else. I knew my brain well enough to know that, if I tried to occupy it simply with breathing, it would move on quickly to other things. Other things, in the tank, meant pain.

So I devised a therapy based on an Adam Sandler movie. I decided that while I was in the tank I would use my imagination to "go to a happy place."

I would call up some joyous experience from the past and go through every detail.

Each memory I chose had a trigger, some strong sensation that I could recall to put me back in that particular time and place.

Sometimes it was a sight. When I wanted to transport myself back to that Gin Blossoms concert at the Basilica in Minneapolis, all I had to think of was Ali's pale golden hair, shining in the light of a sun that was beginning to dip near the horizon. Suddenly I could remember everything vividly. The warmth of a July evening in Minnesota, the lead singer's voice as he crooned, "Till I hear it from you," the impossible smoothness of Ali's skin as I put my arm around her.

Sometimes it was a sound. When I wanted to transport myself back to Venice all I needed was the memory of bells ringing. That semester in Italy I traveled on a jam-packed train through the night to the famous city. Carnival was in full swing and Venice was thick with people wearing porcelain masks and Renaissance-style dresses. I was with another American student, a feisty, bright girl from South Carolina named Curtrice. We arrived in Venice in the early hours of the morning, as the sun was just coming up and beginning to burn off the thick fog that blanketed the canals, and sat side-by-side on the floor of the train station with our backs against some lockers, waiting for the baggage drop to open. Before long Curtrice was asleep, her head resting on my shoulder and her sweet-smelling hair just below my nose. My brain was thick with fatigue after the overnight train ride, but I sat awake, listening to the boats out on the canal ringing their bells to announce their presence in the fog. I fought sleep as long as I could, desperately trying to take in and record every bit of the experience so it would remain in my memory banks forever.

For a less romantic memory, I thought back to the sour odor of my old gym shoes. They were a well-worn pair of silver-and-black Reeboks that brought me back to my senior year of high school. That was the year I assembled a team of fellow junior varsity rejects who happened to be good friends of mine, to play in the city basketball league. We were short, we were slow and many of us were a little pudgy. But we all loved the game and, freed of coaches and any fear of failing, we found that we loved to play together.

Time after time we found that special rhythm that only basketball players understand — that point where every teammate seems to know what the other is about to do, when the team is like five fingers on the same hand, or as the coach in Hoosiers put it, "five pistons, firing as one." We didn't win every game, but we won more than we lost and at the end of the season we opened the playoffs with wins against two more athletic teams to earn a division championship.

I ran through that entire season in my head several times when I was in the tank. I watched our only big man, Chad Boeckers, take over a game in the final minute to lead us to our first win. I watched myself drive and flip a behind-the-back pass — something I'd never have the guts to do in a meaningful game — to Chris Markman. I watched Brett Hansen pass out of a double-team to me for an overtime 3-pointer that turned the playoff opener in our favor.

Those guys were my lifelong friends. But memories of people who touched my life in some very brief intervals also helped out in the tank.

During that semester in Italy the year before, I had set off to climb the relatively gentle Mt. Grappa, which was less than an hour from campus. On the way up I met an Italian family of three: the father was Luigi, the teenage daughter was Cristina and the mother's name I never caught because both of them just called her "Mama." They were the Perizzolos, and they were lost. They didn't have a map and I did, so I told them I would be their guide. I tried not to let on that I was American — the Iraq War had just started, and Americans were not particularly popular right then. But my Italian was spotty, and after about an hour of stilted conversation the jig was up.

"You're not Italian, are you?" Mama Perizzolo asked in Italian.

"No," I sheepishly replied. "Sono degli Stati Uniti."

To my surprise, they couldn't have been more pleased to meet an American. The parents spoke little English, but they pressed Cristina to speak to me in my native tongue. She shook her head timidly, but after a bit of coaxing I learned that she had studied in Britain and was nearly fluent in English. The two of us eventually settled into a half-Italian, half-English mix, as her parents plodded along behind us, looking on proudly. I confessed that my name was actually "Andrew" and not "Andrea," the Italian equivalent I'd initally offered. She tried to explain this to her mother, but the "w" proved impossible for her to handle. "Mama" stumbled over the second syllable several times before finally settling on "Andre-oo," an approximation that made Cristina and I look at each other and giggle. After a few more near-misses, I explained that, because I was in Italy, I would be honored to have her call me "Andrea," even if it was a girl's name in the States. She was pleased.

The four of us spent a near-perfect afternoon on the mountain. Dark-haired Cristina was a classical pianist and, unlike most American girls her age, had no qualms about showing affection for her parents, with both hugs and kind words. I gentlemanly offered my arm to help her step over puddles or branches in the path. In return she gave me shy smiles and batted her eyelashes in a way that made me wish I was younger than 21 or she was older than 16.

The four of us took pictures together at the summit with one blue-tinged vista after another in the background. The entire countryside lay before us, tiny villages dotting wide expanses of green farmland. Flowers poked little buds out above the thin layers of snow that lined either side of the mountain path. With little conscious effort on my part, that striking image of winter and spring intertwined burned itself in my memory.

The Perizzolos bought me a cappuccino in the small mountaintop cafe and, after sitting and sipping in contented camaraderie, we trekked back down. I never saw them again, except in my head, where memories of that sparkling spring afternoon helped keep me sane during the darkest days of my life.

CHAPTER 16

THE VISITORS

As July plodded along, it started to feel as if the walls of my hospital room were closing in on me. The only time I left was to go to the tank, or sometimes to the rehab room. My physical and occupational therapy at that point mostly consisted of stretching because I couldn't yet put weight on my feet and had only one free arm. The television in my room was on probably 10 hours a day, but gradually failed to hold my attention. I found myself staring out the window watching cars go by.

One day there was some activity on one of the rooftops below my window. A group of shirtless men were laying down a new layer of asphalt on the long, flat roof. It was 90 degrees or hotter those days and they were dripping sweat, their hair stringy and soaked. Their backs, bent and straining as they pushed the viscous tar with long squeegees, were tanned to a deep brown. It was hard, messy work, the kind they made the prisoners do in the movie "The Shawshank Redemption." But I found myself wishing I could be out there with them, just so I could be doing something different.

The only thing that broke the monotony was my brigade of visitors, but they, too, reminded me of the life outside the hospital that was going on without me.

A few of the Basehor coaches showed up one day, guys that I used to bother with endless phone calls or postgame interviews after losses they clearly weren't eager to talk about. They brought me up to speed on how all the spring sports teams finished and lamented that there were only a few more weeks before football practice and the start of another school year. That gave me a bit of a jolt as I realized just how much time had passed. An entire class of high-schoolers that I had watched compete was now gone, and everyone else was moving up a grade.

Malcolm and Joyce usually showed up at least once a week and took Mom and Dad out for dinner on other occasions. They were among several KU faculty members who stopped by.

Max Utsler, who taught a sports journalism class, was another. I was taking his class when I fell ill and had been working on a group project with three other classmates — one of the few major academic assignments that I left uncompleted.

"I had barely even started my part," I admitted to Max. "I was planning to really get cracking on it after the Student Senate elections were over and all my *Kansan* stuff slowed down."

Max, a former college baseball player, was a big guy with salt-and-pepper hair and a crooked nose that looked as if it might have come into contact with a ball traveling at high speed at some point.

"I wouldn't worry too much about the project," he said with a laugh. "I'm sure you would have gotten it done, plus I'm pretty sure I gave the rest of your group a break, considering the circumstances. What was it you guys were working on?"

"It was an analysis of fallen sports heroes," I said. "Kind of a commentary on how the media ignored or glossed over their flaws until they were done playing. I was supposed to write a section on Kirby Puckett."

"What?" cried Mom, who was sitting next to Max. "How could you write anything bad about Kirby and call yourself a Minnesotan?"

"He seemed to fit pretty perfectly into our thesis, Ma," I replied. "He was a golden god who could do no wrong during his playing days, but since he retired all you seem to hear about is him pissing in a parking lot or groping a woman in a public bathroom."

"Well, I still think he's a hero," Mom said, feigning indignation.

Max chuckled.

"The first thing I tell kids when they take my class Mrs. Marso," he said, "is that it will change the way they look at professional sports, and big-time college sports. If they want to keep believing in the purity and innocence of the games, they better drop the class the first week. I've had more than one person come up to me at the end of the semester and say, 'Thanks a lot, Max. You ruined sports for me.'"

"Well, you didn't ruin them for me," I said. "I know those guys are overpaid, over-glorified and put on a pedestal they don't deserve. But I'd still love to be at the ballpark right now, especially if it meant I could get out of here."

Max's eyes followed my free hand as I gestured at the drab hospital walls. His grin turned serious.

"You get yourself better so we can get you out there," he said, leaning over to pat me on the shoulder. "You know who John Gordon is, right?"

I nodded.

"The voice of the Twins."

"Right," Max said. "Well, he's a friend of mine, so next time the Twins come to Kansas City I'll call him and see if he can get the two of us up in the press box with him."

"That sounds great," I said, nodding vigorously.

One more reason to push through the tank sessions.

Michelle from the *Kansan* visited almost once a week, often stopping by for an hour or so after work at *The Kansas City Star*, where she was doing an internship. With her dark-rimmed glasses and fashionable clothes, she looked every bit the young metro reporter.

During one visit she brought me up to speed on all the *Kansan* things I'd missed in the last few weeks of school. The Last Night of Production was the highlight. At the end of every semester, the school's aspiring journalism professionals smuggled bottles of champagne into the newsroom (KU was a dry campus) on the night the final issue went to press. When the last newspaper of the semester had been "put to bed," we'd pop open the bubbly and let off the steam of four months of deadlines, critiques and nasty calls and emails.

Then we would cap things off a few days later with the Barn Party — a kegger held at a farm just outside town. By Michelle's account, the latest edition of the Barn Party had been a doozy. She let me know who had been seen making out with whom (shocking!), who had gotten completely plastered (not so shocking) and who was so lame and boring they hadn't even bothered to show up (even less shocking).

I gently reminded her that I hadn't shown up either.

"Well, yeah, but you had a pretty good excuse," she said with a laugh.

"True," I said. "But I should have at least had you guys pour out a little liquor for me."

I enjoyed Michelle's visits and was glad to catch up on all the *Kansan* gossip, but when she left I allowed myself a melancholy moment. I realized that I never said a proper goodbye to people that I'd worked alongside of for the better part of a year. Now many of them were scattering across the country to take their first post-college jobs, while my life remained flash-frozen. Time marched on outside the hospital walls, with or without me.

My Minnesota friends also continued to visit throughout the summer, sometimes driving eight hours on Friday just to spend Saturday in my hospital room and then drive another eight hours back on Sunday.

Tim had an aunt who lived in Kansas City, and she opened her home to anyone who came down with him. There was also that three-bedroom apartment that Randy, Clay and I were leasing. Mom and Dad were paying my share of the rent and using one room as a crash pad for Dan. He stayed there most of the time, but gave way when we needed to host visitors.

A couple weeks after my pouching procedure, Ali and Marie came down again, this time accompanied by two more female friends, Liz and Katie. They would be staying at the apartment because Dan was back in Minnesota at the time. He had taken Randy and Gustavo with him to check on the house, bring back a few things and, as I'd later find out, introduce Gustavo to the American dining experience that is Hooters.

The four girls showed up at the hospital on a Friday night with Clay in tow. I was sitting up in the wheelchair at the time, post-dinner, and the sight of me out of bed was enough to send them rushing in gleefully.

"Hey-y-y-y Andy."

"Oh, Andy, you look so good."

"Great to see you."

"Ladies, ladies," I said, feigning exasperation as they took turns giving me careful hugs. "One at a time. I'm here all weekend."

They giggled as Clay looked on, shaking his head and giving me a little grin.

"You sure you're ready for this?" I asked. "Just you and Randy and all these girls in that little apartment?"

"Actually, Randy went with Dan and Gustavo to Minnesota," Clay said, a bit of red creeping into his cheeks. "So it's just me. Thought you knew that."

I did know that, of course, but I wanted to give Clay a hard time.

"Oh, r-r-really," I said, arching my eyebrows. "Sounds like the recipe for a cra-a-a-azy weekend."

"Don't worry," Katie said, laughing. "We'll be nice to Clay."

"Oh, I'm sure that you will," I said, using my best sleazeball voice. "Hope you girls brought your swimsuits, because the apartment complex has a very romantic little heart-shaped pool. That was one of the big selling points when we signed the lease."

"Ooh, heart-shaped pool," Liz said, turning to the other girls in mock excitement. "We'll definitely have to take advantage of that."

The rest of the evening passed in much the same way — the girls and I catching up on things and ribbing Clay. They returned the next day raving about the pancakes Clay cooked for breakfast and giving me a full report on the heart-shaped pool.

The weekend flew by. The chatty girls kept my mind occupied right up until the pain medicine kicked in and I could no longer keep my eyes open. But after they left I let myself get sad at what I'd missed. That was supposed to be my apartment, and it tore me up inside that they had stayed there without me. That was supposed to be the place where I would spend a year living with two of my best friends, playing tennis, watching movies, having barbecues, telling stories and laughing over beers out on the balcony. We were supposed to host girls there together, in what would be one of the last bachelor years of our lives — at least for the other two. That was my laid-back and lovely vision of life before meningitis. The first few months of that life already had been stolen and I felt the truth closing in: I might never get back there.

If I was being honest with myself, there was no way I was going to be able to grasp that sweet life any time soon. My feet and lower legs were still torn up, and there was no telling when I'd even be able to put weight on them, much less walk. The apartment was on the third floor, in an old building with no elevator. I wasn't getting up there without walking. And if I could get up there, then what? My hands were in a hell of a state. I couldn't wash, eat or go to the bathroom without considerable help. Would I ask Clay and Randy to take care of me? No way. It would be completely unfair to them and, even if they agreed, it would change the dynamic of our friendship in a way I didn't want. Would Mom or Dad or both move in and take care of me? Seemed a little impractical with only three bedrooms. And it would defeat the purpose of spending a carefree year with friends.

In the wake of the girls' visit I came within shouting distance of something I wasn't ready to fully face: this disease had changed everything. I might have to alter everything I had envisioned for myself in the foreseeable future. I pushed the thought away before its implications could sink in.

I prayed: "God, Dr. Lawrence says it might take six months to a year for me to recover. Please just make it six months. Get me better so I can be in that apartment by this winter, please. That's all I ask."

This time I couldn't think of anything to offer God in return.

CHAPTER 17
A NEW POUCH, AND THEN ANOTHER

I went back into surgery on July 19 to lose one abdominal pouch and gain another. Three weeks of holding my right arm stiff had come and gone. The skin and fatty tissues of my stomach had attached themselves to what was left of my right hand. Dr. Lawrence was ready to cut away the tissue, free that hand and then sew me back together. I had never been so eager to have a surgical procedure. Of course, I wasn't so eager about starting the whole process over on my left side, but it had to be done. In the interest of convenience and getting it over with, I had agreed that Dr. Lawrence should just go ahead and pouch the left hand at the same time he released the right.

As a result, I woke up with both sides of my abdomen burning, and both hands stinging as well. My left arm was immobile, which was expected, but I found that I couldn't move my right arm either. I could see that it was freed from my stomach — lying heavily bandaged at my side. But when I tried to lift it off the bed it seemed to weigh a ton. I strained with every bit of muscle I could muster and finally the hand rose a few inches. Satisfied, I let it drop. Everything was OK, relatively speaking. My arm wasn't paralyzed; my muscles were just weak and puny from lack of use. It was an odd feeling, not being strong enough to lift my own arm.

That first day was tough, but the pain again seemed to subside more quickly than in my first few surgeries. It wasn't long before I was sitting up in bed, watching "Jeopardy" with Mom and lifting my right arm periodically in impromptu exercise sessions.

"How's the arm?" Mom asked.

"It's getting better," I replied. "Still stiff, but it's starting to loosen up. Could you scratch my right thigh?"

"Sure," Mom said, reaching over from her chair.

Itching was becoming a problem, especially on the donor sites where Dr.

Lawrence had taken skin for grafting. The itches were deep and impossible to ignore, made even more infuriating by the fact that I had no good hand with which to scratch. That was just one of many things that were starting to wear me down and make me irritable. There was also boredom, constant noise and blood-pressure checks that disturbed my sleep and the helplessness of having one hand in an abdominal pouch and the other nearly immobile because of muscle atrophy. My pain was more or less under control, but the annoyances were starting to build.

I unleashed this growing storm on people who didn't deserve it.

"Do you want me to bring you some Legos?" Mom asked one day. "You used to love them and they might help you work on the dexterity in your right hand."

I rolled my eyes at her, shaking my head in uncalled-for contempt.

"I have no dexterity," I hissed. "Look, why don't you just leave the occupational therapy to the actual occupational therapists, Ma? They have some training, so they might know what they're talking about."

Mom pulled away with a wounded look. She flipped on the TV and we spent the next few hours in uncomfortable silence.

A few days later she was spooning apple sauce into my mouth while a nurse that I didn't recognize put the blood pressure cuff around my arm. I was drowsy from pain meds and, as often happened, was having trouble keeping my eyes open. My head kept dipping and Mom kept nudging me awake so she could feed me more. She had the full spoon at my lips when my head bobbed again, dripping a line of applesauce down the front of my hospital gown.

Mom nudged me and I shook my eyes open just in time to see the nurse stifle a small giggle. Under most circumstances I probably would have laughed too. Here I was, a grown man dozing off in the middle of dinner. But I was past my breaking point.

"Oh this is funny to you, huh?" I sneered. "Well that's just great. Does anybody here know I'm a person, or am I just a fricking joke for you to laugh at? I had major surgery this week. You don't know what kind of pain that is. You have no idea."

The poor girl apologized profusely on her way out the door and Mom gave me a dirty look.

"Look, Andrew," she said. "You can yell at me, that's fine. But you better treat the staff better than that. The people here have been really good to you, to all of us. They've gone above and beyond to make you comfortable. It's pretty obvious that they care about you."

She was right, of course. I was being irrational and a jerk. But I wasn't in the mood to hear it.

"Whatever," I replied, turning my head to let her know that the feeding session was over.

Mom left the room, probably to go apologize to the nurse.

If you believe in karma, my cruelty may explain what happened next. By all measures, the hospital staff had been incredible, including the times when they rolled me over on my side every few hours to prevent bedsores and when they helped transfer me from the bed to a wheelchair. These movements had to be done with the utmost care while I had my hands sewn into my stomach, lest a stitch rip. Because I couldn't put any weight on my feet, I had to do the wheelchair transfers with a sliding board that served as a thin plastic bridge from bed to chair. They slid the board under me and then I shimmied my butt along it until I was in the chair. Once my left hand was pouched this became even more difficult because my right arm was still flaccid and I had nothing to help push me along the sliding board. The hospital staff had to drag me across it until I was in the chair, and yet do it in a slow, delicate manner, especially when they were anywhere near my left arm. I was like 180 pounds of glass.

The nurses and techs handled the transfers with no complaints and usually things went off without a hitch. But one day, during one of those transfers, I felt a tug at my left side, and a new burning sensation where the hand and the abdomen pouch were. I tried to ignore it, to tell myself it was nothing, but there was a sour sense of dread in the pit of my stomach.

Dr. Lawrence removed the many layers of bandages in the tank room the next day. I strained my neck to get a glimpse down there and all I saw was a streak of yellowish-red fluid running down my side. Leakage from the pouch site wasn't unusual, but this looked more bloody than I was used to. Dr. Lawrence waited until I was bandaged up and back in my room to give me the bad news.

"It looks like some of the stitches have pulled free," he said, more somber than usual.

My heart sank.

"Can you just stitch it back up?" I said.

"It's not that simple," Dr. Lawrence said with a sigh. "Your hand pulled loose a little from your abdomen and it's only been nine days since your surgery, so the graft hasn't had nearly enough time to take. I'll have to make a new pouch and start over."

My jaw clenched, my ears buzzed and my eyes filled with water, blurring Dr. Lawrence's face. The thought of starting over and having my hand inside my stomach for 21 more days was almost too much to bear. I just shook my head, the tears starting to pour down my face.

Later that night Harry, the burn tech, came in the room not knowing anything about the pouch debacle.

"How's it going?" Harry said, with his usual bright eyes and big grin.

I couldn't be angry, not at Harry. I was just sad.

"Not so good," I mumbled. "I have to have surgery tomorrow. My hand pulled out of the pouch a little bit and now I have to start all over."

"Oh no," Harry said, his grin disappearing in an instant. "What happened?"

"I don't know," I choked, the waterworks starting again. "Maybe it was during one of my transfers or something. I told everybody to be more gentle, I told everyone that it hurt. I don't know what happened."

Now I was full on sobbing.

"I just can't take this anymore," I blubbered.

Soon Harry was crying too, his chest heaving along with mine and tears streaming down his brown cheeks.

"I'm so sorry, Andy, I'm so sorry," he said. "Everybody here just wants to see you well. None of us ever want to hurt you. I'm so sorry."

I knew it was true. Even though I might snap at them from time to time, I knew my biological family and my burn unit family were both pulling for me, were all doing everything they could to pull me through this. That was the only thing keeping me going. My internal strength was tapped out.

As the days slowly ticked by with my new pouch — just a few inches below where the old one was now stitched back together — I again drew hope from other meningitis survivors.

The burn unit's care coordinator arranged for the prosthetist at KU Med to visit me. He was a quiet, brown-haired guy with glasses, somewhere between my age and my parents' age. He told me a little bit about the replacement arms and legs that he worked with, but, after looking at my hands and feet, said he couldn't do anything for me for quite some time. I had a lot of healing ahead of me before any prosthetics could be attached safely to my limbs. He left me with a stack of amputee magazines.

One of them had an article about a young guy from the East Coast named Nick Springer who had survived a case of meningitis even more harrowing than mine. He was away at summer camp when it happened, far from any major hospital, and he lost both arms below the elbow and both legs above the knee. Yet there he was in a glossy half-page picture, playing wheelchair rugby. He had a navy blue jersey and he wore black rubber sleeves on each of his arm stumps to help him push his chair. His shoulders looked huge and his eyes had the unmistakable intensity of an athlete. He didn't look the least bit worried about getting hurt.

Nick had contracted meningitis when he was just 14 years old.

Dad found another survivor, John Kach, while trolling the Internet and managed to contact him by phone. John was about my age and had contracted meningitis several years earlier as a college freshman. He lost both legs and most of his fingers, so he and I had a lot to talk about when Dad called him from my hospital room and put the receiver up to my ear.

Dad had told me that John had been on the basketball team at his small college.

"Can you still play?" I asked.

"I can still mess around in the driveway," John said, his deep voice tinged with a New York accent. "I've got a little web thing that I can wear on my hands to help dribble the ball."

"But it's not the same, right? I mean, not being able to play in college anymore," I asked. "You must miss it."

"Sure, I miss it sometimes," he said. "But you move on, you know, get into other things. I'm working on starting my own business, I do a lot of motivational speaking and I golf."

"How do you hold the clubs?" I asked.

"My dad rigged up something for that," John said. "I've got these metal cuffs that attach to my arms and the clubs just click into place. I'm going to have him send some drawings to your dad, so he can hook you up."

"I was never very good at golf," I said with a chuckle.

"Hey, neither was I, man," John said. "That's why it's fun, you know. We're not missing out on anything."

Shortly after talking to John, Malcolm made good on his promise to get me in touch with Bonnie Henrickson, the KU women's basketball coach.

He brought her to the hospital for an in-person visit. Bonnie was a tall, slim brunette and it wasn't hard to imagine her running the hardwood. She presented me a gray sweatshirt that said "Kansas Basketball" in blue lettering.

"You can wear that one to men's or women's games," Bonnie said, grinning and giving my shoulder a squeeze.

"Thanks," I said, my cheeks going red. Like many KU students, my attendance at women's games was spotty at best.

"I also brought you a tape of one of Rayna's news reports," Bonnie said.

"How is Rayna now?" I asked.

"Oh, she's doing great," Bonnie said. "Still working on her degree at Virginia Tech, still helping out with the basketball team. She went on a trip to Australia with the team as a student assistant."

"Australia, man, that is a big-time trip," I said.

"Yeah, she's been looking forward to it for years," Bonnie said. "One of the first things she asked when she found out she wouldn't be able to play anymore was 'Bonnie, can I still go to Australia?' I was like, 'Rayna, of course, you can go. We're not going without you.'"

Bonnie was one of the highest-paid female coaches in the country, but her down-to-earth manner was typically Minnesotan. When she gave me her personal phone number at the end of the visit and told me to call any time I wanted tickets, that sealed the deal: I liked her tremendously.

Shortly after she left, Mom popped in the Rayna tape. Rayna was a tall, lanky girl with a smile that split her entire face. It almost seemed like she had too many gleaming white teeth for her mouth. And that smile came back time and again in the minute-and-a-half TV spot. It was there when she wobbled uncertainly on her new prosthetic legs. It was there when she struggled to comb her hair with her temporary prosthetic arms, which were little more than metal claws. It was there when she returned to campus in a wheelchair to watch her teammates play the game she loved, the game that had been taken from her.

When the tape went black Mom asked me whether I wanted to watch it again. I shook my head. I didn't need to hear the story again because I was living it. Besides, I had gotten what I needed from Rayna. If this girl could smile defiantly at meningitis after all she had been through, then I could too.

I would need every bit of strength Nick, John and Rayna could give me in the days ahead. I was going on six straight weeks with my hands sewn inside my abdomen and it was wearing on me.

I started to feel strange things, or at least feel like I was feeling things. Squirming things, moving things. My brain shifted from one explanation to another, each less plausible than the last: there's food shifting around in there, tumors maybe, or maybe I'm infested with some kind of worms.

"Snap out of it, that's crazy," I'd tell myself.

Still, I'd often ask Dr. Lawrence to come in and check the sutures, just to make sure everything was going right. He'd take a quick glance and then reassure me that it was all in place, that he had used more stitches this time and thicker ones at that. I had nothing to worry about.

But I still worried.

One day I was visiting with Joe Fitzpatrick from Pearson, Randy's girlfriend, Hannah, and another friend of ours. I shifted my weight slightly in bed and all of a sudden thought I felt something strange in the pouch. It was something hard, something sharp. A vision of a jagged strip of bone popped into my head.

Once I'd imagined it, I couldn't shake it.

Hannah was telling me about the house the three of them were renting together, but her words were drowned by dread. What if something was wrong with the pouch? What if I had to start over again? What if there really was some bone in there poking and damaging what was left of my hand? Finally, I couldn't take it any longer.

"Um-m-m, guys," I interrupted, forcing a smile. "Could you step out for awhile and send a nurse in here?"

"Sure," Hannah said as the three of them rose from their chairs, puzzled. "Is everything OK?"

"Oh yeah," I lied. "I just need a couple minutes."

Part of me was kind of ashamed of the panic rising inside of me. Part of me just didn't want to alarm them. And I didn't know how to explain this weird feeling, anyway. The three of them had come from Lawrence, so I didn't want to tell them just to go home. I hoped that maybe I could just have somebody look at the pouch and tell me everything was fine.

But even when the nurse came in and told me that, it didn't satisfy me. She peeled away the bandages, peered in and declared everything normal — or at least as normal as it can be when there's part of a hand sewn into an abdominal incision.

"It looks fine," she said. "The hand is secure and there's nothing much leaking down there."

But by that time I was full-on freaking out.

"You don't understand; I need to see a doctor, now," I hissed. If I had had any good hands, that was the point when I would have grabbed her arm in a death grip.

"I really don't think it's necessary," she said, looking vaguely irritated and vaguely confused.

"I'm feeling bone in there," I insisted, my lips tight over my teeth and my eyes starting to bug out. "Bone. Just go get the doctor. Now."

Mom had left about an hour earlier so I could talk to my friends in private. The nurse had no one to help calm me down and eventually she decided to humor me. Dr. Lawrence was in surgery that day, and there was no interrupting him. Instead, she returned with a much younger guy, probably a resident. He took a look at my chart, bent down, peeled back the bandages around the pouch and poked his gloved fingers around in there a little.

"Everything looks fine," he said, straightening up.

"I can feel something in there," I said, frustrated almost to the point of tears. "It feels like bone."

"Right... bone," the doc said, nodding his head slowly. "The thing is, there's not really any bones down in that area. Are you sure that's what you're feeling?"

I wasn't sure. The sharp feeling had actually begun to fade right about the time the nurse left. I wondered whether I'd ever really felt it at all, or just imagined it.

"I don't know," I said, shaking my head. "It just feels weird. I don't know what it is."

The doctor seemed to understand.

"Listen," he said. "We can give you medicine for the pain, but we can't give you anything for that 'heeby-jeeby' feeling. I'm sorry."

Translation: Your hand is in your stomach and it's weird and bizarre, but we just can't take it out yet. Suck it up and deal with it.

"Would you like me to send your friends back in?" the doc asked.

"OK," I said.

Joe and the others returned and took up the conversation about their new place. I nodded and smiled at the appropriate times, but all the while I was wondering whether I could make it through this whole pouch thing without losing my mind.

CHAPTER 18

OF BASKETBALLS AND BLADDERS

Oddly enough, one thing that helped me make it through the last few weeks of the pouch was the 2004 Summer Olympics. The usual daytime television — court shows, talk shows and "The Price is Right" —were starting to annoy as much as entertain me. The Olympics provided hours of live sports all day — a definite step up, even if they weren't all what one would consider spectator sports. I sat through water polo, rowing and archery while eagerly awaiting beach volleyball, softball and basketball.

I watched Misty May and Kerri Walsh leap and run across the sand in tiny bathing suits, spiking one opponent after another. I watched Cat Osterman and Jennie Finch — wearing much less revealing uniforms — hurl riseballs past hopelessly overmatched teams from Latin America and Asia. I watched the USA women run through the basketball competition like the first men's Dream Team did in 1992.

The debacle that was the USA men's basketball team made me forget the pouch through sheer shock. As I watched a ragtag squad from Puerto Rico — Puerto Rico! —run up and down the floor trouncing a bunch of NBA stars, I actually found myself laughing. This was Puerto Rico, a U.S. territory, laying the wood to a team that was supposedly made up of the best players from America at large. I knew even as it unfolded that I was witnessing a historic low point in USA men's basketball.

Doran came in later to change my bandages and I told him about the game. He couldn't believe it.

"They lost by 20?" he said. "To Puerto Rico?"

"Yep," I replied, "and it really wasn't even that close."

"Wow," Doran said, shaking his head and frowning. "Does Puerto Rico even have any NBA players?"

"They've got this little point guard, Carlos Arroyo," I said. "I think he's like third-string for the Utah Jazz. He looked like a Hall of Famer today."

"Geez," Doran said. "What happened?"

"Puerto Rico played like a team and we didn't," I said, falling into the sports cliché of speaking in the first-person plural. "They moved the ball around, helped each other on defense and spaced the floor. Those guys have probably played together for years and it showed. We just jacked up a lot of threes and played 'Olé' defense."

I waved my bandaged arm like a matador to illustrate the last point, reveling in the mundane everyday-ness of talking sports with Doran. It almost made me feel normal, even if he was wearing scrubs and a paper mask and carefully dabbing Silvadene cream onto my open wounds with gloved hands.

A week later the ultimate un-pouching day approached and four Minnesota friends came to visit. Tim and Katie were accompanied this time by two other high school buddies, Brandon and Cheryl. It was a good mix of quiet, laid-back guys and talkative, energetic girls. We watched more Olympics and also played a game of cribbage. Cribbage, a card game that includes a board that teams race wooden pegs around, is generally played by old folks. But we had always been kind of old, even in high school.

So there we were, playing cribbage, me sitting up in bed and the three of them gathered around. We played a three-way game, with Brandon and Cheryl on one team, Katie and I on another and Tim on his own. Katie held the cards in front of me and I motioned to them with my white-wrapped right hand.

"Get rid of this one and this one," I said.

"These two?" she'd ask, letting me confirm every move.

I nodded, then the next phase of the game started and she again let me pull the strings.

"Play that one," I said, turning my hand so I could point with my thumb.

It was awkward, it was slow, but by the end of the game, Katie and I had won. I leaned back in bed and enjoyed that old competitive glow. Meningitis had stolen some things physically, but my mind was sharp. With a little help, I could still win.

Before I got my left hand out of the pouch, I had to go through one more unrelated trial. Dr. Lawrence and many of the nurses had been pushing for me to get my catheter out and start peeing on my own. I was wary. I looked down at my free right hand, still heavily bandaged, and wondered how I could do that, even if someone brought me one of those plastic bottles with the handles and set it between my legs. My right thumb was gradually regaining feeling and flexibility, but I still couldn't figure out how I would hold my penis to make sure I was actually peeing in the bottle and not all over the bed. I also worried that, after more than three months with the catheter, I wouldn't even remember what it felt like to have to go to the bathroom. I was afraid of the humiliation of peeing the bed, especially with friends coming to visit so often.

Then there was my fear of pain. I couldn't stop thinking about a conversation I had with my friend Rick years earlier about when he got his catheter out after his brain surgery. Rick had a horror story about his nurse, a hefty guy named Bud, clumsily trying to pull the tube out. I lifted up my gown and looked at my penis, one of the few areas on my body untouched by meningitis. I silently promised it I wouldn't put it through that until it was absolutely necessary.

I didn't tell Dr. Lawrence that. I told him I wanted to wait at least until Tim, Brandon, Katie and Cheryl went back to Minnesota because I didn't want to pee the bed in front of them. Dr. Lawrence was exasperated, but he knew better than to press the issue too much. I could always call on Mom to put him in his place.

"Well, you know you're going to have to get it out before you can go down to rehab," he said, his last-ditch argument. "You can't go down there with a catheter in."

Going to the rehab unit was like the white whale, or the pot of gold at the end of the rainbow. The sooner I could transfer down there, the sooner I could go home. But I knew I wasn't going to be able to go until the hand was out of the pouch anyway.

"That's fine," I said defiantly. "My friends leave at the end of the weekend, so we can take it out next week, OK? What's the problem with that?"

It was Thursday afternoon, so this would give me four days to come up with another excuse.

"That's OK, I guess," Dr. Lawrence said, shaking his head. "But the longer you have that in, the greater the chance of infection. I want to make sure you know that."

"Well, I've had it in for three months now," I said, my voice rising to match my stubbornness. "I really don't think another few days is going to matter."

This was not technically true, since the catheter had been removed and replaced several times with fresh, sterile ones while I was in surgery under anesthetic. But Dr. Lawrence finally saw that there was no point in arguing any longer. I was satisfied, figuring I had exerted a little control after months of feeling like my fate was out of my hands. Hours later, though, I got a painful reminder of how foolish it was to believe my plans were set in stone.

That night I began to feel pressure in my groin. It was a slight burning sensation that seemed familiar — it seemed as if I had to go pee.

I told the nurse, a short, bespectacled woman named Marta, about the weird sensation. She lifted the sheets and checked the bag at the bedside.

"You're not making any urine," she said. "You could have a urinary tract infection."

That made sense, considering what Dr. Lawrence had told me just a few hours earlier. I didn't mention that. I was hoping we could just keep the whole "infection" thing quiet, and not give the doctor the satisfaction of being right. Marta brought me some antibiotics.

But as the night went on, the pressure in my groin worsened. Dad came and took his shift at my bedside, sleeping in the chair while I tossed and turned, moaning softly. The feeling was unmistakable: I had to pee, as bad as I had ever had to pee before. Marta insisted that sort of pain was also common to urinary tract infections, though she was concerned that there still wasn't any urine flowing to the bag.

Dan arrived in the early morning hours to take over for Dad. By that time I was in agony, biting my lip and fighting back tears. Dad offered to stay but I shook my head — there was nothing he could do anyway.

"All right, I'll go," Dad said. "But make sure you have Dan call me if anything happens."

Dan quickly dozed off, but I remained sleepless. I had been through a lot of pain in the previous months. I thought there was nothing I couldn't handle. But this new feeling, in such a tender area, had me in tears, the blood pounding in my head, occupying every thought. Something was welling up inside me, something was ready to explode.

Suddenly, when I was gasping like a woman in labor, something did burst. A pool of warmth formed around my thighs and I groaned in deep relief. The pressure wasn't completely gone, but it dissipated to about half-strength, which felt glorious. I had no doubt what happened.

"Dan," I said.

He half-woke, mumbled something and rolled over.

"DAN," I said, somewhere between normal volume and a yell.

"What's it?" he said, his eyes reluctantly opening.

"I just peed the bed," I said, lying back and relaxing. I was beyond the point of caring about any sort of embarrassment and, besides, it was just my brother.

Dan's eyes opened wider and his brow furrowed.

"I don't think that's possible," he said. "You've got a catheter in."

"Look, I don't how it happened, but I peed the bed," I insisted. "Feel the sheets."

Dan unfolded his thin frame from the chair and leaned over the bed. He ran his fingers along the sheets between my thighs.

"It is wet," he said, crinkling his nose.

He probably figured I was just having one of my sweating episodes. He raised his fingers tentatively to his nose and his eyes popped open.

"Holy shit," he said. "You did *pee* the bed."

"Told ya," I said, but he had already bolted out the door to get Marta.

When the two of them returned she did a quick test, like Dan's, only she was wearing rubber gloves. Apparently there was now another explanation for my pain more likely than a urinary tract infection.

"Your catheter must be out of place," she said. "It's blocking off the urine stream. It needs to come out now."

I wasn't about to argue at that point. The pain of getting it out could not match the pain I'd just felt.

Marta started swabbing off my private parts to disinfect me. Dan was looking on, fidgeting and suddenly completely awake.

"Do you want me to call Dad?" he asked.

I shook my head. There was no point in waking up Dad and having him and Mom drive down here — there's no way she would have let him go without her. Marta promised me this would be quick.

She gripped the tube a few inches from where it disappeared inside my penis.

"You ready?" she asked, her eyes quizzing me from atop the paper mask. "This is going to burn a little."

I felt that familiar anxiety creep back into my chest. When the medical staff admitted something would "burn a little," that usually meant "you will be in agony." But I nodded anyway. It was time to be brave.

At first I felt just a little tug, which in itself was unpleasant. Then, as the tube began to pull out, I gasped. The slight burning I was supposed to feel was actually like shards of glass being pulled through my penis. My head jerked back and forth and tears again squeezed out of my eyes. I grunted. I groaned. It probably only took about 10 seconds, but it felt like forever. Finally it was over and my muscles, which had tensed up, went flaccid. I sucked in panting breaths, the pain in my groin gradually fading to a manageable sting.

"There, that wasn't so bad, was it?" Marta said.

No, it was excruciating.

"I have to pee," I announced.

I'd emptied a good portion of my bladder on the sheets, but enough had built up in there that I still had more to give. Marta brought a translucent plastic bottle over and held it while I peed on my own. There was some discomfort as the liquid traveled through my traumatized penis, but it felt good to know that I still recognized the feeling of having to pee. And it felt good to have the catheter stage behind me.

Marta helped me into a new gown and changed my sheets. Finally I was able to sleep. After all I'd been through that night, the pouch didn't bother me.

Oddly enough, one of my few reprieves from obsessing about the pouch came when I'd go to the tank to have my wounds washed and my dressings changed. The debridement was nearly done. It was down to a few tiny areas where the skin grafts had not completely taken. But I still got my shot of Fentanyl.

Linda, the pretty burn tech who looked younger than she was, had been working on me for about an hour when the nurse came into the tank and administered the shot a second time. Immediately warmth flooded my body, every muscle went limp and I let out a sigh of deep relief.

"That stuff is amazing," I mumbled to the two ladies. "I don't even care about the pouch right now."

"Well, that's good," Linda said. "You deserve a break from that every now and then."

The drug-induced rapture didn't last long, though. After months of getting the hyper-concentrated painkiller injected straight into my neck, my body was starting to become accustomed to it and it wore off after about 15 minutes. I didn't realize that I was developing a dependency and at the time I probably wouldn't have cared. I just wanted the whole pouch ordeal done with.

"Is there any way you can give me something that could just knock me out for a few days?" I asked. "Just put me out so I could wake up with my hand out of the pouch?"

"You know we can't do that, Andy," Linda said.

Over her surgical mask, I thought I saw concern in her eyes. I only had a few days of the pouch left, and everyone seemed to be holding their breaths, hoping I could make it.

CHAPTER 19

POST POUCH, FAREWELL TO BURN UNIT

The rest of that week is a blurry haze, as if I shut off my brain and did not take in any stimuli. I do recall staring at the second hand on the clock in my room, sometimes for an hour at a time. Perhaps that kept me sane, the revolutions of that little red arm, each getting me that much closer to the unpouching date.

When it arrived I went off to the operating room talking and laughing with the orderly who was pushing me down the hall, and I didn't even mind when my surgery got pushed back five or six hours. I just lay in the prep room with Mom at my side, looking down at the pouch and grinning at the thought that it would be gone before another night passed.

"I'm not sure I've ever seen someone more excited to have surgery," the puzzled anesthesiologist said when he finally came to knock me out.

Over the next few days Dr. Lawrence briefed me on how the unpouching surgery had gone. He cleaned up a few other things while he was in there, removing some final patches of dead flesh from my calves and heels, and repairing a spot on my right wrist where a bit of bone had started to poke through the scarred, stretched skin. A few months earlier the news that a plastic surgeon had filed down one of my wrist bones so the skin could close around it would have been beyond disturbing. By that point I accepted it with barely a nod.

Dr. Lawrence added that he thought the left hand looked pretty good, that the full-thickness graft had taken well and that I would not need another pouch. He would know more, of course, after we took the bandages off for the first time.

When that day arrived, the pain had mostly dissipated. My elbow was slowly starting to loosen up, but my left hand still weighed a ton. I could lift it, but just barely. On the one hand, I was curious to see what was under that bandage. On the other hand, I wasn't sure I really wanted to know.

Cherie was in the tank room with Dr. Lawrence when he took down the bandages. All I could really see of her were the deep, black pools of her eyes above her surgical mask, but they were sympathetic and I wanted to prove to her I could be tough.

It didn't turn out that way. As Dr. Lawrence wound off one layer of bandages after another, he got down to layers that were stained red, black and orange, and stuck to the flesh underneath. He dripped sterile water on them to loosen them and then the final bandages came off and I saw what was left of my hand.

It was a swollen, shapeless blob, ringed with thick black stitches that held the stomach flap on. Yellow ooze dripped out from between the stitches and there were bits of black, dead tissue around the edges of the flap. My stomach turned and I gagged. I could not believe that was my left hand. I still had a thumb on the right hand, so that at least retained some semblance of its former self. The monstrosity on my left side just looked like a fleshy club.

I started to sob.

Dr. Lawrence had taken up his forceps and begun to pluck at the black stuff around the stitches. He stopped and looked down at me, his brow furrowing above the surgical mask.

"Andrew, what's wrong?" he said.

I shook my head, unable to explain myself through the tears and the lump in my throat. It had nothing to do with any physical pain. I was imagining carrying that club-hand around for the rest of my life.

Cherie touched my shoulder.

"It's OK, Andy," she said. "Everything's going to be OK."

Even after Dr. Lawrence re-bandaged my hand and I returned to my room, I spent the rest of the day either in tears or on the verge of tears. Mom, Grandma and Dan all took turns trying to comfort me and, in the end, all ended up just crying with me.

Chris Markman, my friend from Minnesota, had stopped by to visit for a couple days. He was coming from Denver, on his way to North Dakota, where he was studying to be a priest. He had gone several hundred miles out of his way to see me. I was grateful, but swallowed by sorrow and self-pity. I said barely two words to him the whole time he was there.

Chris didn't force any conversation and didn't try to force me to feel better. He sat by my bed and was quietly there, ready if I needed him. I suppose he was praying.

Dr. Lawrence came on his rounds the next day and Mom told him that I was disturbed by how my left hand looked. This seemed to confuse him.

"It's looking much better," he said. "We've removed all the necrotic tissue and the stomach flap seems to have taken."

"I think he was just expecting it to look more like a hand," Mom said.

"Oh, well it will, in time," he answered matter-of-factly. "The swelling will go down and we'll take out the stitches. Eventually, once all the tissue has settled down, I can carve out a little web space there for a thumb."

This was news to me.

"So, it's not done yet?" I asked.

"Well, not completely," Dr. Lawrence said. "There are a number of tweaking procedures we can do down the road. I can even go in and de-bulk some of this if you want me to."

He reached down and gently squeezed my bandaged hand, which was somewhat flabby with tummy tissue.

Far from being afraid of more surgeries, I found the thought that the hand wasn't done comforting. This was just the rough draft. It was ugly and not very useful, but we could polish it up and eventually come out with a better finished product. There was a nagging voice in the back of my head, telling me that this was kind of delusional, that no amount of "tweaking" would make what was left of my hand look the way I wanted it to, but I shoved the voice away. People at the hospital talked about Dr. Lawrence as if he were some kind of miracle worker. Why shouldn't I believe he would pull off some magic on that hand, given enough time?

I set aside my doubts and went to work on my physical and occupational therapy. Rachel and Mylene were still my mentors in that department and they were determined to get me ready to transfer out of the burn unit and down to the rehab ward now that all my necrotic tissue was gone.

They would wheel me down the hall to the burn unit's little rehab room with all the windows, often with Mom in tow. My feet were still too sore to stand and put any weight on them. The heels — grafted and regrafted twice now — were still bleeding, and what was left of each foot was starting to point down, which put all the pressure squarely on the fronts when I tried to put them on the floor. I was told this was called "drop foot." The Achilles tendon in each of my ankles had tightened from lack of use, pulling the backs of my feet up as if I were wearing invisible high heels. The tendons on the top of the foot were shorter now and not powerful enough to counteract the Achilles. Rachel and Mylene were concerned, but there wasn't much they could do. They couldn't put a lot of pressure on the bottom of my feet for fear of tearing my fragile skin and light pressure wasn't enough to do much good — the tendons were already so tight they wouldn't budge without serious force.

My feet were at about a 45-degree angle. To keep them from dropping more I was put in a set of boots with rigid metal frames and thick, woolly padding inside. They were a weird combination of downhill ski boots and Eskimo-style mukluks. Rachel and Mylene called them PRAFOs, which stood for Pressure Relief Ankle-Foot Orthosis. They were designed to prevent permanent plantar flexion, which was apparently what my feet had.

They strapped those boots onto the pedals of the exercise bike in the rehab room and I began the long process of strengthening my lower body. My legs had shrunk to about half their normal width — two flaccid, muscle-less posts that were basically dead weight. After two minutes on the bike, my thighs burned. After three minutes I was dripping sweat. But I didn't care. The burn felt heavenly compared to the pain of surgery or debridement and I was glad to earn some sweat for a change, instead of having it break out spontaneously because I was sick with fever. I pedaled the bike while looking down on the roofs of Kansas City and imagined I was in the street on a real bike, the wind that was gently shaking the trees was blowing in my face and the sun that was shimmering on the pavement was warming my back. I realized that I hadn't been outside for nearly four months. What a strange thought.

The rest of my rehab was mainly stretching, although Mylene had started to work with my right thumb more now that it was loosening up. I still couldn't bend the last joint, but the others were flexible, which meant I could make a pincer-like squeezing motion with the thumb against what was left of the hand. That grip was going to be my lifeline, the one remaining digit that would allow me to hang on to and manipulate objects. Mylene spent hours putting different objects in the web space of the thumb and having me clench and unclench slowly, trying to strengthen my hold. The fresh, pink skin on the underside of the thumb was hypersensitive, so she also had me spend hours running it back and forth across a towel to desensitize it. The towels were soft, but felt prickly as pine needles and the nerves sent tiny electric shocks running up my arm. I started to realize that getting better might take longer than I thought.

One day while I was pedaling the bike, Nurse Bob came in the rehab room on his break.

"I have a new joke for you, but I think maybe this one should wait," he said, glancing at Mom.

"Don't worry, I was just leaving," Mom said. "I need some more iced tea anyway."

Bob had a joke ready nearly every time he saw me. He saved the dirty ones for when Mom wasn't around, so I knew this one was going to be good.

"So, this woman who is totally fed up with men puts out a personal ad," he started. "She's had a lot of bad relationships, so all she writes is, 'Wanted: a man who won't beat me, won't run away and is great in bed."

"Sounds like a lot to ask," I said.

"Well, a few days later her doorbell rings," Bob continued. "And when she opens the door she sees this guy with no arms and no legs. He says, 'I'm here in response to your ad. As you can see, I have no arms, so I can't beat you and I have no legs, so I can't run away.' The woman thinks for a moment and then says, 'OK, I guess that's true, but I also said I wanted a man who was good in bed.' Right away the guy answers, 'How do you think I rang the doorbell?'"

I shook my head, but couldn't keep from grinning.

"Very good, Bob," I said. "Very good."

I trusted Bob. He had seen me go through so much that I knew he truly understood this journey and knew that I had come far enough to laugh at a joke like that.

I got closer and closer to leaving the burn unit. I was informed that I would no longer have to go to the tank room, that my wounds were clean enough that the bandage changes could be done at the bedside. That news was enough to lift my spirits considerably. I could stay on my comfortable air bed rather than the unforgiving metal of the tank. The wounds on my butt had closed up some, but it was still welcome news for that tender flesh.

On one of my last days, the young red-headed wound tech, Jeny, came in to change my bandages with an older male nurse named Manuel. Jeny, who had a thing for nicknames, called him "Manuelo."

"You want some music on while we do this, Andy-Man?" she asked as she pulled on her gloves, gesturing to the small stereo in my room.

"Doesn't matter," I shrugged. "I've pretty much listened to all of my CDs a thousand times now."

Jeny paused in the midst of putting on a surgical mask.

"You like oldies, right?" she asked.

"Yeah, they're all right," I said.

"I may just have something for you," she said, and strolled out of the room, almost skipping.

She returned waving a shimmering CD in her gloved hand.

"I mixed this one myself," she said.

"Uh-oh," Manuel teased. "I don't like the sound of that."

"C'mon Manuelo," she said, giggling and giving him a light shove. "You know you like my music."

Soon they were both busy winding off my bandages to the upbeat tones of Smokey Robinson and the Miracles' "Tears of a Clown," Jeny started to shimmy and soon was incorporating little twirls of the bandages in time with the music. At first Manuel just chuckled, but, after some goading from Jeny, did a silly, half-mocking little jig.

From the head of the bed I watched two vertically-challenged people decked out in blue scrubs and masks, looking for all the world like a couple of dancing Smurfs, and I couldn't help but smile. I was really going to miss the burn staff.

The burn unit threw a party for me on Thursday, August 26, my last day in their care, complete with a cake and card and a gathering in the patient lounge. My parents were there, along with Dan and Grandma. They'd spent most of the morning packing up all the stuff that had accumulated in my room and readying it for the move down to the ground-floor rehab unit. It had taken several boxes, but Room 5211, my home for the better part of three months, was finally cleared out and ready for a new occupant.

As I sat in a wheelchair in the lounge, surrounded by my immediate family and my burn unit family, I felt a little like a kid going off to kindergarten. I was looking up at all kinds of faces that were both teary-eyed and smiling, which is always a strange combination.

I was excited to be going on to the next step in my recovery. I was sad to be leaving people I'd grown to like a whole lot. I was scared of moving to a place where not everyone would fully understand the journey I'd already been through.

Aside from the normal staff that was on duty, several nurses and wound techs showed up on their day off. My two favorite housekeepers, Mary and Javier, also were there. I took pictures with them and with Doran, Bob, Jeny, Louis, Cherie and others, all of them bending down to put their faces next to mine. Mom opened the card, flattened out the crease and put it on the table in front of me so I could read what everybody had written.

One by one the burn unit folks left to go back to work. There were more tears, and several promised to come visit me. I was only moving down to the ground floor of the hospital. But it seemed that they were seeing me off on a long journey. In a sense, they were.

CHAPTER 20
REHAB UNIT

Before I went to Italy in college I attended a lecture on culture shock. The speaker explained our tendency to expect every country to be like our own and the anxiety that occurs when we find that they aren't. I readied myself to accept that Italian buses wouldn't run on time, that I wouldn't recognize every menu item at restaurants and that Italians would talk with their hands more than I was used to. Then I went to Italy, plunked myself down at a school with 120 other American students, and found that life really wasn't all that different.

But that lecture came in handy when I switched from the burn unit to the in-patient rehab ward.

The burn unit at KU Med was in one of the hospital's newer wings. It was brightly lit, modern and impeccably clean. Sterilization was a huge priority. The rehab ward was different.

We exited the elevator at the bottom floor, Mom pushing my wheelchair and Dad pushing a cart stacked high with boxes of posters, videotapes, blankets and other carry-overs from my previous room. We were in the same hospital, but it didn't seem like it. This was one of the oldest sections, lit by long, occasionally flickering fluorescent bulbs. The floor tiles were scuffed and off-color. There were no windows.

Dad pushed a handicapped button and a pair of heavy steel doors opened onto my new home. The rehab ward was one long hallway with rooms on either side leading to an exit to the outside world at the other end. The metaphor struck me immediately — a long, dimly lit tunnel leading to the door, which had a shaft of golden sunlight beaming through its small, rectangular window. My path to recovery.

On the left side of the hallway there was a plain white desk with a computer and a bored-looking male nurse behind it. He was my welcoming committee. Mom signed me in and the nurse led us to my room.

It was tiny. Mom could hardly fit the wheelchair next to the bed. Dad stood outside with his hands still on the cart, frowning at the prospect of trying to wheel it into the already claustrophobic area. I was worn out from sitting up in the chair so long, and was ready to get into bed. But I wasn't ready to accept this as my new living space.

"This isn't going to work," I said, shaking my head.

"It is awfully small, isn't it?" Mom said. "Can you move him some place bigger?"

The nurse, who was wedged in between my wheelchair and the back wall, shook his head.

"We're full right now; this is the only room we've got," he said. "We might be able to move him tomorrow, if someone is discharged."

I sighed and rolled my eyes.

"Fine," I spat, in a tone that I hoped would convey that I thought it was anything but fine. "Just help me get into bed."

Getting into bed was a task. It involved wedging the plastic "bridge" underneath my butt in the wheelchair with the other end on the bed. Then I slid across the bridge, while keeping my bandaged feet off the ground and my bandaged hands in the air. The nurse turned sideways and sucked in his gut so he could slip around the wheelchair and help Dad push me across.

When I finally collapsed into bed I was sweating, partly from the exertion of the transfer and partly because it was just plain hot in the room. More culture shock. In the burn unit the air conditioning was powerful and the ventilation plentiful. The rehab AC was pitiful in comparison. Before long Dad was wiping his brow and Mom was fanning herself with an old newspaper. Neither wanted to leave until they knew I was comfortable in my new surroundings. I made it clear I wasn't.

"God, it's so-o-o hot," I moaned.

"This is kind of ridiculous," Dad said to Mom. "I mean, he does still have open wounds, which makes it hard to regulate temperature."

I used my new call button to summon the nurse and explained to him that I was stifling.

"I'm sorry, the air conditioning is up as far as it goes," he said.

"Can you get me a fan or something?" I asked. "They wouldn't let us have them in the burn unit, but...."

"Oh, they're fine down here," he said.

He left the room and returned a few minutes later carrying a rotating fan mounted on a long pedestal.

"We had this in storage," he said, then left.

For a moment my parents and I just stared at the fan. It was filthy. It had probably been white at one point but had turned gray, with dust bunnies clinging to the spokes on the outside and the fan blades on the inside. Coming from the sterility of the burn unit, our shock was now complete. I half-expected one of us to say, "I don't think we're in Kansas anymore," though we were, quite literally, still in Kansas.

Instead, Dad shook his head, got up and maneuvered around the wheelchair into my little bathroom. He wet several paper towels and spent the next 30 minutes taking apart the fan, wiping down each piece and then putting it back together so I could get some air flow without getting a blast of dust in my face.

After that jarring beginning, my second day in the rehab ward was more encouraging. The first order of business was moving us into a new room down the hall, which was almost cavernous compared to the one I had spent the night in. The bed was against the far wall, with two armchairs at the foot of it, and still about four feet in between. A TV was mounted on the wall above the chairs. There was a small table on wheels next to the bed and the door to the bathroom was beyond that. There was plenty of room to roll the wheelchair up next to the bed and have people walk comfortably around it.

After my usual hospital breakfast of cereal and fruit (the burn unit and rehab ward were served by the same cafeteria), I was wheeled down the hall for my first session of physical therapy. The therapist, Chamiqua, was a broad-shouldered, middle-aged woman with boyishly short hair. She wound a thick nylon belt around my waist, grabbed it with one arm and hoisted me up out of the chair and onto a padded table.

I sat on the edge of the table with my legs hanging off and took in the physical therapy room. It was long but slim, almost like a hallway. The table was at one end of the room and at the other end was a small set of portable wooden steps, about three feet high. Another therapist in light blue scrubs was holding an elderly man's arm as he slowly mounted the steps. I had come in through a door that was now on my right. Opposite the door, running the long way in the room, was a bank of windows and a set of parallel bars for assisted walking. There was a therapist at one end of the bars kicking a small soccer ball to a skinny man who was obviously working on his balance. As he returned the ball with a light kick, he swayed from side to side, his hands spread open over the bars, poised to catch himself if he started to pitch too much either direction.

The man had bushy eyebrows and a thin, black mustache. He giggled almost uncontrollably each time he kicked the ball.

"Oh, my gawd," he said with a thick Spanish accent. "Oh, my gawd."

I watched the man with envy, recalling my days as a mediocre high school soccer player. Sitting in a wheelchair just a few feet in front of me there was an adolescent boy who had suffered some sort of brain damage. He wore a blue plastic helmet and there was a tube coming out one leg of his shorts that wound down to a pee-filled bag attached to his wheelchair. Apparently he still had a catheter in. He looked almost catatonic, staring off into the middle distance while a young female physical therapist stretched out one of his arms. She was undeniably hot, and I wondered whether the poor kid even realized it. She was chatting with him about a picture of a dog that he apparently had in his room, but he might as well have been on Mars. One side of his mouth drooped and drool ran down almost constantly. He reached up reflexively and wiped his chin with the back of his hand, his facial expressions never changing. A few moments later he did it again. And again.

I shuddered, but Chamiqua, who was providing light resistance by pushing on my legs as I tried to lift them, didn't seem to notice. Just another day at the office.

Later that day I tested out of the speech therapy program, proving that I hadn't suffered any brain damage of my own. As I sat in a small office with the speech therapist and accurately repeated a series of numbers in reverse, I couldn't help but grin. Test-taking had always been a skill of mine and it was nice to know I still had it, even if my physical abilities had been compromised. This was a fairly easy test compared to the SAT or ACT, but it was still more mental activity than I'd had in a long time.

That afternoon I also met my new occupational therapist, Stephanie. She was a petite, spritely blonde with a wide smile, only a few years older than I was. She came into my room with a clipboard in hand and was soon chatting with Mom and me.

"So, where are you guys from?" she asked.

"Minnesota," Mom replied.

"No wa-a-ay," Stephanie said. "I'm from Minnesota too — from Bloomington."

"Oh, OK," Mom said, returning her broad grin. "We're just an hour or so north, in St. Cloud."

After the small talk, Stephanie got down to business. Plopping down in a chair next to me, she opened a folder, attached a piece of paper to her clipboard and positioned her pen over it.

"All right Andrew," she said. "Let's set some goals. What are five things you want to do again?"

Oddly enough, this was not a question I had anticipated. There were probably a couple thousand things I wanted to do again. I decided to go as basic as possible. This was no time for pie in the sky.

"Well, I want to be able to write again," I said and watched as Stephanie dropped her head and began scratching notes. "And type too, you know, use the computer. And read. I've always liked reading, so I'd like to be able to hold a book and turn the pages."

I paused, because the next thing that came to my mind seemed pathetic. But it was something that suddenly felt quite important.

"And blow my nose," I said, sighing. "I really want to be able to blow my own nose."

It hit me just how helpless I was, how much had been taken away from me and how hard it was going to be to get it back. A wave of despair came crashing in and, sure enough, I was crying in front of this girl I'd just met.

Mom was at my side, hugging my heaving shoulders.

"What's wrong, honey?" she said.

"I … I can't do anything," I blubbered.

Stephanie, who did not seem uncomfortable with my emotional display, took that as her cue.

"Andrew," she said, reaching out and gently raising my chin with her fingertips until my blurry eyes were looking into hers.

"Andrew," she repeated. "All those things you just mentioned ... those things you want to do ... "

I nodded, sniffling.

"We can do them," she said. "We can do them all, and it won't take you long to get there, OK? ... OK?"

I nodded again, the crying starting to subside.

"If you put in the work, I'll show you how to get there, OK?" she said. "Deal?"

"Deal," I mumbled, giving her a sheepish half-smile.

"All right," she said, smiling back. "Let's get to work."

I thought my goals were pretty basic, but Stephanie added a fifth that was even more mundane: she said that when she came back the next day she wanted to see me in regular clothes. I had gotten so used to wearing a hospital gown that regular clothes hadn't even crossed my mind. But patients in the rehab ward were allowed, and encouraged, to wear clothes from the outside world.

Mom, who had always enjoyed shopping more than I did, took this goal to heart. Stephanie recommended loose-fitting shirts and pants with elastic waistbands rather than buttons or zippers — clothes that would be easy for a person with injured hands to put on. Mom arrived the next morning with a plastic bag that she dumped out on the bed, letting me sift through the spoils. The shirts were standard T's, one with a Kansas Jayhawks logo, another with a picture of Kevin Garnett reaching for a rebound. When I came to the shorts, I paused.

One pair had a gaudy tropical theme complete with palm trees and the other had a Bart Simpson motif featuring his "Eat my shorts, man" catchphrase. I wedged my bandaged right hand under the Bart Simpson shorts and held them up toward Mom.

"You're kidding, right?" I asked.

"What?" she said, her eyes wide and guileless. "They were on sale."

"I can see why," I said with a sigh. I set them down in favor of the tropical shorts, which were the lesser evil.

First I had to wiggle into my boxers. Sitting up in bed, I kicked each bandaged leg inside the underwear and then reached down to try to pull them up. My right thumb was free, but its grip was relatively weak and kept slipping off the waistband when I tried to tug on it. That wouldn't work. So I bent over farther and stuck one hand on each side of the waistband, trying to form a two-handed vise. This worked a little better, but I still had to wriggle my hips back and forth while I pulled in order to move the boxers up a few inches at a time. I repeated the process with the tropical shorts.

Having covered my lower body, I slipped each arm out of my hospital gown and lay back on the bed, panting, sweating and shirtless. Getting half-dressed had taken 20 minutes.

Few things came easy in occupational therapy, but Stephanie was knowledgeable and creative. She brought in a small stand that would hold a book upright, and was working with me every day on turning pages with my thumb. Mom brought in the first Harry Potter book as a test subject. I had previously scoffed at the ultra-popular series, deeming it childish, but once I gave it a shot I found it was exactly the kind of escapism I needed.

Stephanie also rigged straps for my wrists that could hold pencils and encouraged me to use the erasers as posts for typing. We logged into the laptop Josh and Lori had brought for me and Stephanie showed me how to use the built-in Windows software to turn on a handicapped setting that would allow me to type capital letters without having to hit two keys at once. I soon got good enough that I was able to participate in a fantasy football draft with Rick, Greg, Tim and several other guys from high school, and even chat online with them a little.

By turning the pencil around in the wrist strap so the pointed end was facing down, I could also work on my writing. I started by painstakingly trying to sketch out gigantic letters, then gradually incorporated my thumb grip and let it take over while using the wrist strap only for support. That made the writing more precise and legible.

Stephanie also had me doing exercises to strengthen that thumb grip in preparation for heavy work. It was all I had left for dexterity, so it would have to hold up under lots of daily stress. She had a wooden box with large screws protruding from all sides. On those screws were large bolts. I sat in my wheelchair with the box on a table in front of me, unscrewing the bolts one after another for a half hour. Once I'd unscrewed them all I took a moment to admire my handiwork. Then I set about screwing them all back in.

It was dull, tedious work, but I was glad to be doing something to take control of my recovery.

"You know the only thing probably more boring than me doing this?" I said one day to Stephanie, who sat by my side throughout the exercises.

"What's that?" she said.

"Watching me do this," I said, and she laughed.

My daily routine soon included two sessions of physical therapy and a couple hours with Stephanie. The physical therapists tried to get me to put weight on my legs, but that was complicated by the severe downward angle of my foot stumps, as well as their still-tender flesh. Stepping down directly on the unforgiving linoleum of the hospital floor was just not possible, but one of the physical therapists came up with a brainstorm.

He brought in a yellow foam mat, about a foot-and-a-half wide and long, and a little less than a foot deep. By putting my feet down on that soft, forgiving surface I could tolerate standing for a few quick seconds, long enough, at least, to get out of bed and into a wheelchair. This made the transfer process much easier because I no longer needed to scoot along the plastic bridge. It also made it practical for me to get out of bed and use a portable commode rather than pooping in a bedpan. This was quite a milestone. I found it a little disgusting to poop in the same place I slept.

Soon we were incorporating the pad into my physical therapy. The therapists placed it on the floor in front of the padded table. With their help, I'd slide to the edge of the table and set each foot gingerly on the pad. Placing a hand underneath each of my armpits, the physical therapist would hoist me and then help support me while I stood, trying to make it through a 10-second count. Even with the thick padding the pressure on the front of my feet was excruciating, but it felt good to stand for a few seconds. I was still only about 5-foot-8, but I felt tall.

My standing world was limited to the few square feet of the pad, though, and I started to think about ways to extend it. My first idea was to cover the floor of an entire room with padding, but the impracticality of that soon became obvious. Then it struck me — why not take the foam with me?

"What if we were to cut some of this foam into little squares the size of my feet," I asked Chamiqua, "and then put it inside those PRAFO boots? Do you think then I could maybe use the boots to try to walk?"

She looked down at the pad and then at my stumpy feet, dangling in front of the table.

"We could certainly try," she said.

Within the first few days of in-patient rehab I had thrown myself into my work. It was not easy — every time I was hoisted upright my feet pounded with pain and my poor, overworked right thumb cramped up more than once while loosening one bolt after another. But even the simplest victories, like being able to wedge that thumb under the next page of a book and flip it, or scratch out my name in big, block letters, gave me a rush of pride.

There were other rewards too. After three days down in rehab I was cleared to go outside. As Mom pushed the wheelchair toward the outer door, my heart thumped with excitement. It was a quiet Sunday, and relatively cool for late August in Kansas City — which is to say, not in the 90s. My eyes instantly squeezed into slits as we emerged from the building and into a small green space between the hospital and one of its parking ramps.

"My God, it's so bright," I said, shielding my face with a right arm that was still covered in bandages.

"I'm sure it seems that way," Mom said. "You've been under nothing but fluorescent lighting for four months."

My eyes adjusted and I dropped my arm to marvel at a world that seemed new. The grass had never looked greener, the sky had never looked bluer, the breeze that tickled my neck hairs had never felt fresher.

"Wow," I said, slowly swinging my head from side to side and taking it all in.

Mom couldn't stop smiling. There was a small, rock-ringed pond out there and she wheeled me to it, reached down to apply the brakes and then sat on a bench next to me. I watched rainbow-colored koi swim around each other, their curving bodies carving bright lines through the water like an ever-changing painting. I heard a dull roar and looked overhead to see a large, white jet cut across the sky and blend in with the marshmallow clouds behind it. I listened to birds chirping. They were so much louder than I remembered, but it was still a more pleasant cacophony than the beeping of machines and clanging of rolling beds hitting metal doors that I'd grown accustomed to.

I felt the sun on my face and thanked God that he'd brought me through this alive.

CHAPTER 21

IN THE CUCKOO'S NEST

The person in charge of my rehab was Dr. McPeak, a middle-aged brunette. After a week, she told me she was impressed with my progress, especially that I was able to stand and even walk a couple of steps using a platform walker and the padded PRAFO boots I'd helped design. But my mobility was not where it needed to be for me to leave the hospital. I was not a functional walker, not even close, and with my hands still healing, I was not able to push a wheelchair either. She told me she'd work on getting me a motorized wheelchair so I could be discharged.

I nodded and smiled and tried to seem excited. Truthfully, I had mixed feelings about leaving the hospital. People weren't supposed to leave until they were "better" and I didn't feel "better." How would I function in the outside world? How would people treat me? What would my life be like?

After months of pushing these questions down, I was finally letting them surface, and I was having trouble dealing with them. I was losing sleep over it.

At night, when the room was dark and quiet — or as quiet as it ever is in the hospital — I had time to ponder what lay ahead. My time in the hospital had been full of pain, but at least I usually knew what was coming. My future outside the hospital was full of uncertainty and that scared me even more.

During those nights I leaned on Dad. We talked ourselves to sleep, me in the bed and he in the chair. I had always loved my dad, but we had rarely talked like this, sharing so much of our feelings. On one of those nights I told him something he probably suspected, but couldn't have known for sure: I was a virgin.

Yes, at 22 years old I had never had sex, and I wasn't quite sure how to feel about that. I wasn't ashamed of it, but I wasn't particularly proud of it, either. I was a practicing Catholic, and the Church's teaching was very clear: Thou shalt have no sex until after your wedding vows (or something like that). On the other hand, the conventional wisdom secularly was that at my age I should be having as much sex as humanly possible, especially if I happened to be on Spring Break.

My own convictions landed somewhere in the middle. I wasn't explicitly saving myself for marriage, but I was at least saving myself for a serious relationship. That relationship had not materialized and, consequently, I had never had sex. But I didn't feel like I had any right to be super-proud of living up to my convictions because it had never been all that difficult. Girls weren't exactly knocking down my door begging for sex. Perhaps I never went to the right place for Spring Break.

There were a couple opportunities, though, situations where I could look back and say, "You know, I bet she would have had sex with me." Lying in that hospital bed, those opportunities began to haunt me. So I told Dad I was still a virgin and tried to explain how I was feeling.

"You know, it's just that, I had this body before, and it wasn't perfect, but it was pretty good — maybe better than I realized at the time," I said. "And now sometimes I think, you know, I kind of wish I'd had sex back when I had that body, cause now it's gone."

Dad's conversations with my brothers and me about sex had mostly consisted of: don't do it. He never seemed particularly comfortable talking about it and that was fine with us. We didn't particularly want to discuss it with him, either — or with Mom.

But things were different in the hospital. The awkwardness of the conversation didn't scare me compared to trips to the tank room or putting weight on my ravaged feet. Also, I felt I had earned some major "adult points," so Dad and I could talk man-to-man. I just hoped he would understand what I was saying on an emotional level and not think I was just horny.

"I think I get it," he said. "You want to sow some wild oats."

OK, so no one had used that metaphor since probably the 1960s, but at least he was trying. He still wasn't quite grasping what I was feeling, though.

"It's not even that," I said. "It's just that before, there were a few girls who I knew were attracted to me. I knew I could have had sex. And now...."

I trailed off and turned my head away from Dad. I wished he would just figure out what I was driving at without my having to say it out loud. I knew I couldn't do that without breaking down and crying. It wasn't really about sex at all, or at least not about the physical pleasure of it.

It was about looking at my new body — stumpy, discolored and patched together with thick, ropy scars and blotchy skin grafts. It was the about the question lurking in the back of my mind, one that I desperately wanted to keep back, that I simply couldn't deal with, that I didn't want to ask out loud because I knew it would hurt too much:

How will any girl ever want me now?

After a few moments it finally sunk in for Dad, probably when he saw the tears forming at the corners of my eyes. He reached out and put his hand on my shoulder.

"You'll still be able to do that," he said. "You'll find the right girl."

I nodded. I wasn't fully convinced, but at least I had shared my fear and I wasn't facing it alone. I could finally roll over and at least try to sleep.

Leaving the hospital was scary, but the alternative — staying there — was not only expensive and impractical, it also had its scary aspects. Foremost among them was Brian.

Brian was one of the other rehab patients — a rail-thin guy in his thirties with a brown mullet and a scruffy mustache. He had been in a serious car accident and, though his physical injuries were nearly healed, his mental state was highly questionable. Brian had apparently suffered brain damage that made him aggressive and prone to anger. He scared the hell out of me.

I was in the PT room doing leg lifts one day when Brian decided he wanted to open one of the windows. This was strictly forbidden, I guess because the air conditioning was constantly running. Still, without reason or warning, Brian left the physical therapist he was working with, limped over to the window, and started trying to heave it open from the bottom.

"Brian, get away from the window," the male PT said in a reasonable tone of voice.

Brian ignored him.

I stopped my leg lifts and looked over at Chamiqua, who had turned to watch what was unfolding.

"Brian," the male PT said, raising his voice. "I said, get away from the window."

Brian grunted and redoubled his efforts. Apparently he didn't realize that the window was locked with a metal latch in the middle. It was kind of funny, watching him strain like that when all he had to do was reach up and flip the lock. But my chuckle turned to a rush of panic as Brian began to punch the window with his bare hand, screaming in frustration.

"Holy shit," I hissed, sliding my butt across the padded table to try to get as far away as I could.

A flurry of action followed. The male PT rushed over and grabbed Brian around the waist, trying to drag him away from the window. He was stocky and muscular, but Brian thrashed against him like a rabid dog, gnashing his teeth and swinging his elbows dangerously close to the PT's head.

Chamiqua and another PT rushed over to help, and the three saviors in scrubs dragged Brian out of the room. The other patients and I were left alone briefly, staring at each other, shell-shocked. Finally the skinny guy, who was again kicking a soccer ball in the parallel bars, broke the silence.

"Oh my gaw-wd," he said.

Having Brian around drove home how helpless I was. The rehab unit was understaffed compared to the burn unit. There were only one or two nurses on duty at night and they couldn't keep an eye on the guy constantly, which was the kind of supervision I thought he needed. Sometimes Dad and I would hear him roaming the halls, muttering creepy, angry things.

"Treat me like I'm sick," we heard him say one night. "Treat me like a fucking dick."

The bitter rhyme sent a chill down my spine.

"Geez," Dad said, leaning out the door of the room to take a look and then shutting it quickly behind him. "That guy should be in a psych ward."

I nodded. Dad was in his mid-50s, had a pot belly and had probably never fought anyone in his life. But at that moment I was glad I had him standing between me and the hallway. I lay in bed, wondering how I would feel if I was alone with Brian just outside the door. What if he decided to come in and confront me about some imaginary wrong I'd done? The door didn't lock, so that would be no help. I was physically unable to run, and trying to fight him with my still-healing hands would hurt me more than him. My only recourse would be to hit the "call" button and hope the nurse got there in time.

One night Brian was roaming the halls again when the male nurse on duty caught him.

"Brian, go back to your room," Dad and I heard him say.

Brian broke into a screaming, expletive-filled rant that included more versions of "Treat me like I'm sick."

Dad and I looked at each other. He crept toward the door, opening it a crack to hazard a glance down the hall. Outside, the male nurse seemed incredibly calm.

"Do you want me to give you your meds now, Brian?" he said, which sounded like more of a threat than a friendly offer.

Yes, yes, give him his meds now, I silently implored. Medicate him into a stupor, please!

The next thing I heard was a Brian scream, followed by a loud crash and the unmistakable sound of glass shattering. I sat up in bed, shaking.

"What the hell was that?" I hissed.

"He took a picture off the wall and smashed it on the floor," Dad whispered, glancing back at me.

"That's it, Brian," I heard the male nurse say. "I'm calling security."

Dad shut the door and we listened to the screaming and scuffling on the other side until it finally died out. Dad sat back down in his chair and I let my head drop back onto my pillow. After about 20 quiet minutes, Dad was snoring. I lay awake, staring at the ceiling and shaking a little.

"I've got to get out of here," I whispered to myself.

CHAPTER 22
ONE LAST SCARE

While I went back and forth about whether I was emotionally ready to leave the hospital, I made steady physical progress. That, of course, couldn't last forever.

I first noticed a problem with my left hand when I was sitting on the white, padded bench in the rehab unit's shower room. It was crowded in there, with me naked except for my bandages and Mom, Dad and Dr. McPeak huddled around. Part of my transition from the burn unit to rehab was learning to use a shower again. At first the rehab staff would bring me in, strip off my bandages, wash me and then re-bandage all the open spots. But after a couple weeks Dr. McPeak told Mom and Dad they had to learn how to help me in the shower, to prepare for when I was discharged.

Mom and Dad were happy to do this, but it was a stressful operation. They had to wet down my bandages to keep them from sticking, then peel them off slowly. The tug of fragile flesh sometimes caused a sharp intake of breath from me, and Mom or Dad would pull their hands back.

"Am I hurting you?" they'd ask.

"No," I'd lie, gritting my teeth. "Just get it done."

They knew they were hurting me, and I knew it hurt them to see me in that condition. After four months I still looked like I belonged in a MASH unit. Blood oozed from slow-healing wounds on my heels, knees, buttocks, elbows and wrists. It mixed with the various ointments that were applied daily, turning into a sickly gray mush. The open areas were too fragile to be scrubbed, so Mom and Dad wrung out washclothes over them, dripping soapy water on me as I held my arms straight out from my sides.

During one of those sessions I noticed that the palm of my left hand stump looked a little dark right where the original hand met the full-thickness tummy graft. It was hard to tell for sure through all the blood, ointment mush and soapy water, but there was a dusky oval of skin that looked a lot like the damaged and dying tissue that was debrided from my arms and legs.

I didn't bring it up while I was in the shower. Back in my room, lying in bed with fresh bandages and my tropical shorts on, it started nagging at me. Mom and I were watching Ken Jennings win yet another episode of "Jeopardy" while waiting for my dinner to be delivered.

"Hey Ma," I said. "Did you notice anything weird about my left hand in the shower?"

"Not really," she said with a frown. "It looked swollen and it was bleeding a little bit, but you just had surgery a couple weeks ago."

"I thought I noticed some change in the color on the palm," I said. "It almost looked kind of ... necrotic."

The last word was hard to say out loud. I thought I was done with all the debriding, all the scalpels digging into me. What if more dead tissue meant another trip to the tank room? Worse yet, what if the full-thickness graft wasn't actually taking? Could I be in for another three weeks with a stomach pouch, or have my left hand amputated altogether?

I preferred to think that I was just imagining that the hand looked necrotic and there was really nothing wrong. But I had also learned to trust my instincts: if there was something wrong, it would be best to address it sooner rather than later.

Mom felt the same way. As soon as I said the word "necrotic" she announced that she was going to get Dr. Lawrence to come and take a look at the hand. After going down the hall and talking to the nurse, though, she found it wouldn't be quite that simple. Dr. Lawrence was on vacation in Brazil for a week. The best they could do was send one of his residents.

The resident was a young, brown-haired guy we'd never seen before. He came in with my chart under his arm and a stethoscope slung around his neck, looking like an extra from "ER."

"Looks like you've been through quite an ordeal," he said, tapping the chart.

"Yep," I answered curtly. *Thank you, Mr. Obvious.* My anxiety was growing by the minute and I wanted to get down to business.

"I think there's something wrong with my left hand," I said. "It looks like there's some discoloration around the graft."

"All righty, let's have a look at it," he said.

The resident pulled on some gloves and started winding off bandages. After all the wraps were gone he took a clean square of gauze, dipped it in sterile water and began to gently wipe away the ointment and ooze to get a better look at the area in question. He bent down momentarily, then quickly straightened up and looked me in the eye.

"I don't think it's anything to worry about," he said. "There's some discoloration there, but a lot of times that happens with Acticoat bandages. It has silver in it to help with the healing and that can stain the skin."

It seemed plausible. I still had wide swaths of grayish skin on my legs from when they had been wrapped in Acticoat more than a month earlier. Dr. Lawrence had assured me the stains would fade with time. I thought the discoloration on my hand looked different, but who was I to question this resident? He had been to medical school and, ostensibly, had looked at several samples of necrotic skin. I had only seen it on myself.

"So you don't think it's necrotic?" I asked, just to make sure.

"Oh, no," he assured me with a quick shake of his head. "I think it's something that will resolve on its own."

Exactly what I wanted to hear. If this guy said I didn't have to go back to the tank, that was good enough for me.

The situation did not resolve on its own. The offending oval grew and turned darker until it got black in the middle. Five days after that meeting with the resident, I was sitting in the wheelchair with my arms up on the book stand, reading, when I noticed a foulness in the air, a nasty, pungent odor that I couldn't quite place. I caught brief wafts of it every now and then, and cast about the room looking for the source.

"Did you fart?" I asked Mom, who was sitting nearby, doing the crossword.

She shook her head.

I raised my left arm in front of my nose and gave a good sniff, then almost gagged. The stench of dead flesh was unmistakable, even through three or four layers of bandages.

My heart skipped.

"Oh God, oh God, oh God," I moaned.

"What's wrong honey?" Mom asked, dropping the paper to the floor.

"My hand ... it reeks," I said, holding it in front of her.

Mom took one brief sniff and turned away, squinting her eyes and placing her own healthy, pink hand under her nose.

"I'll get Dr. Lawrence," she said.

I sat gritting my teeth. Dr. Lawrence hadn't seen me for a while but Mom obviously briefed him on the situation — probably a bit heatedly — on the way to the room. He came in ready to work.

"Could you get me some gloves and sterile water?" he asked the rehab nurse who entered with him.

The nurse's name was Kathy. She was a slim brunette approaching middle age. My family liked her. No matter how busy the unit was, she always seemed to answer the call button promptly and then stayed until she was sure I was comfortable. I was glad she was the one who was there, dripping sterile water on my bandages and helping Dr. Lawrence peel them off.

When all the bandages were removed the smell was almost overwhelming. Dr. Lawrence's nose crinkled under his paper mask, causing it to bounce up and down on his face.

"Well, it's definitely necrotic," he said.

"Damn it," I choked, trying not to burst into tears. "I knew it. I knew it. I told the guy that's what it was ..."

Dr. Lawrence let me rant until I ran out of steam.

"I think it's fairly superficial," he said finally. "I can debride the necrotic part right now if you want."

"In here?" I asked incredulously. My eyes flitted over the dust bunnies in one corner of the room and a faded and peeling section of paint near the door.

"Unless you want to go upstairs to the tank room," he said with a shrug. "We can do that, too."

I shook my head. I was willing to trade a little sterility if it meant not having to return to that place.

My rehab room was quickly prepped for wound treatment. Nurse Kathy rolled my dinner tray in front of the wheelchair and covered it with a paper mat and a clean towel. I placed what was left of my hand on top of the towel, palm up. Dr. Lawrence peeled the cover off a fresh set of metal tools and laid out a small scissors, forceps and scalpel next to each other on the paper mat.

He picked up the scalpel and was poised to start cutting into my hand when Nurse Kathy stopped him.

"Wait a sec," she said. "Should he have some pain meds for this?"

Dr. Lawrence paused, shrugged and turned his bespectacled gaze to me.

"Do you want some?" he asked.

"Uh, yeah," I said, as if it were the most ridiculous question I'd ever been asked.

Nurse Kathy administered a shot of Fentanyl in the open port that was still taped to my neck. Then Dr. Lawrence was off and cutting, using the scalpel to slice a ring around the blackened area and then tugging away the loose, dead skin with the forceps. As he suspected, it was superficial necrosis. The graft had not taken 100 percent, but only the top layer of skin was affected. Blood ran down the sides of my hand and soaked the towel below, which Dr. Lawrence noted was a good sign. It hadn't taken much cutting to get down to bleeding, living tissue.

He tossed the small patch of black, shriveled skin into the trash can below and let Nurse Kathy re-bandage my hand while he removed his gloves and pulled down the paper mask from his mouth.

"There you go," he said with a smile. "It should heal on its own, now, but keep an eye on it. If anything looks odd, have them page me."

I nodded and managed a weak smile, a tiny bit queasy from watching him slice into my hand yet again.

That night started with a simple fever. Dad and I were watching TV as I tried to sleep when I felt a familiar warmth gathering in my head and chest.

"Dad, I'm hot," I said, turning to look at him in the adjacent chair. "Could you help me take some of these blankets off?"

Dad nodded and helped me wriggle free of the white sheets and light green comforter. Stripped down to my T-shirt and boxers, I still felt warm. Little beads of sweat gathered on my face. Dad put the back of his hand on my forehead, wiping away the sweat and gauging my temperature in one motion.

"Yeah, seems like you've got a bit of a fever," he said slowly. "I'll try and get you some Tylenol."

He left the room and returned a few minutes later with Nurse Kathy, who held a paper cup with two little white pills in one hand and a digital thermometer in the other.

"Your dad says you're feeling a little warm," she said. "Is that right?"

I nodded.

"All right, open up and let's see what we've got," she said, removing the plastic cover from the thermometer and placing one end under my tongue.

I clamped my mouth shut around it and the three of us waited, looking at each other. After a few seconds the thermometer beeped and she removed it.

"Yeah, looks like you're a little over 100," she said. "You feel any pain or discomfort anywhere?"

"No more than usual," I said. "I used to get these fevers all the time in the burn unit. They usually pass after a little bit."

"According to your chart you haven't had one for awhile, though," Nurse Kathy said, frowning.

I shrugged.

"That's true," I said. "I don't know what to tell ya."

"Well, I'm on all night," she said. "If you need anything, hit your call button."

I smiled, she tipped the cup of Tylenol into my mouth and then brought my water bottle over so I could suck from the straw and swallow it all. She left and I fell asleep with the bed covers piled at my feet.

In the middle of the night I woke up, freezing. The pendulum that was my body temperature had swung completely in the other direction and I was shivering uncontrollably.

"D-d-d-dad," I said, my lips quivering. "I'm really cold."

Dad shook himself awake, rose from his chair and started replacing my blankets. As he pulled the last one over me he looked at my still-shivering frame and his foggy eyes began to clear, then narrow with concern.

"Is that any better?" he asked.

I shook my head.

"S-s-s-still c-c-c-cold," I answered.

There was a cabinet next to the bathroom with linens in it and Dad took more blankets from there and covered me with them. I could feel their weight but not their warmth. The shivering got worse, until my legs were kicking several inches up in the air and the whole bed was shaking. I tried to take deep breaths and calm myself, but chills ran up my back one after another and I could feel a sheen of sickly sweat forming on my neck and chest.

Dad grabbed the electronic strip from the side of my bed and hit the call button. Nurse Kathy came in a few moments later, her eyes widening when she saw me thrashing under the mountain of blankets.

"How long has he been like this?" she asked Dad.

"Just a few minutes," he said, his voice cracking with a hint of panic.

I tried to take deep breaths, but each one caught halfway through and ended in a pathetic wheeze. To compensate I started breathing faster, one wheeze after another. What the hell was going on? Could it be meningitis all over again? Was that possible? Tears welled up in my eyes. Had I survived the trauma of the past few months just to die in a dingy rehab room?

"H-h-help," I said through chattering teeth to Nurse Kathy, who had pulled the covers down to my waist and was quickly running her gloved hands over my chest and forehead. Her brown eyes met mine for a moment and she stroked my hair.

"Don't worry Andrew," she said. "I'm going to take care of you, all right? I'm going to get help."

She rushed out of the room and returned minutes later with a taller, younger nurse who was pushing a cart loaded with monitors and an oxygen tank. The familiar plastic mask was placed over my nose and mouth, the strap digging into the back of my scalp as the younger nurse pulled it tight around my head. Nurse Kathy lifted my shirt and placed sticky electrodes on my chest. Then she wrapped the blood pressure cuff around my right arm and began inflating it. Dad looked on, helpless, one hand over his mouth, the other wrapped around his midsection.

The blood pressure cuff beeped and Kathy looked over at the other nurse, her lips pursed.

"One-eighty over one-twenty," she said calmly.

I moaned. My blood pressure had been taken often enough in the previous four months for me to know that was way out of the normal range. I was too busy gasping for air to ask for help again, but I stared at Kathy, asking her as best I could with my eyes.

"Isn't there anything you can do?" Dad said, pushing himself between the two nurses next to my bed. "I mean, his lips: they're *blue*. Can't you get a doctor in here?"

"I'll page the resident on call," she said.

"I'm calling his mother," Dad said. There was nothing else he could do.

For the second time in four months I found myself drifting out of consciousness, not sure of what I'd wake up to.

I woke up a few hours later in the same bed. A relatively young guy in a white lab coat was leaning over me and smiling.

"Hello," he said. "I'm Dr. Chi. Are you feeling better?"

I nodded. I was feeling much better. Almost normal, in fact. I wasn't shaking, I wasn't sweating, I wasn't gasping for breath. I just felt tired. Mom and Dad were standing at the bedside just behind Dr. Chi, looking concerned. I smiled to reassure them.

"What happened?" I asked the doctor.

"Well, you had some kind of infection, in your blood," he said.

"Sepsis?" I asked.

"Yes, a form of it," he said.

"But it wasn't meningitis again?" I asked.

"I really don't think so," he said, smiling and shaking his head. "We've taken some cultures and sent them to the lab for analysis. In the meantime I've got you on broad-spectrum antibiotics, and they seem to be doing some good."

I nodded. They had done a world of good actually. I was amazed at the roller coaster I'd been on in the past eight hours — going from feeling pretty good, to wondering whether I was dying, to feeling pretty good again. The speed at which these infections could strike was incredible and the effectiveness of the antibiotics was almost equally so.

"I've scheduled you for a consult with an infectious disease specialist tomorrow," the doc said. "He should be able to tell you more about this."

Satisfied that I was stable and improving, Dr. Chi left. A few minutes later Nurse Kathy came back in, approaching the bed slowly and putting her hand on my shoulder.

"You doing all right now?" she asked, her eyes never leaving mine.

I nodded.

"Good," she said. "You gave me quite a scare. The doctor first suggested that I just give you some Ativan or Demerol to calm you down. But I was like, 'No, I think this is more serious than just anxiety. You better come down and look at him.'"

I shook my head, remembering how scared I'd been.

"I'm glad you insisted," I finally said. "Thank you."

The following afternoon we met with Dr. Luchi from Infectious Disease, who looked like your stereotypical guy-who-spends-a-lot-of-time-in-a-lab-looking-through-a-microscope. White coat, non-descript, single-color tie, thick glasses and carefully parted brown hair. He introduced himself in a soft, almost timid voice.

The previous night's unscheduled visit had left Mom short on sleep, but she didn't seem tired. She was on the warpath. It was very suspicious to her that I had crashed with some sort of infection on the same day that Dr. Lawrence had cut into my left hand. She conveyed those suspicions, rather loudly, to Dr. Luchi, who calmly absorbed them, occasionally pursing his lips and nodding.

"... and he, rather cavalierly, I might add, cut away the necrotic tissue right here in this room yesterday," Mom said in her best courtroom voice. "Tissue, you will recall, we wanted to have examined for an entire week. Tissue, you will recall, his resident said a week ago wasn't necrotic but just stained from the Acticoat."

She was really worked up. Dr. Luchi waited patiently for her to finish before offering his own measured view of the situation.

"We have taken a culture from that hand and, while it is possible that is the source of the infection, it seems unlikely," he said. "From the looks of his chart, Andrew had much more necrotic tissue on his body in the previous months without any sort of episode like last night's."

There was no denying that.

"As far as Dr. Lawrence opening up the wound yesterday, my guess is that was probably also unrelated," Dr. Luchi continued. "It's unlikely that an infection would incubate and manifest itself so severely in so short an amount of time. Besides, the wound on the hand was superficial, while this infection appears to have taken hold deep in the circulatory system. He has other openings that are far more likely conduits for such an infection."

"Like what?" I asked.

"Well, like your PIC line here," he said, taking one hand off his chart to point to my neck, where I still had a port for intravenous drugs that was covered with tape when not in use. "That opening is connected to a tube that runs into one of your veins and then almost to your heart."

"My heart?" I said, a brief, involuntary shiver running through me.

"Uh-huh," Dr. Luchi answered. "Of course, we do our best to keep that line sterile. But, when you've had a line in for months, like you, there's always some risk of exposure to bacteria and infection."

"So you're saying what happened last night isn't unusual?" I asked.

"Well, it's unusual to have such a severe reaction so quickly," he said slowly, measuring each word. "But your body has been through a lot and is still rebuilding some of its defenses. As far as getting an infection while in the hospital, though, that's not unusual, especially for someone who has been here as long as you have."

"I thought hospitals were supposed to be super-sterile," I said.

Dr. Luchi gave me a smile and a knowing nod.

"Well, we certainly try to be," he said. "We take all kinds of precautions, especially with our most vulnerable patients. But, the fact is, we have a building full of sick people here, and a small group of people going from bed to bed taking care of them and often carrying bacteria from one room to another. It's very hard to keep germs from spreading. Nearly everyone who is in the hospital for an extended period of time gets some sort of infection, which is why we generally try to send people home as soon as possible."

I had always thought of hospitals as safe havens from disease — protective bubbles. Now I was looking around my room imagining all the malevolent little bugs that were hanging out in there, left by prior patients.

"I'm supposed to be discharged soon," I said. "Is this infection going to keep me here?"

"You should still probably be able to leave on time," Dr. Luchi said. "You seem to be responding well to the broad-spectrum antibiotics. Once we get the lab results back, we'll be able to scale those back and give you more specific, targeted antibiotics. If those come in oral form, then we'll just send you home with some pills. If they require an IV, it's a little trickier, but we can usually arrange for a home health nurse to come out and administer those once or twice a day."

"Wait. So, speaking of the IV, I still have this PIC line in," I said, gesturing up to my neck. "Isn't that dangerous?"

"I've arranged for you to have it replaced, and a fresh one put in," he said, nodding. "Obviously, we'd ideally like to get you to the point where you don't need one, but right now we still need quick access for IV meds."

A few days later Dr. Luchi came back with the results of my labs. As he had anticipated, the source of my infection was the PIC line. I had been invaded by the MRSA bacteria, another bug I had barely heard of, though it's infamous in the medical community.

"M-R-S-A, what's that stand for?" I asked.

"Methicillin-resistant Staphylococcus aureus," he rattled off at lightning speed.

"Right," I said, nodding in mock comprehension. "What's that?"

"It's a staph infection that, through genetic mutations, has developed resistance to penicillin," he said. "Very common in hospital settings."

"Jeez," I said. "That doesn't sound good."

"Oh, don't worry," he added quickly, pushing his glasses up the bridge of his nose with his index finger. "We have several types of antibiotics that are effective in treating it. I've written up orders for Vancomycin. Unfortunately, that can only be administered intravenously."

"So that means I have to go home with a tube running into my body?"

Dr. Luchi nodded.

"Doesn't that put me at risk for another infection?" I asked.

"Well, it's not ideal, but I'd say you're at less risk of infection in a clean home environment than lingering in the hospital," he said.

"But what if what happened Tuesday night happens again when I'm at home?" I asked. "What if I get really sick and just kind of crash all of a sudden and there's no doctors or nurses around?"

I thought back to that helpless moment when I lay gasping for air, and begging Nurse Kathy for help. I imagined what it would have been like if Nurse Kathy wasn't even there. I shuddered.

"I don't think it's likely to happen again," Dr. Luchi answered. "MRSA is much more common in a hospital environment and .... "

"Yeah, but I've beaten those kind of odds before," I broke in. "Remember? I got a disease that you guys said only like one in every 200,000 or 300,000 people get. So what if something goes wrong when I'm at home?"

"Then you call 9-1-1," Dr. Luchi said with a shrug. "The paramedics know what to do."

I sat in my wheelchair and pondered that. That is what "normal" people do when they get really sick. They don't hit a "call" button or send their parents down the hall to get a nurse. They call 9-1-1. I would have to get used to that again.

CHAPTER 23

THE OUTSIDE WORLD

Despite the MRSA episode, I kept creeping toward my "go-home" date. The weekend before I was to be discharged I got permission to leave the hospital grounds for a few hours. Until then, my trips outside were limited to the koi pond on the back lawn or a small courtyard with a fountain in the middle of the hospital. I was pretty much OK with those limitations. It was September in Kansas City and it was oppressively hot.

I was also unable to dress properly for summer, and not just because of those ridiculous Bart Simpson shorts. Tucked under the sleeves of my T-shirts and extending down to each wrist, I wore tightly woven compression garments designed to flatten the scars on my arms. I was only allowed to take them off to shower. I even had to wear them to bed. I had similar form-fitting leggings on my lower half to minimize scarring on my legs as well. Where they ended, the several layers of bandages on my hands and feet began. So I sat out by the pond or fountain covered pretty much from neck to toes, or at least where my toes used to be, despite 90-degree temperatures.

I kept the trips outside fairly short because of that, and also because I didn't want to be seen. My scars were covered, but I felt sure the "different-ness" of my stumpy hands and feet was painfully obvious. People strolled down the sidewalk behind the hospital wearing suits and skirts, often swinging briefcases, and I was sure they were stealing quick glances at the crippled kid in the wheelchair with the gimpy arms and legs. Did they pity me? Were they afraid of me? Were they just morbidly curious?

I was apprehensive about my first trip off the hospital grounds. It was not an ambitious plan — Mom insisted we head down the block and grab lunch at a place called Minsky's, which she said had the absolute best pizza. She was bubbling with pride and excitement and had invited nearly everyone in town we knew to come along. When the day arrived we had about a dozen hungry people jockeying for space in my rehab room. Greg and his parents were visiting from Minnesota. Malcolm and Joyce had come in from Lawrence. Clay and Randy were there representing Pearson, along with Jason and his mom, Melva. The family was all there too — Mom, Dad, Grandma, Dan. Even Josh and Lori were in from Chicago. As nervous as I was, there was no way I was backing out and disappointing all those folks. So I put on a smiley face.

"All right Andy, you ready to go?" Mom asked.

"Sure, I'm waiting on you," I said.

We all moved out into the hall. I pushed my right thumb against the joystick attached to my new electric wheelchair. A vendor had brought it to the hospital for me and dropped it off for an extended test drive. It was a sleek, black, modern machine, with a mesh back for better ventilation and a seat that could go up and down about two feet to help reach things. The control panel on the end of the right armrest had a short joystick for going forward, backward and turning and several backlit buttons including on/off and a "horn" that was actually an annoying, high-pitched buzzer.

I buzzed it playfully a few times as we traveled down the hall and my entourage parted in front of me. With a couple of gentle pushes of my thumb the chair whizzed ahead until it was even with the frontrunners.

"You gotta really open that thing up when we get outside," Clay said. " See how fast it goes."

"I don't know, it seems a little touchy and I don't wanna break it," I said. "It costs like 20 grand."

"C'mon, that's nothin'," Randy said. "I'll trade you my Buick for it, straight up."

"You mean the one with the peeling paint?" I asked.

"Oh-h-h-h yeah," he answered.

"I'll think about it," I said.

Someone hit the metal button and then I was wheeling out the door and into the big, wide world. I felt conspicuous. I was wearing nylon athletic pants, the kind that snapped all the way up on each side. That was relatively normal, but the goofy PRAFO boots on my feet stuck out, their furry padding out of place in the summer heat. The tight fabric sleeves on each arm also looked kind of silly — like I was a gimpy version of Allen Iverson, on my way to a wheelchair basketball game. It wasn't till then that I thought maybe I should have worn a long-sleeved shirt. But my heavily bandaged hand stumps would still have given away that there was something wrong with me. As would the wheelchair, of course. It made only a faint whirring noise as the pavement rolled by, but it seemed deafening to me. It also seemed I was taking up the entire sidewalk. My face burned as pedestrians going the other direction stepped onto the grass to give me a wide berth. The crowd walking with me was a mixed blessing — it provided a bit of coverage and a screen from staring eyes, but the size of it also drew attention.

As we crossed the street to the next block the high-rise hospital buildings on the right were replaced by squat, one-story shops and restaurants. The area directly east of KU Med was like a small town's Main Street, but more Bohemian, with ethnic restaurants and tattoo parlors alongside pizza places and Chipotle. Under other circumstances I probably would have found it charming and inviting. But on that particular day I wondered how much longer it would take to get to Minsky's. I was ready to get inside and get the public scrutiny over with.

In my rush, though, I made a wheelchair rookie mistake. Tired of dodging people on the sidewalk, I steered out into the street at the next intersection. I was fine for a while, hugging the curb and taking it slow. But when I arrived at Minsky's it was in the middle of the block, and I had no way to get there. There was no curb cut in front of the pizzeria, or the shops adjacent to it. I turned the wheelchair so I was facing the curb and lightly pushed the joystick, trying to force my way over the four-inch barrier. No luck. The wheels ground into the curb and stopped dead. By this point Dan was holding the door to the restaurant and the rest of my crew had gathered around him, waiting for me.

"Maybe if you back up and try to go over it with some speed," Malcolm suggested.

"I don't want him tipping over," Mom said quickly.

I rolled my eyes.

"I'm not going to tip over," I snarled.

"Maybe we can lift the chair a little, or just tilt it so the front wheels are up on the curb," Dad said, reaching an arm down and grasping one of the wheel wells.

"It weighs like a thousand pounds, Dad," I said, shaking my head and swatting his arm away. "Just get out of the way."

I spun the chair around and took off down the street again, heading all the way to the end of the block. There I finally found a ramp and was able to roll up onto the sidewalk. I backtracked all the way to Minsky's, where everyone was still gathered outside the door, waiting. It was a short trip, but I was boiling with frustration.

There would be more little indignities. Minsky's was all on one level, so it was wheelchair-friendly in that sense. But it was cozy inside and the tables, chairs and booths were crammed in relatively tight. Mom and Dad walked in front of me, pushing in chairs and generally trying to clear a path, but my vehicle still banged and knocked into one thing after another. Getting to our long table was like several sessions of parallel parking, with me getting stuck in tight spots and then having to back up and try again. Fortunately we had the place mostly to ourselves, so I was only hitting furniture and not people.

Finally we sat down to eat. Everyone else at the table was picking up their pizza and eating it with their hands, or deftly paring it with knife and fork. I sat watching like an infant while Mom reached over and cut mine into small pieces for me. Then she attached a fork to the Velcro strap on my right wrist and kept an eye on me as I stabbed awkwardly at each piece. Half the time they fell off the fork before they reached my mouth.

"Do you want me to feed you?" she asked, leaning toward me.

"No," I snapped. "I can do it myself."

I did, but not without dropping several pieces of pizza in my lap. The food lived up to Mom's hype. The company was also good — Randy and Clay had me laughing several times in spite of my mood. But I was still glad to be back in the safe cocoon of my hospital room an hour later.

A few days later, Dr. Stiers suggested I ditch the power wheelchair.

The psychiatrist had asked for a special meeting, which I thought was odd. I had made it abundantly clear in our regular meetings that I didn't want to talk to him. Still, we found ourselves in my room, me sitting up in bed, Mom sitting in a chair next to me and Dr. Stiers sitting in another chair facing us. He had one leg draped over the opposite knee and a clipboard in his lap. Usually Mom was not in the room for our sessions. I wondered why he had asked her to stay this time.

"Some of the staff have asked me to speak with you about this wheelchair you're considering buying," he began.

That seemed strange. What would a psychiatrist have to say about my mobility? Was he going to talk about the social stigma of using one of those chairs at my age?

"They think it's an unnecessary cost," he said.

Apparently not. Now I was really confused, and so was Mom.

"Our insurance covers it," she said, frowning. "We'd only pay a tiny portion out of pocket and we're more than willing to do that. Andrew will have everything he needs."

"There may be an alternative," Dr. Stiers said to mom, then turned to me. "Do you recall the consult with the orthopedic surgeon that you had a few weeks ago?"

I nodded. I'd seen several doctors from several different specialties when I moved to rehab. I hadn't really paid much attention to them.

"Well, that particular surgeon thinks ... and many of the physical therapists agree with him ... "

Dr. Stiers slowed, as if measuring each word.

"... that you should consider further amputation of your legs."

"What?" I said, recoiling. "Why would I do that?"

"They believe that with below-knee prosthetic legs you would be up and walking very quickly," he said. "Then you would have no need for the wheelchair."

Then I realized why Dr. Stiers was really there and I saw white stars of anger. This orthopedic surgeon, who had seen me just once, had talked to some of the PTs and they decided he should cut me. But they didn't have the courage to tell me themselves, so they had sent the shrink with the walrus mustache.

"Why the hell are you the one telling me this?" I asked.

"They thought it would be better coming from me ...," he began.

"Because we have such an awesome relationship?" I sneered. "Please."

"You should have come to me and my husband first," Mom said, leaning forward in her chair angrily. "We should be the ones telling him these kind of things."

"Well, I wanted you to be here, but your son is an adult and he needs to have all the information so he can make his own decisions," Dr. Stiers said.

"Look, there's no decision to make," I broke in. "The wheelchair is just a temporary thing until I can walk again. Then we can sell it, or donate it, or whatever."

Dr. Stiers paused for a moment, then slowly opened his mouth again.

"Your lower legs are severely damaged," he said. "The orthopedists aren't sure you will be able to walk again."

I had known, on some level, that might be true. I had looked down at my toothpick-like lower legs, almost hairless and covered in tender skin grafts and then down to the swollen, bulbous knobs that were all that was left of my feet and wondered just how strong they would be. Would they support my weight? But I knew there was at least a chance they would, and I was holding on to that.

"Dr. Lawrence thinks my legs will heal up more," I said defiantly. "That they'll get stronger as I get more active."

"He does," Dr. Stiers nodded. "But the orthopedic surgeons disagree. Several of them said they would have recommended below-knee amputations months ago."

A new, unexpected emotion welled up alongside my shock and anger: a fierce gratitude for Dr. Lawrence. I realized just how close I had come to losing both legs. If someone else had been named my primary surgeon when I moved to the burn unit, I might have been sitting in that bed with two stumps that ended just below the knees. Dr. Lawrence at least had given me a chance. He at least had given me a choice. He could have lopped off both my legs, but instead he was willing to go through all those sessions with me in the tank and in the operating room for the possibility of saving them. I wasn't willing to throw away all that work. Not for some knife-happy ortho.

"I'm not giving up on my legs," I said, staring into Dr. Stiers' eyes.

"Andrew, let me tell you a story," he said calmly. "At one time I worked with a soldier who had lost a leg in war and it was very traumatic for him. In fact, he told his friends in his platoon when he first enlisted that if he ever lost any of his limbs, they should shoot him right there on the battlefield because he didn't want to live like that."

"Are you sure this story is appropriate?" Mom asked, reaching over and rubbing my shoulder.

"Let him go, Mom, I don't care," I said.

Dr. Stiers continued.

"This soldier was initially very angry with his friends for not carrying out his wishes. But as time went on he realized that his life was still very good. That he could still enjoy a pizza, or sit on his porch and watch a sunset. Eventually he thanked his friends for not doing what he'd asked of them."

I sat there for a second with my mouth open. Wasn't that a subplot from the movie "Forrest Gump"? Wasn't he basically describing Lieutenant Dan? Even if it were a true story, I failed to see the relevance.

"What the hell's your point?" I demanded. "The guy lost a leg, so what? He was in a war zone, it obviously could have been a lot worse. He's still got two good hands and one good leg, so he'll pretty much live almost exactly like he did before. What was even the point of that story?"

"The point is that your limbs don't define you, Andrew," he said.

"I know that," I shouted. "Look at me, do you think I'm not aware of that? But they sure as hell are a part of me and I'd like to keep as much of them as I can."

"They may just be holding you back at this point," he said.

"Maybe they are, but I don't know that, you don't know that and none of the doctors know that," I said. "All I've been hearing since I've been here is, 'You're not a textbook case, we don't know precisely what to expect, we don't know just how long your recovery time will be.' So nobody knows for sure what my legs will be like in the end."

Tears were now dripping out of my eyes and Mom was squeezing my shoulder tighter.

"I can't believe you would come in here and tell my son he needs to accept that he's going to lose his legs after everything he's already been through," she said, choking back her own tears.

"I'm not saying he needs to accept it, I'm just saying he should consider it," Dr. Stiers said.

"Well I don't accept it and, right now, I'm not going to consider it," I said. "I'm going to put in the work and I'm going to do what I have to do and I'm going to see how far I can go. If it's biologically possible, I will walk on these legs."

I stared at Dr. Stiers, now blurry because of my tears. I pointed down at what was left of my feet with what was left of my right hand, and repeated myself.

"If it's biologically possible, I will walk on these legs."

Suddenly Mom's hand was off my shoulder. I turned to see her stumbling to the bathroom on the right. The rush of emotions — mine and hers — had overcome her and she was doubled over, kneeling on the floor. Her curly, salt-and-pepper hair was all that was visible of her head over the rim of the toilet. I heard the unmistakable splash of vomit hitting water from close range.

Fumbling around, I positioned the electronic stick on the side of the bed where I could see it clearly and pressed the "call" button with my palm.

"I think you'd better get out of here," I said to Dr. Stiers.

He nodded and gave a little sigh.

"I'll send the nurse in," he said.

CHAPTER 24

THE FINAL CHOICE

I ignored Dr. Stiers and the orthopedic surgeons and kept working with my ravaged legs in physical therapy. There was one more hoop to jump through before I could leave the hospital for good: a day-long home stay.

This meant spending the day at the apartment a few miles from the hospital where Mom, Dad and Grandma were living. There was some discussion of moving back home to St. Cloud, but in the end we all agreed it would be better to stay near KU Med. Our house in St. Cloud was a split-level and would have taken a lot of renovation to be wheelchair-friendly. The apartment was a ground-floor handicapped unit with wide doorways. I would be able to continue my recovery at KU Med on an outpatient basis, with doctors and physical therapists that knew my case inside and out.

So Mom and Dad told the apartment landlords they'd like to continue renting the place on a month-to-month basis, and weren't sure how long we'd need it. The landlords had seen me on TV and said our family could consider the complex home for as long as we needed, and then move out penalty-free any time. Dad told his bosses he needed to extend his leave of absence indefinitely. They told him his job would be waiting whenever he could come back. Mom decided to close her law office after months in limbo. Other lawyers in town shuffled their own schedules to take on her clients, her former employees sold the office equipment and her friends carried boxes of files — which she was legally required to keep — out of the office and brought them to our house. Given the lost wages, transportation costs, rent and out-of-pocket medical bills, my parents lost more than $100,000 on my illness, despite having excellent insurance.

Grandma said she wasn't going back to St. Cloud until I did. Dan also pledged to stay and help out as much as he could. He transferred from St. Cloud State to KU for the fall semester. Having enrolled too late to get a housing assignment, he moved in with Malcolm rent-free. Josh had a job and a serious girlfriend in Chicago, but he pledged to visit often and lend whatever help he could. There would not have been much room in the apartment for him anyway. It had two bedrooms, and the plan was for Mom and Grandma to share one room and Dad and I to share the other, so he could help me go to the bathroom in the middle of the night if I needed to.

Everyone had prepared to make that quiet suburban apartment my temporary home. All it needed was me.

On a hot September morning, Mom wheeled me outside for the day trip and my first car ride in more than four months. We couldn't take the electric wheelchair home until we had a ramp to get it in and out of my minivan, so I was relegated to the old-fashioned push chair. Dad walked ahead to where our dark green Cadillac Catera was parked in a handicapped spot. He opened the passenger door and waited for Mom to roll me up alongside it. I held the white, plastic transfer bridge and the yellow foam pad on my lap.

It was hard enough to transfer from the wheelchair to a bed and vice versa, but adding a car door as an obstacle made things even trickier. Dad dropped the foam mat on the ground in front of the wheelchair. It was weird to see it lying on the filthy asphalt. I knew it was just the underside getting dirty, and that it was already dirty from being on the floor of the rehab unit. But something still seemed incongruous about my yellow mat sitting on the ground. It didn't fit outside the hospital walls.

Dad wedged himself between me and the car door and helped me scoot along the plastic bridge. With the mat I was able to use my legs to push myself along a little, and that helped. Eventually I was sitting comfortably in the passenger seat, positioning my foot stumps carefully on the floor.

"Are you in?" Dad asked.

I nodded, and he eased the door shut.

My next trial was the seatbelt. I reached back with my right hand and was able to hook the belt in the webbing of my thumb. But as I swung it across my body I reached my limit. What remained of my left hand wasn't able to steady the seatbelt clasp down by my hip. I pushed the buckle onto it, fruitlessly trying to get the two to click together. Soon Dad had gotten in, started the car and buckled his own belt.

"Can I help you?" he asked.

"Yeah," I said, and yielded to his hands.

Dad reached over and clicked the buckle instantly, doing with one hand what I couldn't do with both of mine. I slumped back in my seat.

"You want windows down, or AC?" he asked as he pulled out into the side street behind the hospital.

"AC," I mumbled.

It was definitely warm enough for air conditioning. But I also wanted isolation, a little protection from the outside world. If the windows were tinted I would have felt better. Instead I kept my stumpy hands at my sides, out of sight, and watched as the world went by. At first I saw a lot of people wearing familiar, reassuring blue scrubs or white lab coats. As we pulled away from the hospital grounds, the characters changed. There was a jogger in a sweat-soaked gray T-shirt, a wire running from his ears to the music player strapped to his arm. There was a man in a dark suit, holding a briefcase in one hand and cupping his cell phone under his ear with his shoulder so he could use the other hand to open his car door. There were two teenage girls in tank tops, chatting animatedly as they strolled down the sidewalk side-by-side. One of them tipped her head back and erupted in silent laughter.

"Do you want to stop at Sonic?" Mom asked from the back seat. Her voice was sing-songy. She was excited.

"Naw, let's just get there," I said.

We passed the usual trappings of suburbia: big SUVs, a book store, a restaurant, a high-end grocery store. The people milling around seemed interchangeable, unremarkable. I felt tense, conspicuous, out-of-place, even in the safe cocoon of the car. Eventually we turned off the busy street and onto a narrow, tree-lined lane that led to the apartment complex There was a pool on the right and several swimsuit-clad people sitting in lounge chairs and splashing in the water. A lot of smooth, tanned skin. I looked down at my body. I was again wearing those long nylon warm-up pants that snapped up the sides and my scarred arms were covered with black compression stockings. I couldn't imagine wearing a swimsuit.

We passed several brown and tan two-story apartments. The ground-floor units all had walk-out patios and the upper floors all had small decks with brown wooden railings. It was a large complex. Dad made a left and eased the car into a handicapped parking spot in front of one of the buildings.

"Well, here we are," he said, cutting the engine.

I tried to press the button to release the seatbelt, but my left hand was too tender. I couldn't manage enough force. I turned to the other side, hooked my right thumb in the door handle, and was able to pull just hard enough to open the door a crack. Then Mom was there to swing it open from the outside. I heard Dad grunt as he hauled the folded wheelchair out of the trunk. He was closer to 60 than to 50 and had a bad back. Playing the odds, it should have been me doing that for him, given our ages.

Transferring from the car to the wheelchair was more difficult because the wheelchair sat up considerably higher and we had to work against gravity. As Dad helped me scoot up the plastic bridge, a sedan pulled into a parking spot nearby and a young couple got out and started walking toward one of the apartments. The guy looked our way, then turned, put his arm around his girl and kept walking. It was just a quick glance, but my face burned. I wondered whether they were talking about me, making their own little guesses about what could have happened to the handless freak in the wheelchair.

Mom and Dad didn't seem to notice. Dad pushed me up the concrete path leading to the apartment and Mom started talking about the neighborhood. There was a Chipotle just down the road, a Target not far from that, and the post office in between. The complex was quiet, you really couldn't hear much street noise and each building had its own hot tub, though of course she wouldn't recommend going in it until all my wounds had healed up. Those things can be full of bacteria, you know.

I kept nodding, wishing the door was closer. Finally we were there and Mom led me into my new sanctuary. It was a normal apartment — carpeted floors, low ceiling, few windows — but cleaner and newer smelling than the place where Randy, Clay and I had signed our lease.

"Want me to give you the tour?" Mom asked.

"OK," I said, figuring it wouldn't take long.

"Well, this is the kitchen and the dining area," she said, gesturing to our left.

There was a tiled floor with a round, wood table and four chairs around it. Next to it was a long countertop and behind the counter I could see the top half of a refrigerator and a microwave mounted on the wall.

"There's a stove and a sink back there too, but it's kind of a tight squeeze," she said, then turned the wheelchair as if she was going to try to roll me back there.

"That's all right, I've seen a sink before," I said, waving her off. I wondered how I would wash my hands with three or four layers of bandages on.

"OK, well this is the living room," she said, gesturing to the right.

This was the largest open area of the apartment, probably a 10-foot-by-10-foot square. In the corner there was my old 19-inch TV from college, now serving the whole family. Dad grabbed the remote, clicked it on and dropped heavily onto the couch. It looked comfortable.

"Where'd you get that couch?" I asked.

"Catholic Charities," Mom answered. "They brought over most of this stuff. The table, the chairs, the lamps, the couch, the TV stand."

"All free?" I asked.

"All donated," she said. "There's a lot of people who care about you."

I couldn't fully appreciate that. It was all great stuff, but it wasn't my stuff. It wasn't something that I'd picked out, bought and arranged myself, the way I'd envisioned for my first apartment.

The rest of the tour went fast. At the end of a long, dimly lit hallway was a bathroom and a bedroom on the left. Those were for Mom and Grandma. Dad and I were in the master bedroom on the right. Most of the space in there was taken up by our two twin beds. Dad's was donated, a regular, worn spring mattress. Mine was a top-of-the-line Sleep Number model. Again, it occurred to me that this probably should have been the other way around.

Dad and I had our own bathroom with a wide door for the wheelchair, a high toilet to make transfers easier and a bench that took up most of the bathtub/shower. Between the bathroom and the bedroom there was a little nook with a mirror. It was probably meant for applying makeup while someone else was in the bathroom. Dad had made it a computer area, setting up the laptop Josh had brought me.

"There's a nice little park not far from here," Mom said. "Want me to take you down there?"

"No," I answered. "I think I'll take a nap."

I was tired — the two transfers had taken a lot out of me — but I also didn't want to go out in public again. Mom called Dad in and he helped me transfer, this time from the chair to the bed.

Dad closed the Venetian blinds on the room's one window and it got pretty dark, considering it was the middle of the day.

"Is it cool enough for you?" he asked.

I nodded.

"All right, well just yell if you need anything," he said.

I nodded again and he left the room. It was quiet in there — much quieter than the hospital. I drifted off to sleep almost immediately.

I woke up a couple hours later with a familiar burning in my groin. I had to pee. I tried to ignore it, roll over and go back to sleep. No good. I pushed myself up on one elbow and looked at the bathroom. It was about 10 feet away. I looked down at my still-bleeding foot stumps. It might as well have been 10 miles.

"Hey, Dad," I said.

Nothing.

"*Dad*," I yelled, twisting my neck so my head was pointed back toward the living room on the other side of the wall.

There was an indiscernible rustling noise.

"Coming," he said, his voice slightly muffled by the walls.

He opened the door and poked his head in.

"What is it?"

"I have to pee."

"Oh."

He came in all the way and shut the door.

"Do you want me to get you on the toilet or do you want to just use a bottle?" he asked.

He had brought one of the plastic urinal bottles home from the hospital. My feelings were mixed. I wanted to go sit on the toilet like a normal human being, even if I could no longer stand and pee like a normal human male. But that would entail at least three transfers — one to get me out of bed and into the chair, one to get me out of the chair and onto the toilet and one to get me off the toilet and back onto the chair. Then, if I wanted to sleep some more, there would be another transfer to get me back into bed. Seemed like a lot of effort just to pee.

"Let's use the bottle," I said.

I stared at the white, popcorn-style ceiling while my dad helped me pee in a bottle. Then I rolled over and went back to sleep and he went to empty the bottle.

I slept most of the day, until Dad woke me up and wheeled me back to the main room for dinner. Mom had gone all out for my first dinner in the new place. Steak, mashed potatoes, corn, rolls and fruit salad. Dan had come in from Lawrence after class so there were five places set. There was hardly a speck of the table's pale wood visible under all the plates and food.

As it turned out, I wasn't actually able to eat at the table. When Dad tried to push the wheelchair up to it he found that my knees were knocking up against the wooden edge. Either the table was too low or the wheelchair was too high. In any case, there was a tray that attached to the armrests of the chair and I ended up eating off that while sitting next to the table. Which was fine. It created a little more room for everybody else. Finally everyone was seated and ready to eat.

"Shall we pray?" Mom asked.

Everyone else bowed their heads and clasped their hands together. I kept my hands in my lap. I had no fingers to interlock, but I pressed one gauze-covered palm up against the other gauze-covered palm.

"Bless us, O Lord, and these, thy gifts, which we are about to receive, from thy bounty, through Christ, our Lord. Amen."

After we ate Dad rolled me five feet into the living room where we all watched TV. I stared at the screen, but didn't pay much attention to what was going on. Something was building up inside me — a feeling I didn't want to face. I focused on the screen. I tried not to let my mind wander.

Eventually it was time to go back to the hospital for the night. I rode back silently, with Dad in the driver's seat next to me and Mom in the back again. I thought about that other apartment, the one that Clay and Randy were living in. I wondered what they were doing at that moment. The sourness in my stomach grew.

We rolled back into the rehab unit and Nurse Kathy was there to greet us, smiling and asking how the home visit went.

"Good," I said, mustering a smile.

I was glad to see her, glad she was the one on duty. But that half-smile was all I could give her. Something bad was creeping up on me. We rolled back into my dingy little room and Dad helped me get into bed. I lay there on my back for a few minutes, breathing in and out slowly. Then I started to weep.

"Andy, what's wrong?" Mom asked.

I just cried.

"What is it? Are you hurt?" she asked.

I shook my head.

"What's the matter?" she asked.

I huffed and sniffed and caught my breath long enough to choke out a few words.

"I ju... I jus... I just thought I'd be better," I said.

"What do you mean?" she said.

"I thought... when I left the hos... the hospital... I'd be better," I said through the sobs.

"Oh-h-h-h, Andy, you're going to get better," she said. "You've still got some healing to do."

"I kn... I know, but... but, I didn't think everything would be so d-d-different," I choked.

And there it was, out in the open. Until that moment I had not truly faced what this whole meningitis experience meant. I had looked to that hospital discharge date as a sort of golden ticket. People didn't leave the hospital until they were "better," which I thought meant they could go back to their normal lives. So, against all logic, I kept telling myself that when I left the hospital I would pick up the pieces and jump right back on the old track. But the home stay forced me to realize this was not true. Everything was different now. I had to take all those visions and hopes for my future and, if not throw them out, at least modify them to match my now fingerless, toeless existence. Nothing would be quite the same as before. No matter how desperately I wanted that old life, I couldn't have it. It was gone. There was no going back.

I realized that I could never be completely anonymous again, that I would no longer be able to walk through a crowd, or eat at a restaurant and blend in with all the other people. Even if I had the most realistic prosthetics known to man, eventually I would have to do something with my hands, and then everyone would see that I was different. Horribly, achingly different. What if kids were scared of me? What if some people couldn't look beyond my deformities? Would I always be defined by my scars, my stumps, my disfigurements?

"People are going to treat me like a f-f-freak," I sputtered, then broke out in a fresh wave of sobs.

"Oh, no, Andy, no, no, no," Mom said.

She was leaning over the bed now, stroking my hair. Her own tears were dripping down her cheeks and she used her other hand to take off her glasses and wipe her eyes.

"No one's going to think you're a freak," she said. "They're going to see your smile and your brown eyes and all they're going to think is, 'What a handsome guy.'"

That was not a very convincing argument right about then, especially coming from my mother.

"I don't think I can do it," I said. "I don't think I can go on."

Now Dad was also standing next to the bed, hugging Mom. His chest heaved and he frowned and blinked repeatedly. I had only seen my father cry once or twice before in my life, but the drops started to roll down his quivering, weathered cheeks.

"Andrew, the first few weeks we were here, I was having a lot of trouble with this," he said. "I was angry, I was depressed, I'd lie awake at night just thinking about how unfair it was that this happened to you. I couldn't understand it. But then you woke up and one of the first things you said was, 'What's the plan now?' And you were always looking forward and your attitude was so incredible as you went through all this misery. And that's the only thing that's kept me going. You've been so strong. You can't give up now."

I had rarely heard my dad open up like that. I wanted to tell him that I had been strong only because I was in denial. I wanted to tell him that my attitude had been a farce, a front, a shallow pool of clear water atop a mucky, weed-ridden set of emotions that I hadn't begun to deal with.

But I also didn't want my parents to be sad anymore. They had done so much for me. I loved them so much. They would do anything to take the hurt from me. I had to hurt, at least for awhile. But I didn't want them to hurt. I reached out my bandaged arms and we all hugged. And I cried. I cried and cried until I fell asleep.

A few hours later I woke up in the middle of the night. Nurse Kathy was trying to take my blood pressure as gently as possible, but the compression on my arm was enough to bring me to consciousness. I moaned.

"Sorry," she whispered in my ear.

I looked over past the foot of the bed. Dad was sprawled out in one of the chairs, snoring softly. Mom was gone. I suddenly remembered everything that had happened earlier in the day, the painful realization of how different my life was going to be running back through my synapses at light speed. The tears flowed again.

"What's wrong?" Nurse Kathy whispered quickly. "Are you in pain? Am I hurting you?"

I shook my head.

"I'm... I'm just... severely depressed," I said, tasting salty tears on my upper lip.

Her brown eyes grew impossibly soft and she seemed to bite the side of her cheek.

"Do you want to talk about it?" she said softly.

I shook my head.

"Do you want me to give you something to help you sleep?" she asked.

I nodded. I knew there wasn't really a pill for what I had right about then, but anything was better than nothing.

"I'll be right back," she said.

She left and I cried softly. I didn't try to stop the tears, but I did my best to muffle my sobs. I didn't want Dad to wake up.

Nurse Kathy returned with a pill in a paper cup. She tipped it into my mouth, then grabbed my water bottle and gave me the straw. I swallowed, then set my head back on the pillow, tilting it slightly to the right so my tears could run down and stop stinging my eyes.

"Do you want me to stay?" Nurse Kathy asked.

I shook my head.

"OK, well be sure to call me if you need me," she said.

She pursed her lips, put her hand on my shoulder and gave it a squeeze.

"You're going to be OK," she said slowly. "You may not think so yet, but you will."

Four days later, on Thursday, September 16, 2004, Dad pushed my wheelchair down the hall as I left the hospital for good. There was no send-off this time, no group of teary-eyed people watching me roll away as there had been in the burn unit. But that was the way I wanted it. Some local TV stations asked to film me leaving the hospital, but I had declined. I knew how they would frame the footage. I knew roughly what the narrative would be:

"Here's Andy Marso, the meningitis kid from KU, on his way home after 141 days in the hospital, his battle with the deadly disease finally over."

They would frame it as an ending. I knew it was actually a beginning.

After crying myself into exhaustion twice, I woke up the next morning to find that the sun had actually come up. The world was still spinning and I was still alive. Going back to my old life was not an option. There were only two options: keep crying, or make the most of my new life.

As we rolled toward the hospital doors, there was a slow-burning pain in the pit of my stomach, a deep melancholy, a deep sense of loss. I had loved my old life, after all. And it was daunting to think that, going forward, hardly anything would ever come as easily as before.

But by acknowledging that my old life was gone, I gained a measure of control over my new life. No matter what befalls us, no matter what harm is done to us, our response to it is in our own hands. We can choose to fall back in despair or keep trudging doggedly forward. I had all the support I needed to ease the way. But ultimately I had to make the choice.

Dad stopped the wheelchair and hit the metal handicapped plate on the wall. The heavy glass door in front of us swung slowly open and the sounds of birds and traffic mixed with the beeping, banging hospital noises. From the doorway I could see our car in the parking lot with Mom in the back seat. The engine was on, the AC was humming.

"It's hot out there," Dad warned. "You ready?"

I breathed in through my nose, taking in an outdoor scent heavy with grass clippings. I let the air flow back out of my mouth, squinting against the brilliance of a midday sun.

"Yep," I replied. "Let's go."

CHAPTER 25

GOING HOME

From the day I left the hospital I was on a new path and there was no doubling back. Emotional recovery generally moved forward, with a few setbacks. I was slowly weaned off the Fentanyl patches, but my first few weeks without painkillers were still a shock to my system. My physical pain was manageable, but losing the drug temporarily sucked out my spirit. For a week I didn't want to get out of bed.

Sorrow sneaked up at strange times, too. One day, Mom and Dad and I were in line at the hospital cafeteria, waiting to get lunch between outpatient rehab sessions, when I spotted a young guy I recognized. He was wearing a white lab coat, but I knew I didn't know him from the hospital. I had seen him somewhere else, but it took me a minute to remember where. Then it came to me: he had been a regular in the pick-up basketball games at KU — a gym rat like myself. I realized he must have graduated and gone on to med school and I suddenly felt weirdly disoriented. It was another reminder that the world had moved on without me during those endless months in the hospital, that the future remained boundless and bright and easy for some of the people I used to associate with and that, but for a twist of fate, it might have been me standing up and chatting breezily with other smooth-skinned, vital young people, instead of confined to that wheelchair with my parents accompanying me everywhere.

There were those bad times. But they were never quite as dark as that night of despair I had shortly before leaving the hospital. That was the low point and from there I began to dig myself out. As the days went on there were more and more good times, as I focused less on what I had lost and more on how much I could get back.

I also had a new mission: to try to keep others from going through what I went through.

A month after I left the hospital, Dr. Luckeroth threw a party at her house. We invited several media outlets to come for part of the day and so her dining room was filled with TV cameras and reporters clutching notebooks. I sat at her table to address them, a pale, drawn specter of my former self despite a month of outpatient rehab. I wore a gray and blue T-shirt that read "This is Jayhawk Country," but that was the only part of me that looked like a normal college student. My arms and hands were still wrapped in tight black sleeves to restrain scarring and my wrists were strapped into heavy braces to keep the tendons stretched. It would take several more months of rehab before I could regain movement in my wrists.

I cut a striking figure and I was determined to use my time in front of the cameras to shame colleges into requiring meningitis vaccinations, if that's what it would take. I had no notes in front of me, but as I spoke off the cuff everything seemed to flow. I was not nervous, I was not emotional, I was just adamant and reasonable. It was one of the few times in my life when I had no doubt that I was doing exactly what I was supposed to do, exactly what God intended me to do at that moment to make the world he created a better place.

"It needs to be mandatory: you don't enroll until you are vaccinated," I said. "It only makes sense. The shot is $70. All of the medical things that I went through were millions. Millions and millions of dollars."

I pointed out that college students were six times more likely to get meningitis than the general public and that the military had all but eliminated its meningitis problem decades earlier through comprehensive vaccination.

"College kids are the ones who are most likely to get it, because they live in close quarters," I said. "It's the same concept with the military. Those people also live in close quarters, so they're required to get the shot."

KU's chancellor helped fast-track a new university policy requiring all incoming freshmen living in student housing to get the meningitis vaccine or sign a waiver indicating that they understood the risks of the disease but chose not to get the shot. A year later the rest of the public colleges in Kansas followed KU's lead and the percentage of vaccinated students in the state rose dramatically.

That made me feel good, but what made me feel even better was learning how my story affected people in ways I never anticipated. One day I ran into Jeny, the red-haired tech from the burn unit. She told me she was in the midst of a home health rotation and one of the homes she visited regularly was that of a husband and wife in their 80s who both had serious health problems. As Jeny leaned in to look at a framed newspaper article hanging on their wall, she was shocked to see that it was a *Kansas City Star* article about me.

"I know him!" she squealed.

"Every time I want to complain, I read that and think about what he went through," the wife said.

Life at the apartment quickly settled into a new routine: breakfast, then off to the hospital for physical therapy, then lunch, then occupational therapy, then dinner, then TV until bedtime. There were also daily scar massage sessions, in which Mom rubbed greasy moisturizers into my arms and tried to stretch and knead the tissue so it wouldn't tighten up and restrict my movements. I took more tentative steps on the foam pad, used my right thumb to screw and unscrew the bolts on Stephanie's wooden board and moved toward physical recovery bit by bit, day by day.

When my feet finally healed, the KU prosthetics guy came by again and he was shocked to see me walking on the foam pad despite my extreme drop-foot.

"Let me see what I can build for you," he said.

He took molds of my legs and came back days later with two hard, black braces with huge platform heels on them to compensate for the odd positioning of my feet. There was a front and a back piece that clicked together snugly around each leg and then several thick straps to hold it in place. They looked a bit like something out of a twisted S&M fantasy, but they allowed me to walk short distances, slowly, with a walker. I began trudging down the hallway from my bedroom to a chair in the TV room for practice.

This opened up a new world for me. Clay and a couple of other friends wanted to go see the movie "Sideways" and asked me to go, too. It was playing at an old, independent theater and I'd have to go up a few steps. I did that, picking the heavy boots up one step at a time while leaning heavily on the railing. Clay was waiting at the top of the stairs with the walker. The tilt of the boots was so severe and the heel so high, that I could not keep my balance without it.

I could feel some eyes on me as I shuffled down the aisle to a seat next to Clay. It was unusual to see someone my age using a walker, after all. But I was with friends, so I had a buffer — some social protection. And once the lights went down, nobody could see me. I laughed at melancholy Paul Giamatti and clueless Thomas Haden Church along with everybody else.

On New Year's Eve I finally got into that third-floor apartment that Randy and Clay and I had rented. Dad helped me up one step at a time, while Clay carried the walker up behind us. Then Dad left. It was not the same unit that we'd looked at before signing the lease, but it still seemed familiar — dingy, off-white walls, unused wood fireplace, stalactite-style ceiling.

Randy was not there; he and Hannah had gotten pretty serious, so he was now spending most holidays with her. But Clay and I sat out on the balcony and watched amateur fireworks shows off in the distance. I told him I felt that I was gaining a new normalcy — that every day now I was getting more of a sense that, even though life was different, it could still be good.

Late that night I called Dad, and he helped me to the car under the watchful eye of a police officer parked downstairs. We joked that he was probably wondering just how drunk I was, and probably making sure I wasn't going to get in the driver's side. We drove home, smiling, and I realized it had been awhile since I had cried.

The big, black braces were useful and taking any kind of steps was good, but I was not satisfied. I had started watching this new TV show, "Lost", about a plane that crashed on a mysterious island. One of the characters was a crash survivor named John Locke. He had been in a wheelchair before the plane went down, paralyzed below the waist. After the crash he miraculously stood up on the sandy beach where he had been thrown, and walked. The look of wonder on his face — the smile in the midst of devastation and fiery chaos — I wanted that.

For me there would be no miracle moment. Rather, there would be external fixators — heavy steel devices with about a dozen metal pins drilled into the bones of my lower legs and what was left of my feet. My stumps had healed enough that now there was a new medical opinion. Dr. Greg Horton, KU's top orthopedic surgeon, told me the fixators might be able to correct my drop-foot and get my stumps back into a flat position that would give me a chance to walk somewhat normally again. He also mentioned below-knee amputations as a possible solution, but said he was willing to try the fixators first if I was willing to let him drill them onto my legs.

So I let him do it, one leg at a time. I woke up from the surgery with several pounds of steel attached to my throbbing left leg and wondered briefly what the hell I was thinking. Then I remembered John Locke.

For the next two months Dad was in charge of cranking the fixator's screws a few millimeters a day, slowly pulling my foot back up against the stubborn resistance of my Achilles tendon, which Horton had loosened with a V-shaped incision. Mom said the fixator looked like an instrument of the

Spanish Inquisition. At one point I had to have more pins inserted because the force of the tendon was still so great that it was bending some of the metal. It was painful, and in order to stave off infection Mom and Dad had to apply Silvadene ointment to the many sites where the pins entered my legs and the gaping hole in my heel that Dr. Horton had created to get at the Achilles. But it was my only option.

Walking was out of the question at that point, even with the platform walker and my one "good leg" encased in the black, high-heeled boot. Having the one leg to plant did make transferring much easier, though. So I spent the months mostly in a recliner, with my fixated foot resting on pillows to keep the swelling and the throbbing to a minimum.

I spent some of the down time learning to use my hands again. Showering, dressing, cooking, cleaning, writing, typing, driving — it all became a trial-and-error process of just figuring it out. There was frustration and there was rage. Things I used to be able to do without even thinking took twice as long. Picking things up involved actively thinking about mass, force, pressure and friction. It was a constant physics lesson, and I had never been good at physics. I was fitted for a prosthetic hand on my left side, but it proved more trouble than it was worth. It hung off my left arm cartoonishly, unnaturally long, heavy and cumbersome. It also covered my palm and therefore robbed me of my sense of touch, which was crucial to determining things like pressure and friction. I learned to function without any upper-limb prosthetics instead.

After two months the fixator finally came off my left foot, which went into a cast so the bones could heal before I tried to walk. My right foot was fixated in the same surgery and so I had two more months of heavy metal and painstaking screw-turning on that side. Still, having seen how much better my left foot looked, I was not complaining.

By then winter had melted into spring, the weather was getting hot and I was yearning for Minnesota. In early June, before the second fixator came off, I decided it was time for the family to move back to St. Cloud. It had been more than a year since I almost died and I knew that Mom and Dad had to get back to work. I also knew that we all needed more space. We were getting on each other's nerves in that little apartment.

So there I was, stretched out in the backseat of the Catera with my fixated leg on a pillow while Dad and Grandma followed with the minivan and another car full of our accumulated stuff. We were going home.

Days later I sat in the wheelchair in our backyard, the air filled with the sound of the creek running over rocks. The little waterway was high up on its banks, still swollen with snow-melt and spring rains. My brothers and I used to play down there. I spotted the big rock in the middle of the water that we waded out to and sat on sometimes. I remembered the time when I was young and the creek was particularly high, and I had looked down from that rock at the water and suddenly been too scared to wade back to the bank. I thought of the trials I'd been through since then and shook my head, wondering how that scared little kid grew into someone who withstood the amputations, the tank room, the despair. I was in a wheelchair and my muscles were still pathetic, but I felt tough. I felt proud. I had beaten a disease that tried like hell to kill me.

Home felt spacious and reassuring, if a bit musty. I wouldn't be taking back my old room, because it was downstairs and the living room and kitchen were upstairs. I was OK with that. The old room was from my childhood — my other life. I wanted to move forward, so it didn't matter if I was upstairs or downstairs; it was only going to be temporary anyway.

One of Dad's friends installed a stair chair so I could ride up from the ground-floor landing to the living room, as long as someone was there to bring my wheelchair to me when I got there. The heavy power chair would have to stay in the minivan; there was no way to get it up and down stairs easily. I told Dad I wouldn't need it, or the stair chair for very long. I was going to walk.

The house seemed empty without Shaggy and Dad was in no position to deny his wheelchair-bound son a new dog, even if he'd have to put off that new carpeting he'd been promised. Mom and I went back to the same Humane Society where we had adopted Shaggy some 17 years earlier. I found another mangy, mixed-breed mutt with a sweet disposition. His name was Bear, but I decided to call him Baxter, like the dog from the movie "Anchorman." We brought him home and when we got up to the living room, I pushed myself out of the wheelchair with my good left leg and collapsed into a more comfortable couch. He immediately jumped in my lap. From then on, we were best buds.

The move back to St. Cloud accelerated everything. A new rehab clinic had opened less than a mile from our house. It had state-of-the-art equipment and exercise machines, and I made steady progress in building strength in my arms and the grip of my right thumb. Dad went back to work, which forced me to be more independent and learn to do things on my own. It was maddeningly difficult at first, but eventually things became routine again, even if the new routine was totally different from the old one.

Dr. Horton was not thrilled to see me move 500 miles away with one of his creations still drilled into my leg. But a surgeon he trusted in St. Paul removed the fixator a few weeks later and Horton's work was extraordinary. In defiance of the prognoses of many of his peers, I was up and walking at the rehab clinic with just a single forearm crutch within a month and was able to ditch the crutch and walk unassisted a few months later. I had to wear orthotic braces that came up almost to my knees for balance, but that seemed a small price to pay for keeping my legs. Dr. Horton had done the final step, but Dr. Lawrence had made the difference. Many surgeons would not have given my legs a chance and some would likely have amputated my left hand as well.

Almost exactly one year after hearing the message from the dubious doctors and physical therapists, I walked down the aisle as a groomsman at Josh and Lori's wedding under my own power. "Hobbled" might be a more accurate word than "walked," but I was upright. And, as if to stick it to those doubters a little more, I even swayed through a couple of slow dances at the reception. That was early September 2005, and I was well on my way to ditching the wheelchair permanently.

A few weeks later I was invited to speak at my old high school, St. Cloud Cathedral. The principal, Mrs. Grewing, was my junior high English teacher and played a key role in persuading me to pursue this whole writing thing.

Cathedral students had kept up with my status throughout my hospitalization and had been praying for me and raising money for my family ever since. When I was introduced to a packed gym at an all-school assembly the kids gave me a standing ovation that put a warm feeling in my chest and made my eyes well up. For one, brief, shining moment I tasted what it would have been like to be the coolest guy in school.

I don't remember exactly what I told them, except that they should be thankful for their wonderful, perfect bodies, which allow them to do so many things. I also told them that they need not feel sorry for me, that I was still committed to "living the life I'd imagined" — an homage to Thoreau that I hoped would put a smile on the face of my old AP literature teacher.

CHAPTER 26

THE NEW LIFE

About three months after returning to St. Cloud I woke up one morning, sat up in bed and put what was left of my feet on the floor. It was a big day, and for once I didn't want to linger under the covers.

I looked down at my stumps, running them back and forth along the carpet slowly. I was still getting used to them being flat after the ankle surgeries, and the nerves along the bottom were still getting used to touching ground. Tiny electric shocks ran up my legs from the hypersensitive areas. Other spots had no feeling.

Using my right thumb, I pulled two socks onto each leg. Then I slipped my foot stumps inside my new leg braces. They were made of soft plastic — more comfortable and much less noticeable than those black models with the huge platform heels that I'd worn when I had the horrible drop-foot.

I reached for the silver crutch that was propped up against the nightstand next to the bed, nestled my forearm in its slot and gripped the handle with what was left of my right hand. Pushing my weight through the crutch, I flexed my knees and jolted into a standing position. At first I swayed, struggling to find my center of balance even with the leg braces. But I leaned on the crutch until I was sure of myself, then began to walk the few steps from the bedroom to the bathroom.

There was something exhilarating about being upright. Sure, I was using a crutch and my feet needed to build up a lot of strength. But after nearly a year in the wheelchair, I felt tall, mobile, able to go wherever I wanted.

In the bathroom I sat down on a bench that Dad had installed in our shower and removed the braces and my clothes. I swung my legs around, pulled the shower curtain closed and turned on the water. I let it run over my hair as I held a loofah between my knees and used both my mangled hands to squeeze liquid body wash into it. Before meningitis I'd never used a loofah – I found them unmanly compared to an old-fashioned bar of soap. But since leaving the hospital I'd found that gripping soap was a task my thumb and hand stump weren't well-equipped to handle, and retrieving a wet bar of soap from the bottom of the shower while sitting on a bench was near impossible. So I started using the unmanly loofah, and found that I actually liked its lather. I also liked being able to wash myself, after months of having other people do it for me.

After the shower I dried off and dressed, using a small, plastic button-hook to help me fasten my jeans. This little device was my ticket out of sweatpants and nylon warmups. It was made for people with arthritis who had trouble gripping small objects, but it also worked perfectly for people with just one thumb and a stump of a hand. We sold them at the drugstore where I'd worked in high school, so when we returned to St. Cloud, Mom and I went there and bought up every one they had in stock.

I also used the hook to button a fresh, new shirt and then looked at myself in the mirror. I liked what I saw. There was something about being able to wear whatever clothes I wanted.

"What do you want for breakfast?" Mom asked when I emerged from the bathroom. "I could make you pancakes."

But I was already headed for the cupboard next to the refrigerator, propping my crutch against the kitchen counter behind it.

"I'm just going to have some cereal," I said. "I want to get out on the road as soon as I can."

Squeezing the box of cereal under the crook of my left arm, I took up the crutch again and walked to the dining table, where I dropped the box. Then I turned around and retrieved a bowl and spoon, carrying it to the table the same way. Then I made a third trip for the milk.

"Do you want me to do that for you?" Mom asked, watching me from the kitchen with a cup of coffee in her hand.

I smiled, but shook my head.

"I'm going to have to do this on my own, you know," I said.

"Well, you'll be living with Malcolm and Joyce so they could help you," Mom said. "Besides, you could let me do it for you one last time."

"Don't need help," I said, as I used both of my hands to tilt the cereal box and pour it into the bowl, then hooked my thumb into the handle of the plastic milk jug.

Baxter was under the table, whining. He often whined when there was food around, but it seemed more urgent than usual. We'd become pretty attached to each other, and he'd already developed an uncanny sense of when I was about to leave the house.

"He's going to miss you," Mom said.

"I'm going to miss him, too," I said. "But I'm still trying to figure out how to take care of myself. Once I do that, then I'll come back and get him."

After I ate, I carefully went down the stairs, putting my crutch down first, then planting each foot next to it before proceeding to the next step. Grandma met me on the landing, a plastic bag full of cookies in her hand.

"Here," she said, hooking the handles of the bag around my left arm. "Don't want you to get hungry on the road."

"Not much chance of that with all these," I said, smiling and pretending to struggle under the weight of the cookies.

Outside, my new Toyota Corolla was stuffed full of bags and boxes. Well, it wasn't quite new, but it was new to me. Mom and Dad had helped me buy it as soon as I was cleared to drive. That actually came back fairly naturally. The physical therapist had a steering wheel hooked up to a rather primitive computer program of a car on a two-dimensional road. Once I proved I could keep the cyber-car in its lane, I was told it was fine for me to try with the real thing. I briefly tried out a steering wheel knob, but found that actually made things more difficult. I would no longer be able to drink a 40-ounce Coke and talk on the phone while behind the wheel, but I drove just as safely as before — if not more so.

To go along with the safety theme, Mom and Dad wanted me driving something more reliable than a 12-year-old minivan with nearly 200,000 miles on it. The Corolla was a shiny deep maroon with sleek curves and a tiny spoiler on the back. I loved it.

Dad was at work the day I left, but in typical Dad fashion he had gotten the oil changed and made sure the tires were inflated the night before.

"It's a long drive," he explained, giving me a hug before he went to bed. "If you get tired, pull over."

I was far from tired. I was ready.

I placed the bag of cookies on the passenger seat, then turned and saw Mom and Grandma standing outside. Mom was holding Baxter by his leash. I walked over, leaned down and gingerly placed a still-sore left knee on the pavement, getting eye-to-eye with my dog. I stroked his head a few times with my right hand, then hugged him around his neck.

"You be a good boy, OK?" I said.

He whined and tugged at the leash.

I stood up and saw that Grandma and Mom both had watery eyes.

"All right, no tears now," I said with a smile.

They nodded and we hugged.

"Goodbye," Grandma said.

"I love you," Mom said.

"I'll see you soon," I said. "I'll call you when I get there."

Then I got back in the car, placing the bottom of the crutch on the floor of the passenger side and resting the top of it against the door. I turned on the radio with my right thumb, gently turning the dial until it was at the right volume.

Then I gripped the steering wheel with the thumb and what was left of my right hand, and pressed the stump of my left hand up against the wheel as well to steady it as I looked over my shoulder and began to back out of the driveway.

Turning into the street I paused, opened the car window and gave Mom, Grandma and Baxter one last wave. Then I put the car in drive and pulled away from the house where I had grown up and pointed myself toward Kansas, where a bedroom in Malcolm and Joyce's basement and my old part-time job at the *Basehor Sentinel* were waiting.

I put the stump of my left hand out the window, moving it up and down in the wind and grinning. I was at the beginning of an eight-hour drive, and the start of a new journey.

EPILOGUE

When I look back at my time in the hospital, I find myself oddly glad that it lasted as long as it did. I had 141 days in that emotional cocoon to puzzle out what had happened and what it would mean for my future before I re-entered the "real world." I realized later that I had gone through all of psychologist Elisabeth Kubler-Ross' five stages of grief: denial, anger, bargaining, depression and acceptance.

When I left, I was somewhere between depression and complete acceptance. I had been to my lowest point, but I wasn't completely ready to let go of my old life.

Clay was interviewed by a local TV station shortly after I got out of the hospital. He said a lot of nice things about my emotional strength, apparently having missed many of the days when I was a broken-down, blubbering mess. But I was most struck by the last thing he said, which went something like this:

"He may not feel this way yet, but some day Andy is going to look back on this as one of the best things that ever happened to him."

Sitting in a wheelchair, with what was left of my hands still bleeding and bandaged, I was skeptical, to say the least. But time would prove that Clay, as usual, was right.

Meningitis took some things from me, but with time I realized that the experience, the trial, had given me things that were more important. It was worth the pain, for several reasons.

Perseverance

About 18 months after leaving the hospital I was back at my old job in Basehor, covering a girls' basketball game when I noticed blood seeping through the thin bandage on my left hand. I was using my right thumb and hand stump at the time, scratching out game moments to remember in my spiral-bound notebook with handwriting that was becoming increasingly legible — to me at least.

The left-hand stump by that time had a small web space, created by Dr. Lawrence, in which I could grip a pen or other small items. But it was out of commission. In his quest to save as much of my hands as possible the doctor had missed a small chip of dead bone that had caused a localized infection. An angry, reddish-purple blister was bubbling out from the stump and I had wrapped a strip of gauze around it to give it a bit of coverage. But at some point during the game the blister had popped and now, in the middle of a crowded, noisy high school gym, I was doing wound control.

I remembered that I had some Kleenex in my pants pocket that were, fortunately, clean. Setting my notebook down on the bleacher beside me, I rooted around for them and pulled out several, laying them in my lap temporarily. Then I loosened the gauze on my left hand enough to slip several Kleenex underneath, soaking up the goopy fluid that was leaking out of the deflating blister. I also surreptitiously wiped clean a line of more watery blood that was running down toward my wrist.

I glanced over my shoulder quickly to see whether anyone was watching, but they seemed focused on the game, which was wrapping up.

The makeshift bandage held long enough for me to do my post-game interviews and drive home. There, I unwrapped the whole thing, washed out the wound, including the tiny piece of blackened bone that my body had pushed out, and applied a clean piece of gauze. I sat down and gingerly typed out a game story using my right thumb and the stub of a left thumb Dr. Lawrence had shaped.

It wasn't until I went to bed that night that I stopped to think of what I was willing to do, matter-of-factly, to stay on the job. Meningitis had made me much tougher than I was before.

It was a good thing, too, because those first few years outside the hospital were not always a smooth line to recovery. I was back to see Dr. Lawrence several times for numerous surgeries he called "tweaking" procedures. Shave back a bit of bone protruding from my hand stump here, cut open a thick scar that was pulling my thumb in an unnatural direction there, insert a wire into the thumb to hold it together when it became clear that the joint was hopelessly damaged.

There were other difficulties. Once I started walking, I ran through boxes of Band-Aids and tubes of Neosporin trying to mend sores on my foot stumps until my skin stabilized through a combination of the tissues toughening up and my finding the right prosthetic technician.

But by that point challenges that previously would have driven me to tears of frustration seemed like minor annoyances.

I kept going back to work, covering high school athletics, and I appreciated it more than ever.

The community of Basehor welcomed me back to work warmly. For weeks, a near-constant stream of students and parents came up to me at games to tell me they were glad to see me again. Their support helped ease my transition into public life. It was hard to leave when, in 2006, I got my first full-time job writing sports for a newspaper in another Kansas City suburb, Olathe.

I would spend two-and-a half years there, among a great group of young journalists who became my friends. Rarely did a day of it feel like work. That ended in 2009, when our paper downsized to the bone and nearly all of us became victims of a Great Recession that hit our industry even harder than most.

The day when I and two of my colleagues got the news, I needed the emotional fortitude I had gained through all those difficult days in the hospital. I went out to the parking lot, kicking pebbles and feeling that I deserved better, that I was entitled to more. I was feeling sorry for myself and, to some extent, wondering what I was going to do in a fast-tightening job market. But as I looked down at my orthopedic shoes I remembered the foot stumps inside them. The ones doctors had said I'd never walk on.

You are entitled to nothing. But you can accomplish anything.

It was a long but rewarding journey back to full employment — a journey I might not have had the courage to take had I not already plodded through a two-steps-forward, one-step-back rehabilitation. I spent a year back in Minnesota, working part-time for my hometown paper and tutoring in a local school through AmeriCorps, where I got used to giving a reassuring smile when elementary students came up to me with a mixture of fear and wonder and asked, "What happened to your hands?"

"I got sick a long time ago and the doctors had to take off some of my fingers so I could get better," I took to answering. "But don't worry, it doesn't hurt, and I can still do pretty much everything I used to do."

For some kids, that was sufficient, and they'd skip off on their merry way. Others had a laundry list of things they wanted to ask whether I could do: drive, eat, write, ride a bike, etc.

Yes, yes, yes, yes and yes.

"I just do some things a little different than I used to," I said, parroting the words of Mylene, my former occupational therapist.

I used my AmeriCorps grant to go back to school, packing up and heading to the University of Maryland to learn about covering government for a master's in journalism. There, I toughened my foot stumps even more with days walking on Capitol Hill and standing in line outside the U.S. Supreme Court. I also worked part-time on the sports desk for *The Washington Post*, where they even let me go out and cover a few dozen high school and college games for them on a freelance basis. Seeing my byline in that venerable paper was something else.

After getting my second degree I had a brief stop covering courts in Baltimore before heading back to Kansas to take a job writing about the statehouse for *The Topeka Capital-Journal*.

After my first year there I won several awards and my editor said multiple people had described my reporting style as "persistent." Months of debridement, surgeries and physical therapy had helped make me that way. I still had that old sense of entitlement in my reporting — I felt entitled to information, and indignant when it was not forthcoming. But after meningitis I didn't give up as easily.

It's very possible that none of the professional success I experienced after getting laid off would have happened without the tolerance for pain and long-term work that meningitis gave me. I might very well have quit. But meningitis taught me that if I didn't quit, if I kept plugging away day by day, good things would happen eventually.

After I got laid off in Olathe, I took my severance pay and used it to go back to Europe for a few weeks. On my way to the Swiss Alps I chatted with a beautiful girl on a train who was impressed by the way I handled food, drink and a book at the same time with my mangled hands. When she started up a conversation by leaning across the aisle and shyly asking what happened to me, I realized my physical differences could be an ice-breaker rather than a liability in the dating game.

In time the concerns about my physical experience that I expressed to my dad would prove unfounded. I did better with the ladies after meningitis than before it — although admittedly I had set the bar awfully low.

But that too was a lesson in perseverance, and also in knowing when to get off a train and when to stay on. I got off in Interlaken, as planned, after saying goodbye to the girl, who was heading on to Zurich. It was only after the train pulled away from the station that I realized I was on a daily Eurail pass and could have made an instant change of plans and told her that I, too, was heading to Zurich. Still, I had a date with the Alps.

I would need my newfound perseverance there because I broke one of the cardinal rules I was taught as a Boy Scout: I set off on a hike without telling anyone where I was going. I'd picked out a downhill hiking trail that I expected to be a nice, easy slope. For some reason I did not anticipate that "downhill" in the Alps meant something very different from "downhill" in Kansas or Minnesota.

When I set out, the difficulty of the journey was more than offset by the scenic rewards and I reveled in just being out there with my stumpy feet. I was letting nothing stop me. But after a few hours of bracing each step to keep from tumbling down gravelly declines, sweat glued my clothes to my body and my quadriceps started to burn.

After another hour or so my leg muscles were cramping and I had to sit down on the trail and take long pulls from the water bottle I was carrying. Afternoon was turning to evening and the sun was getting lower. For the first time I began to wonder how cold it would get at night and how long it would take someone to find me if I missed a step and twisted a knee. I had seen only a few other hikers on the trail.

The hard truth was that I was alone on that mountain and no matter how much it hurt I was going to have to keep putting one foot in front of the other until I got to the town down in the nearby valley, where I could catch the funicular back to my mountain hostel. No one was coming to rescue me from the pain.

Before meningitis I might have panicked. After meningitis I knew what I had to do and approached it with reluctant resolve. I got up and trudged on, side-stepping the most treacherous declines and slowly moving onward, onward, onward. Another hour crept by and my thighs began to twitch, begging for a break. I ignored them and thought of other things — basketball and women and thin-crust pizzas smothered in melted cheese. The sun was setting and I didn't want to get caught trying to navigate those declines in the dark.

When a shadowy dusk started to overtake the mountain trail and I thought I could ignore my aching legs no more, the path leveled off, the trees opened up and I could see lights, houses and farm fields. A few dozen more minutes of swinging one leg in front of the other and I was on a paved road. I'd never been happier to see a city bus.

Personal relationships

Nurse Bob and I eventually did get out to that Royals game together and I was even at his wedding. I also made good on my pledge to see Keith Langford in his last season as a Jayhawk, getting courtside seats because of my wheelchair-bound status. He had 17 points, five assists and four rebounds and KU handed Texas coach Rick Barnes his worst-ever Big 12 loss, 90-65. A pretty typical stat line for "K-Freeze."

Dr. Luckeroth became like a surrogate mom once I returned to KC, checking in on me periodically and taking me to dinner often. I also met her daughters, Tina and Sabrina. Like my brothers and me, their personalities could hardly have been more different. Tina, the younger one, was a ball of energy — bubbly, outgoing, talking and giggling a mile a minute. Sabrina was serious and shy, occasionally rolling her eyes at her sister's antics. But both were intelligent and kind-hearted and I felt privileged to play a role in their lives. Meningitis led to my meeting them and others, like Matt Bellomo and Mike Nolte.

It also deepened my relationships with those closest to me. For years after I turned 16 and got my driver's license, my parents and I had a near-nightly ritual. I would tell them where I was going before rushing out the door to a restaurant, a bowling alley, or a movie theater where I would meet my friends and hang out before trying to determine what to do next.

Every night without fail, Dad would advise me, "Be careful," before I was out the front door. It became something of a running joke; Mom and I could finish the words almost as soon as he'd started them. The ritual continued on my trips home from college and I wondered whether Dad didn't realize that, when I was away at school, I was being relatively careful even without being told. But on my trips home after meningitis I realized Dad was letting me out the door without the reminder. Finally I tried to prompt him, stopping in front of his living room chair before going out for the night.

"What is it you always tell me before I leave?" I said.

He looked up from his computer screen and gave me a little smile.

"I don't need to tell you that any more," he said.

Sure, part of it was that I was getting older. But part of it was that meningitis had changed my relationship with my dad. After that it was never as hierarchical, with him as the authority figure and me trying to evaluate my actions based on not disappointing him. After that we were on a similar plane, able to exchange ideas and commiserate like friends.

I had never known how to talk to my dad about anything emotionally substantive before that. Death, love and pain were things neither of us were comfortable discussing. But on those long nights in the hospital, and then in our shared apartment during the recovery year that followed, nothing was off limits. We talked, we shared, and we got close in a way we never would have otherwise. In the years since, I've been comfortable going to him for advice about relationships, finding fulfillment on the job and other things that I would have previously kept to myself.

Meningitis also changed my relationship with my mom.

We had always been close, but in a different way. I was a mama's boy growing up and she was my fierce protector, going all the way back to first grade when she stormed onto the bus to confront the driver whose somewhat raunchy choice of music had disturbed me the day before. She was still playing that role while I was in the hospital, but it was there that I learned when I had to tell her to back off and give me the space to fight the battles I needed to fight without her. That was growth for me, growth I needed to vault me into manhood and a wide world that would care little who my mom was, or how smart and talented she knew me to be.

While Mom's influence within the hospital was a little overbearing at times, her heart was in the right place and she was aggressively protective when I needed her to be. Hospitalizations are fraught with danger, even when the staff has the best intentions. Infections are common, doctors of different disciplines have disagreements and communication breakdowns sometimes leave patients as the last to know about plans for their care. And that's not even mentioning health-insurance complications. Every long-term hospital patient needs a hawkish advocate, and Mom was that for me. It certainly didn't hurt that she was licensed to practice law.

But at some point I had to accept that at times I was going to face pain that she couldn't take away. Once I demonstrated that I could do that, it allowed our relationship to mature to one of mutual respect rather than co-dependence.

She still needs a reminder once in a while, but I'm more comfortable letting her know.

Meningitis also changed my relationships with my brothers.

Sure, we still drive each other crazy at times and any discussion of politics steers us right toward an argument that will temporarily derail any holiday gathering. But I think we're probably not unlike many families in that regard. At least now those arguments are undermined by the first-hand knowledge that there are more crucial things in life than politics.

I know that some day Mom and Dad will be gone and my brothers will be the closest family for me to lean on. I know that when those days come I will be there for them and they will be there for me.

Through meningitis, I learned that I am supported unconditionally. I learned that the Marsos, despite our disputes and differences, will band together to protect a hurting member of our family, forming a phalanx against the attacks of the outside world.

I also learned that my family extends far beyond those whose genetic material I share. Years after meningitis I found myself in a Laundromat, wearing short sleeves that bared my scars to the few other people who were there. One of them, a middle-aged man with a short beard, asked me what kind of accident I was in.

I explained my appearance with a now-familiar Cliff's Notes version of the story: rare form of bacterial meningitis during college, cut off circulation to my extremities, lots of skin grafts and amputations.

"Oh," he said, taking a second to process all that. "So, do your friends not hang around you any more?"

That took me a second to process. Was he asking whether my friends thought I was still contagious? Then I realized he was assuming that perhaps my friends shunned me in public because of the way I looked. I laughed, because the idea seemed preposterous by that point. Their reaction had been the polar opposite.

I recalled a time years earlier when I was still in my wheelchair and had gone out to dinner with Clay, Randy and some other guys. An older lady at a nearby table spotted us and, as she was walking out, leaned down to my friends and talked to them as if I wasn't there.

"It's so nice of you all to take him out like this," she said, giving me a slight nod and smile. After she left I rolled my eyes and we all laughed about it.

I never got to live in that apartment with Clay and Randy. But I did spend several years living with Matt Unger from Pearson Hall in a house he'd bought in Olathe. We had lots of goofy, random, occasionally drunken fun together, leading one of my *Olathe News* co-workers to comment that Matt and I had an "epic bro-mance."

After meningitis, I knew that it was a friendship much deeper than that. Matt was a friend I could always count on, like so many from Minnesota I had known far longer — including Ali.

About three years after meningitis, Ali married the guy she had been dating when I was hospitalized. He was a friend of a friend and I knew him pretty well — well enough to know that he was a gentle and decent man who would treat her well and make her happy. I went to the wedding and was mildly surprised when even watching her say her vows didn't elicit a strong emotional reaction.

Seeing her in her wedding dress just gave me a general tinge of nostalgia; a mental nod to when I was 15 and the future was boundless and a pretty girl paid attention to me for the first time and I had this silly certainty that she would be just the first of many and that life would always be free and easy.

At the reception, during a quiet moment, I made a point to seek out Ali's dad. He had made a generous donation to a fund that my parents set up to help with my medical bills. I tried to thank him, but he smiled and shook his head.

"You've got Ali to thank for that," he said. "She wanted us to do whatever we could to help you out. I know she would have liked to do more, but we're all just glad to see you up and around."

I looked across the room to where Ali was laughing and dancing with her bridesmaids. There was a warm sensation in my chest, but it was different from the one I used to feel when I saw her. Now, it was a feeling of intense gratitude and friendship.

Purpose

My emotional reaction to promoting meningitis vaccinations before the TV cameras — that feeling of being exactly where I was supposed to be and doing exactly what I was supposed to do — has never left me.

Some people spend their entire lives searching for some purpose more meaningful than going to work every day and contributing to the Gross Domestic Product. I got such a purpose at the age of 22, and I have meningitis to thank for that.

With vaccination legislation proposed almost annually in statehouses across the country the opportunities for advocacy are many, and the stakes are literally life and death.

Soon after returning to Kansas to rejoin the sportswriting ranks I found myself in the state Capitol, testifying before a Senate health committee on behalf of a bill that would require doctors to distribute information about meningitis during high school physicals. I told the senators that, although I thought the bill was inadequate, it was a good step because I had little knowledge of the disease when I caught it. Then I recounted to them some of what I went through — the hours in the tank room watching my flesh scraped away, the excruciating days waking up after amputation surgeries, the nights when I lay awake wondering whether my new life would even be worth living. By the time I was done, tears were streaming down my face, and though I was somewhat embarrassed I also knew those tears would help get my point across.

Upon returning to Kansas I also started visiting high school health classes several times a year to talk meningitis. When I told the story of my illness, I stressed three take-home lessons: the importance of getting vaccinated against meningococcal disease, the importance of practicing good hygiene to prevent the spread of the bacteria and the importance of knowing the symptoms and getting to a hospital immediately if they appeared.

Although some of the high school kids predictably tuned out my messages — or even fell asleep at their desks — one or two typically came up to me after the bell and told me they were going to get vaccinated as soon as possible. That was always nice to hear, but my visit to their class was as much for my benefit as theirs. Part of my emotional recovery relied on putting meaning behind the tragedy — doing something to turn it into a positive.

I had to add a caveat to a lot of those high school talks: "The vaccine actually wouldn't have helped me because I had the type of meningitis the vaccine doesn't prevent, but it's effective against nearly all other types of meningitis, so it can significantly reduce your risk."

That caveat could be eliminated soon. Multiple type B meningitis vaccines were in development in 2012 and one, Bexsero, was approved by the European Union at the beginning of 2013.

We're getting closer to having a comprehensive vaccine that could wipe out bacterial meningitis. Developing the shot is the scientists' job. Persuading everyone to get it is where I come in.

We have a problem in this country with declining vaccination rates — a problem that is growing and fraught with tragic consequences. Discounting all data to the contrary, there are those who stoke fear through unproven anecdotes about what can happen if you vaccinate your kids. I am walking and talking proof of what can happen if you don't — an antidote to the anecdotes. I'm not alone, either.

Meningococcal disease is rare, but by getting involved in groups like Meningitis Angels and the National Meningitis Association I saw its full cost firsthand. At the NMA conference in Orlando I met parents who had lost children to the disease.

Several pulled me aside and asked the same question: "How much pain were you in?" By the third or fourth time I realized why, and my heart broke for them. It was hard enough to accept that their children were gone. It was harder still for them to not know whether it was a peaceful or painful passing. I told them that there was significant pain on that first day, and that I'd never felt so sick in my life. But I also told them about the tremendous sense of peace that I felt when I blacked out on the helicopter pad at KU Med, and that my most painful experiences happened after I woke up. I told them that there were times in the months that followed when I wished I hadn't woken up at all. Whether that was comforting to them or not, I don't know. But I felt compelled to tell the truth.

The people at the conference who had lost loved ones seemed to draw comfort from the camaraderie and spirit of the survivors, including Nick Springer and John Kach, two who had inspired me months earlier when I was in the hospital. What did we discuss when we got together? A lot of things. Some were practical, such as wound care, state vaccination laws and going through airport security quickly with a metal leg. Some were profound: near-death experiences, dealing with tragedy, adjusting to having a body that suddenly looks markedly different than most of those around you. We came from all sorts of backgrounds and from all corners of the U.S., but we had an instant connection. We'd been through something hardly anyone else could understand.

Appreciating the people I'd met, the strength I'd gained and the relationships that deepened got me closer to Clay's prophecy about one day looking at my experience with meningitis as one of the best things that ever happened to me. Then I figured out how the experience fit with my Christian faith.

One day I was sitting in church with Dr. Luckeroth and her daughters when a gospel passage from John, Chapter 9, was read. To Jesus was presented a man blind from birth and his disciples asked him, "Teacher, whose sin caused him to be born blind? Was it his own or his parents' sins?"

I leaned forward in the pew, eager to hear Jesus' answer, for this was my own question, the one I had been struggled with: Why had I been saddled with this rare disease and its rare deformities?

Jesus answered: "His blindness has nothing to do with his sins or his parents' sins. He is blind so that God's power may be seen at work in him."

That floored me. With 12 years of Catholic school under my belt, I'd probably heard the passage dozens of times. But I'd never really listened, never really tried to understand what it meant.

I thought of all the people who came to my aid when I got sick. I thought of my family, friends, nurses, doctors, other hospital staff and people outside the hospital who had gone out of their way to help my family though some of them didn't even know us. I thought of all the people who had shown the best side of humanity: our instinctive desire to ease the suffering of others. I couldn't imagine anything that would glorify God more than the love that was poured out toward me. If there were no suffering in the world, there would be no need for that love, that compassion. Someone had to suffer to bring it out, so why not me?

In time I would realize that I had been given a miracle, though not the one I prayed for in the hospital. My miracle was a glimpse of the divine side of humanity. Amidst all the suffering in the world, it is this instinct that gives me great hope for the future.

Meningitis gave me a story that can spread that hope to others, and that's worth the pain.

On May 21, 2005, a year after I missed my own graduation ceremony, I was invited back to KU for another graduation, this time as the School of Journalism's commencement speaker. Still in a wheelchair, I spoke to a group of more than 1,000 grads that included hundreds of friends and supporters, some of whom I was meeting for the first time. This is what I told them:

> *I'm not going to talk much about meningitis because honestly, I'm really tired of talking about it. Instead I'm going to talk about plans.*
>
> *Most of us out here probably have plans for the future, some of them big, some of them small. And this ceremony today is a milestone for all of us; we've taken a big step toward turning those plans into reality. We're now on the freeway to our dreams, we've got our route all*

MapQuest-ed out, sitting on the passenger seat next to us, and now we just have to put our foot on the gas and keep moving forward.

But as we head toward our dreams, there's something we need to remember: our lives are not entirely our own. There is a force outside our control. Some call it God, some call it fate, some simply call it luck. Whatever we believe it is, we know it has a hand in our lives. At any moment this force could block that smooth freeway to our dreams.

These roadblocks can take many forms. They could be simply unexpected events, like the loss of a job or an unplanned pregnancy. Or they could be something truly tragic, like a traumatic illness or the death of a loved one. Whatever they are, once they have blocked that straight path we had planned, we have no other choice but to take a detour.

Once we're on that detour, there are different ways we can approach it. We can get angry and bitter and rail against God or fate or luck for having betrayed us. These are natural reactions. After all, some of these detours are quite difficult. They are bumpy and windy and they may never actually lead back to the freeway and the plans we made before.

But if we refuse to be discouraged, and instead embrace these detours, there can be great rewards. For it is off the freeway, off the well-traveled path, that we often find the most breath-taking, jaw-dropping scenery. And it is there that we also meet the most interesting and generous people.

I have learned that, no matter what dark and difficult roads we are forced to travel, there are always people who will reach out to us. They will offer us directions, help us refuel, fix us up and get us on our way again with a kind word and a gentle touch. If everything went according to plan we would never have the privilege of meeting these people.

And so, the road to our dreams is rarely smooth and straight. But when we come to a detour, we shouldn't lose heart or get angry. Instead we should embrace each detour, live it and explore it to its fullest. Because if we travel each road as far as it goes, then no matter where we end up we will look back on a successful journey.

ACKNOWLEDGMENTS

There are so many people to thank for making this book possible, but fortunately, if you've read this far, you've already "met" many of them.

There were several formal and informal editors though, who believed in this story and helped me do it justice. Last and foremost was Monroe Dodd, who made the final polishes, but specific mention also must go to University of Maryland journalism professor Carl Sessions Stepp. Carl spent as much time with the manuscript as anyone, helping hone the craft and inspire a little bit of magic — especially at the beginning and the end.

Special thanks go to Doug Weaver at Kansas City Star Books for taking the final leap and turning this story from a Word document into a paperback.

I wouldn't have been around to write this if not for the doctors who saved my life and the KU Medical Center staff who helped make it worth living. That includes nurses, techs, PTs, OTs, custodians, dieticians, social workers and chaplains. For four months, you were my second family.

To my friends, those of you who were there for me throughout the hospital experience and those who accepted me afterwards, thank you, thank you, thank you. Sometimes you can't say it any better than James Taylor: "You just call out my name, and you know wherever I am, I'll come running, to see you again."

Then there's my family. The people who took shifts at my bedside so I'd never have to wake up alone.

Dan and Josh: I love you guys. We never say it to each other and sometimes we have a funny way of showing it, but I know I can count on you when the world looks grim and I want you to know that you can count on me.

Grandma: You are the most unselfish person I know. You taught me how to live for others. I love you.

To mom and dad: You are the best. I don't really know what else I can say. I love you.

To all the strangers who helped me and my family during my hospitalization: You renew my faith in humanity. I can never repay you, but every day I strive to live up to the sacrifices you made.

22938729R00152

Made in the USA
San Bernardino, CA
28 July 2015